MW00426881

To Linda Garcia Shelton

FAMILY IDENTITY

Ties, Symbols, and Transitions

To remember Milan
and our "Postgraduate School
Apostino Gemelli"

[signature]

Milano 15. luglio

FAMILY IDENTITY

Ties, Symbols, and Transitions

VITTORIO CIGOLI
EUGENIA SCABINI
Catholic University, Milan, Italy

with Foreword by
Robert E. Emery
University of Virginia

LEA

LAWRENCE ERLBAUM ASSOCIATES, PUBLISHERS

2006   Mahwah, New Jersey   London

Lawrence Erlbaum Associates, Inc., Publishers
10 Industrial Avenue
Mahwah, New Jersey 07430
www.erlbaum.com

Cover design by Tomai Maridou

Library of Congress Cataloging-in-Publication Data

Cigoli, Vittorio.
    Family identity : ties, symbols, and transitions / Vittorio Cigoli,
    Eugenia Scabini : with a foreword by Robert E. Emery.
        p.   cm.
    Includes bibliographical references and index.
    ISBN 0–8058–5231–X
    1. Family. 2. Family—Psychological aspects. 3. Identity
    (Psychology) I. Scabini, Eugenia. II. Title.
HQ723.C484 2006
306.85—dc22   2005040146

Books published by Lawrence Erlbaum Associates are printed on acid-free
paper, and their bindings are chosen for strength and durability.

Printed in the United States of America
10 9 8 7 6 5 4 3 2 1

*To our family tree, its living branches
and those stunted by pain and bereavement,
in the hope that the sap will flow
once more and generate new life.*

Contents

Foreword

I am delighted to have the opportunity to write a few words to introduce the family theories, perspectives, and methods of Vittorio Cigoli and Eugenia Scabini in their first, major translation into English. Cigoli and Scabini are psychologists and family scholars at Catholic University of Milan. Their fresh and insightful ideas, as well as their extensive writing and research, rank them as leading family systems theorists not only in Italy but also throughout Europe. I know this both from their reputation and writing, and also through my fortunate personal experiences of joining them in various meetings and presentations throughout Italy.

To my American eyes, this book, and Cigoli and Scabini's family scholarship, is quintessentially Italian: intellectual, historical, emotional, cultural, human, multigenerational, a bit mysterious, charming, and engaging throughout. This is a book packed with ideas, and as I read it, I found myself reflecting on its meaning not only for my own work but also for much bigger issues—the value of theory (American psychology is dominated by analysis at the sacrifice of synthesis), the value of family (including the lessons taught by my own family experiences), and the implications of our psychological theories of family for social policy and for society (read on).

I will not (and cannot) give a PowerPoint version of Cigoli and Scabini's ideas. As but one example, their breadth (chapter 1) ranges from discussing the family in ancient Greece to the family according to Spike Lee. (You can easily snap one twig in half, but you cannot break a bunch of twigs. "And that is what family is.") What I can do is to highlight a few of their key concepts and contributions in the hope that these illustrations will serve as a "teaser" that draws you, the reader, into this wonderful book.

One captivating set of ideas stems from Cigoli and Scabini's central focus on intergenerational relationships and family values. (They do not use the latter term, but I do to distinguish their high-minded focus on values like trust, loyalty, hope, justice, and obligation in intergenerational family relationships from current American debates about "family values" which sadly are more political than aspirational.) In elaborating upon their theories of family, Cigoli and Scabini gently but incisively critique economic models of relationships, like social exchange theory, and argue that family relationships are—have to be—much more. At the base, their premise is that biology (child bearing) and lineage make all family relationships about more than moment-to-moment or even broader social interaction. Family relationships, in their view, are also very much—and very much should be—historical.

This perspective came alive for me, personally and intellectually, in Cigoli and Scabini's discussion of the *gift,* an unconditional giving of time, emotion, and energy that is, by definition, an act of trust (chapter 2). Probably the most basic gift in families is the unconditional love and extensive care that parents offer to children. (I should note, however, that these authors also rightly criticize contemporary parental overinvestment in children, a pattern that can serve parental needs more than children's). Family gifts like caring for children are given freely; however, the gift is more complicated than that. The recipient of the gift encumbers an *obligation,* an obligation to reciprocate.

Cigoli and Scabini's view of *reciprocation* transcends ideas about social exchange in the moment—exchanging "reinforcers" with the giver. Rather, the obligation to reciprocate that results from giving and receiving can and should involve "paying back" by giving to others, perhaps most notably by giving to future generations as the child becomes the parent. This makes reciprocation something more than social exchange, even social exchange with an exceedingly long time horizon. In Cigoli and Scabini's view, *reciprocation is a value, a moral commitment, not a commodity.*

The ideas of obligation and reciprocation, in some ways, are simple ones. These are values I was taught as child, and ones that I have tried to *act on,* but perhaps a value that I have not tried hard enough to *pass on.* Why? I think the answer is because, like many contemporary parents, I failed to appreciate the value's importance—and perhaps the importance of values.

In fact, Cigoli and Scabini's bringing forth of the idea of the *gift* (along with their many other keen observations) made me wonder more broadly about the impact of psychological theorizing on families and society. Description, it seems, quickly becomes prescription. If relationships are based not only theoretically but also *morally* on social exchange, is it not only justifiable but somehow right if one leaves a relationship because "I'm not getting what I should get out of it." This rather frightening view of social exchange seems to apply not only to marriage today (divorce is far more acceptable when marriage is viewed as a contract rather than as a social, religious, and/or moral obligation), but perhaps also to parenting, much of which necessarily is (and must be) hard work and one-sided.

This book is directed toward students, practitioners, and researchers interested in families and family relationships. Yet, in its text and subtext, this book has value and implication far beyond family scholarship. I have offered you my brief introduction to Cigoli and Scabini. You will gain much more by introducing yourself to them as you read through this engaging, insightful, and complex book.

—*Robert E. Emery*

Preface

Genders, generations, and lineage; faith, hope, and justice; gifts, duties, and debts; affection, responsibility, and generativity; values, secrets, and objectives; transmissions and transitions: These are the main family themes. This refers to what the family relationship builds in terms of organization structure, motives, and objectives. It assumes different forms and attire according to culture and the passage of time, but there are seeds that pass constantly through the millstone of family relationships and make up its identity.

This book is the fruit of many years of research and of the fruitful exchanges we have had with researchers all over the world, through personal contact as well as through their writings. Its aim is to bring into focus all the many themes that help to construct family identity.

We do not believe that researchers start from definite ideas; we believe that ideas are discovered and then ripen with time and through personal encounter. This has certainly been our own experience since we began our research in the late 1980s. We come from different backgrounds and sensibilities—one of us is female, the other male; one is a philosopher by training, the other a literature specialist; one is involved in social psychology, the other in clinical psychology—and we have brought our respective strengths and weaknesses to the banquet. The core of our study is family psychology, so it is no accident that philosophy, literature, history, art, and anthropology are its kindred disciplines. We have also brought our fears and our limitations to the feast, but it is our shared passion for family studies that has been and continues to be the bond that unites us as authors and coresearchers. We hope and believe that this passion is also shared by all the researchers who bring their ideas and enthusiasm to the Center for Family Studies and Research at the Catholic University in Milan. Research without passion is a soul-destroying business. The social psychologists, clinical psychologists and sociologists who work there are engaged in areas of research concerned with "family-ness" and are in constant touch with colleagues throughout Italy and elsewhere in the world. We thank them for the input and suggestions they have offered us over the years.

We also owe a major debt of thanks to the authors whose ideas we have drawn on in writing this book. Our citations in the text itself show how, and to what extent, we are indebted to them. At a more personal level, we offer our warmest thanks to Robert Emery for his faith in our work and his unfailing support, as well as for the ideas he has so generously shared with us. We also thank Frank Fincham, whose studies on forgiveness helped us to focus on this crucial dimension of family relationships. Finally, we thank Sara Molgora, PhD, who treated the editing of this book with carefulness and loving dedication, and Stephen Thorne, who has taken care of its translation, sharing with us the key concepts and the most important clinical and psychosocial constructs.

The publication of this book received the 2004 Catholic University Grant for research on the basis of empirical results therein stated.

—*Vittorio Cigoli*
—*Eugenia Scabini*

CHAPTER ONE

The Gallery of Time: Picturing the Family

The family is an exceedingly complex living organism, a social entity and psychological subject that both mirrors and meshes with its environmental/social context and the cultural history it is steeped in. When viewed across the centuries, the family's ability to transform itself is truly surprising. A temporal perspective as long as this is essential if we are to avoid the foreshortening effects of a merely descriptive approach and instead arrive at a deeper understanding of the family as a phenomenon that satisfactorily explains both the varying and the permanent features that constitute what we call the "family-ness."

This brief though necessary excursus through time will be more meaningful if it encompasses not only history as such, but also mythology and art. The latter two especially are symbolic distillates of ideas and representations of extreme interest to anyone involved in family studies and, in particular, clinical and social psychology.

FAMILY MYTHOLOGIES IN GREEK AND ROMAN CULTURE

In Ancient Greece, marriage was a formal public contract drawn up under the aegis of Zeus and Hera (the divine couple), whose aim was the perpetuation of paternal lineage through the union of two families. Sexual seduction was considered necessary only as a means of achieving this—on their wedding day, the young couple wore crowns of myrrh and anointed themselves with perfume—but in all other respects, eroticism was regarded as extremely dangerous. Greek culture made a clear distinction between courtesans, who were there for pleasure, and wives, who were there to ensure the legitimacy of offspring and to act as faithful custodians of the hearth. Thus marriage, insofar as it meant foregoing the pleasures and seductions of eroticism, was considered a pure state (Detienne, 1972; Guthrie, 1968).

1

Hermes and Hestia were the Olympian divinities who shaped and guided family life. Hermes, a polymorphous divinity, was by turns the messenger of the gods, a phallic divinity, a healer, and the protector of wayfarers (including merchants and thieves) who possessed talent and cunning in equal measure. However, one image of him is crucial: He was also presented as the "lord of the heap of stones" that was used to mark boundaries, whether between the home and the polis, or the polis and wild, uncultivated, alien nature. Thus, Hermes, as the guardian of boundaries, thresholds, and doorways, was the god who kept danger at bay.

However, the "heap of stones" also served to signpost roads and connect places. It was no accident, then, that images of Hermes were erected at crossroads, and that he was depicted in frescoes and on vases as Psycopomp, the Guide of Souls on their journey to the underworld. Thus, Hermes not only performed the masculine role of guarding and defending the boundary; he was also a link between the living and their ancestors.

By contrast, Hestia had a quintessentially feminine role: As the keeper of the hearth, she ensured the continuity of the family lineage and therefore the perpetuity of its offspring and name. In Greek culture, a child was not born of woman. The womb was regarded as a cold receptacle for the male seed, which was warm and fertile. Conception was a kind of plowing, in which the woman was the furrow and the man the plow. It was a father's duty to acknowledge the fruit of the seed that he had sown by plowing the woman. He did so by raising (cultivating) the child, thereby acknowledging its status as a descendant of the family. Interestingly, the English noun "husband"—the man to whom a woman is married, but literally a dweller in a house (OE: *hus*, house, *buandi*, present participle of *buan*, to dwell)—can also mean "a thrifty manager," while the related noun "husbandry" means "the business of a farmer," "tillage," and "economical management," and a "husbandman" is a working farmer.

Let us return to the notion of woman-bride. She is "ground corn"; that is, a product of fertile, cultivated earth. Marital code and crop code (the tilled earth is no longer wild) go hand in hand. As Homer says, man eats bread, while woman is both the promise of and trust in a good harvest (offspring). She was also mobile, in the sense that she could pass from one family to another as a gift. In ancient cultures, however, a gift had a price that had to be paid—it had a trading value—and so was not totally free. This tradition lives on in some cultures today, although it was the opposite of what would happen in Western culture, where the woman had to be passed on with the assurance of a dowry, the value that alone made her marriageable. In any case, creating a family was inseparable from the principle that exchanges had to be properly regulated, meaning that the woman had both the mobility of moveable property that could be passed from family to family (she could be traded) and the immobility that came of tending the hearth, the symbol of eternal regeneration.

However, there is another figure in the Greek pantheon—Heracles Epitrape-zius, that is, Heracles of the table—who is of special interest in family studies. As portrayed by the sculptor Lysippus, he is very different from the traditional Heracles, the hero of the Twelve Labors performed in expiation of the crime he committed against the family by killing his own children in a fit of madness. In Lysippus' very different representation, he is the guest who may knock at the door of any house and for whom a place should always be reserved at table. Lysippus goes so far as to reserve the seat at the head of the table for him.

The importance of hospitality (responsiveness to other people and their needs) would be taken up and enhanced by Christianity as a family value. The pilgrim who may knock at any door and expect to be admitted and find a place reserved for him at table is an image of Christ who begs hospitality. It is no accident that in times gone by, especially in the homes of the poor, an extra chair was always kept in readiness for an unexpected guest. A home that was unwilling to welcome a guest was not a home, but a refuge, and therefore pathological in the sense that it was symptomatic of a rigid division between the family's interior and exterior worlds.

Obviously, it was through the guest and the pilgrim that the theme of rela-tions with the outside world made its entrance on the family stage. An outsider could as easily be a foreigner (barbarian) or dangerous enemy as a fellow human being who expected to be welcomed and listened to. Indeed, the family itself could be seen as a meeting of strangers who have agreed to draw up contractual bonds. The identity of the family cannot, therefore, be understood unless this profoundly important underlying theme is also taken into account.

However, Lysippus goes even further in his portrayal. Heracles does not just occupy the place of honor at table; his head is also turned in the manner of someone who is playing an active part in the conversation around him, which is as much as to say that words, like food, are common fare passed around from a single dish. This is the principle of companionship at table (*com* and *panis*, sharing bread) that established the rules of exchange within the family. Words, like food, had to be passed round; no one could keep them entirely to them-selves. Communal sharing and offering (of food and words) created a bond of association between people. By contrast, refusal to participate in shared meals signified opposition to and hatred of the family community. It is also the mean-ing underlying anorexic and bulimic pathologies.

Finally, there is one other principle of exchange—the exercise of *charis*—that has come down to us from ancient Greek culture. The Greeks were fully cognizant of the violence and hatred that can also be a feature of family rela-tionships. Indeed, the literary genre of tragedy was based on the vicissitudes of a set of families—the House of Atreus, to which Orestes belonged; the House of Perseus, to which Heracles belonged; and the House of Cadmus, to which Oedipus belonged. In Greek tragedy it is as if the family relationships that unravel across generations harbor a sort of "tragic soul," an irreducible core of violence, hate, abuse, deceit, and mortal envy that can develop and spread at any moment, contaminating family relationships and leading family members ineluctably toward violent death, ignominy, and horror. It may manifest itself as hatred between siblings, hatred between generations, contempt for the gods and their will, unbridled lust, or an all-consuming desire for material possessions.[1]

However, the actions of families could produce not just tragedy but also comedy—integration as well as destruction. For this outcome to be possible, the exercise of charis was needed. As Aeschylus demonstrates in *Eumenides,* charis opposes the logic of the blood feud according to which injustice is repaid with injustice, violence with violence. Instead, he proposes the new logic of the rightful act, performed to reinstate justice, that necessitates a genuine desire for reconciliation and a willingness to take the first step in trusting others. Acting against charis are the deceitfulness and violence that break the circuit of exchange and, not surprisingly, join forces to destroy marital and family bonds.

The mythical figure of Ixion is a good example of how Greek culture symbolized the pernicious transgenerational outcomes of family relationships based not on charis, but on hatred, envy, and ingratitude. Ixion was a man who held the family bond in contempt. He lied to his wife (employed duplicity and deceit), resorted to murdering his son-in-law, and even attempted the chastity of Hera, the Great Mother. In reality, however, he ended up embracing Cloud, a deceptively convincing phantom of the goddess Hera. The coupling of Ixion and Cloud generated the Centaur, a bastard child of the universe and a nonexistent entity in the order of affiliation because it had no real ancestry. It is as if sexual union without charis was an illusory game, a kind of pretending that could never generate offspring in the true sense.

Christianity would develop on the concept of charis and make it, as St. Paul said, the greatest of all virtues. Without charity, faith and hope are deprived not only of meaning, but also of their ability to bind people together ("religion" is related to the Latin *religare,* to bind) in meaningful relationships.[2]

To summarize, the concepts of maleness, femaleness, and lineage (the *ghènos* linked to a progenitor/ancestor) were fundamental to Greek culture and were contextualized within a framework of sacredness attributed to a world perceived as more divine than human. The principles of family functioning were exemplified in the lives of gods like Zeus and Hera, Hermes and Hestia, whose principles of relationship and rules of exchange were reproposed in the human family. The most important of these principles were companionship at table

[1] In *Nichomachean Ethics,* Aristotle (2002) uses the lives of families to illustrate the notion of *praxis,* that is, action and its consequences.

[2] St Paul, *First Letter to the Corinthians,* 13: 4–7. "Charity suffereth long, and is kind; charity envieth not; charity vaunteth not itself, is not puffed up, doth not behave itself unseemly, seeketh not her own, is not easily provoked, thinketh no evil; rejoiceth not in iniquity, but rejoiceth in the truth; beareth all things, believeth all things, hopeth all things, endured all things."

(exchange of food and talk) and charis, deployed to oppose the core of violence ("blood cries out for blood") inherent in the family relationship.

Etrusco-Roman culture, following after the Greek, transformed the mental picture of the family and its affairs. The family as such became sacred and constituted the foundation of social life. During the Etrusco-Roman era, the *gens* was the fountainhead of social relationships. Roman Law is a summation of the rights of each individual gens. Each gens (Giulia, Claudia, Cornelia) had its own mythical progenitor, deified hero, Hellenistic prince, or god-like presence on earth, as well as its own household gods (Lares et Penates)[3] and Genius of the House. These divinities were the focus of domestic worship in the home and accompanied the families on journeys in the form of statuettes. There is a fine example of this in the Vettii House in Pompei, where a wall painting shows, in its center, framed by an altar, the Genius of the Master of the House, flanked by the Lares et Penates. At his feet, a snake, symbol of the Earth's fertility, is moving toward an altar laden with various kinds of food. This painting illustrates two fundamental themes: the home as sanctuary and the home as palace. The latter sought to create the illusion of living in a Hellenistic palace—the illusion of a Greek lifestyle—whereas the aim of the former was to celebrate the home as the center of religious worship. The Ara Pacis Augustae in Rome, a remarkable artistic and religious object, also points to the religious significance of the family and its continuity down the centuries.

Thus, the family and the family home became a holy place. The figure of the paterfamilias was central to this concept: The only legitimate children were those which he himself acknowledged, and only the paterfamilias could run for political office. Legitimate children could be adoptive as well as biological, and even freed slaves could be added to the family tree with full legal and moral rights. When this happened, they were duty-bound to worship the ancestors of the house.[4]

Everyone belonging to the *gens* shared tasks relating to religious worship, feasts, and festivals, just as they shared obligations toward each member of the gens when the need arose. In this way, the gens exercised material and religious power over its members and the people associated it (*liberti* and *clientes*). Moreover, it was the *gentes* that ruled the city of Rome and even the Empire.

---

[3] The *Penates* took their name from the word for pantry (*penus*), a symbolical indication of the sustenance they gave to the family. Offerings of salt and spelt were made to them. The religious core of the Roman family included the notion of some mythical ancestor, belief in generative and protective presences (the Lares and the Genius), and the expectation that basic needs of life would be satisfied (the Penates).

[4] It should be remembered that the word *family* derives from *famulus* and includes all the slaves and servants subject to the authority of the paterfamilias and matron. There is a fine example in the Sutoria Primigenia House in Pompei, where a painting shows an entire family that has come together to eat in a food-filled kitchen. The matron is in the center, surrounded by family members with their hands raised as a sign of devout participation in the ceremonial event.

On one hand, then, the notion of genealogy (for which the Romans had a genuine passion) became increasingly tied to the family as such; on the other, those looking to enhance their social standing either by amassing wealth or by waging war had to boost the status of their family tree by finding some mythical or otherwise exemplary ancestor. This gens-induced change in family culture also generated alliances and power struggles between families, as happened with Ancient Rome's patrician families and, later, the families of the European princes who for centuries fought to be elected pope. Sixteenth and seventeenth century painting offers countless examples of popes surrounded by members of their families who have been appointed to important religious and social positions. One is Titian's portrait of Pope Paul III Farnese with his grandchildren; another is Bugiardini's portrait of Leo X de'Medici.

There is another aspect of family life in Ancient Rome that interests us here, namely the dowry given to the woman by her paterfamilias (the origin of "patrimony"). Getting married was, first and foremost, a duty on the part of each citizen, but a woman could become a bride only if she possessed a dowry. This was an inflexible principle in exchanges between families, but it also guaranteed the woman's power. She had the same status as a man in the law of succession (i.e., the naming of heirs) and could dispose of her goods as she wished. Marital love, where it existed, was expressed through the respect, willingness to help each other, and loving friendship that had already been described by Homer. However, sexual desire was unseemly and had always to be kept at bay. According to Veyne (1985), the Roman era saw a shift from morality founded on citizens' rights to an internalized morality based on the private life of the couple, although it should be noted that this happened precisely because women were accorded greater power and social prestige. Moralists of the day claimed, for example, that by learning to put up with the character defects and changing moods of their wives, husbands would be able to cope better with the adversities of life. A good wife was also important for a successful career in politics.

We have seen how the Roman family corresponded to the gens, the broadly constituted domestic unit headed by the paterfamilias and symbolized by its mythical ancestors. However, the gens was also one with the social structure of the time, and therefore easily confused with it. Deciding where the family ended and the outside world began is no easy task, therefore.

THE CHRISTIAN INFLUENCE ON FAMILY LIFE

The family as we now understand it—a distinct entity emerging clearly from its social background, and composed mainly of married couples and their children—started to appear in the 12th century as the domestic social unit gradually detached itself from the social community and began asserting its independence. More specifically, it was the value of the married couple that became—albeit slowly, and with no true equality of the sexes—the linchpin of the modern concept of the family. Moreover, for several centuries the family successfully combined the two distinct concepts of "living under the same roof" and "living under the same head of household." That this social definition of the family was still valid in the mid-18th century can be seen from definitions of "family" in the English dictionaries current at that time. For example, Johnson (1755) defined "family" as "1. Those who live in the same house; household. 2. Those that descend from one common progenitor; a race; a tribe; a generation. 3. A course of descent; a genealogy. 4. A class; a tribe; a species."

According to Herlihy (1985), as early as the High Middle Ages, kinship ties were more clearly defined and families, both rich and poor, obeyed (more or less) the same sexual and household rules, although rich families were always larger and more complex than poor ones. By this time, monogamy, exogamy, and the end of slavery, all of which were championed by the Church, had narrowed the range of variation that characterized families in the societies of the Ancient World. Based on precepts of the Old and New Testaments, the rules were as follows: A husband's duties to his wife take precedence over his duties toward his parents, although he is obliged to respect his parents and help when the need arises; the family estate remains in the father's hands until his death; sexuality is synonymous with the duty to reproduce; marriage is monogamous and eternal; divorce is prohibited except when the wife is unfaithful to her husband.

Underlying this new similarity between families of different social classes is the Pauline family model. The family, and the man–woman relationship especially, acquired a new sacrality based on the analogy of Christ's relationship with His Church. What now guided the family was a principle of love (*charis*): "So also ought men to love their wives as their own bodies. He that loveth his wife, loveth himself" (Eph. 5:28, King James Version).

There was, however, another way in which the Church promoted the idea of the holiness of the family: the representation and worship of the Holy Family in which the Madonna and Child were obviously the center of attention. The Holy Family had already been depicted on sarcophagi and in mosaics of the 4th and 5th centuries (there is a stunning example in Santa Maria Maggiore in Rome), but the practice really took hold in the stained glass windows of European cathedrals, the paintings of Giotto and other unknown artists of the 13th and 14th centuries, and then right up to the 17th century through such painters as Beato Angelico, Piero della Francesca, Filippo Lippi, Hans Memling, Benozzo Gozzoli, Giorgione, Tintoretto, Georges de la Tour, and many others.

What happened to the notion of offspring and the male–female relationship with the advent of Humanism and the Renaissance? One indication comes from the typically Florentine "family books" that many historians have pored over. These were domestic record books in which the father also noted down "remembrances"—concern about offspring and their moral behavior was as constant a worry as the family's economic affairs. There was real passion here—passion for the continuity of the family, now represented by the family name—so there was also an impelling need to pass on to future generations everything that might help the family group to survive, starting with precise knowledge of its shared ancestry and progenitors. The family's origins were researched and genealogies were carefully drawn up. In short, the past was reconstructed and reinvented; even commoners tried to trace their family trees back to ancient times.

Women figured only marginally in this obsession with genealogy; the maternal line counted for little or nothing compared with the paternal line (patrilineage). In other words, women were not worth recording because the core (soul) of household was male, not female! However, the household that people actually lived in was not a genealogical House with its constraints and ideals (family name and honor). As Klapisch-Zuber (1985) points out, more than the traditional rules regarding the separation of sexes and roles were needed to handle relationships effectively. At home, people showed themselves as they really were, and there were frequent crises in marital and kinship relations. A whole range of shifting sentiments was involved, and it was these that the family books (written by males!) lingered over most.

So we have to take into account the relationship between family ideals and family life; although they may well have been complementary, they were also a source of much antagonism. We also need to take into account different kinds of family organization. Although it was rich families that left us records of what they were like, it is also possible to know something about other types of family. The variety of different family organizations is not a prerogative of the present days.

There were, for example, during the period in European history we are considering, not only patrilinear families organized to safeguard the family patrimony, but also families organized in such a way that their goods could be shared among their children. In the former, the guiding principles were upholding unity and hierarchy and, as Alberti (1960) well demonstrates, restricting the claims of descendants over the sharing of the inheritance, which was either handed down in its entirety to a single heir (who also, however, inherited well-defined obligations toward other family members) or shared out among a small number of heirs. There were also families consisting of people who worked as share-croppers, artisans, and even as occasional laborers, which only goes to show that owning or not owning property—and the type of property involved—did not always mean the same thing.

The size of the family depended on demographic, economic, aspirational, and circumstantial factors. For example, from studies of the famous land register of 1427, Herlihy (1985) has shown that countrywomen and wealthy townswomen had more children than both poor and middle-class townswomen, indicating that the latter were more likely to use contraceptive methods or have abortions. The reasons for having numerous offspring were obviously different: Poorer families wanted to increase their working resources, whereas the chief concern of wealthier, middle-class families was to produce enough children to ensure the continuation of the family line.

FAMILY PAINTINGS: RELIGIOUS AND SECULAR VIEWS

It is at this point that family portraits come to our aid in reconstructing how families have been perceived across the centuries. It is no accident that family portraits began to appear in the 16th century and became increasingly important over the following centuries, offering glimpses of major relational changes within the larger family relationship, as well as some of the crucial themes inherent in the family relationship. Naturally, our approach to these paintings will not be that of the art critic or historian; our aim is to gauge emotional and ideational changes in relation to family size.[5]

Maerten van Heemskerck's, *Family Portrait* (c. 1530) was one of the first family portraits.[6] As we have seen, the date is not accidental because the family as a social entity comprising parents and children achieved autonomous definition through a lengthy process of cultural and social development, and it was only at this particular stage in the process that it became possible to portray the family as a distinct object.

The father, in patrician attire and holding a goblet of wine, is looking directly at the viewer. On the table in front of him there is food (bread, fruit, cheese) and a number of other objects, a veritable still life, in fact. To his left, in the center of the painting, a boy and girl are smiling as they play with some grapes. On the right, her eyes averted as a sign of humility, the mother is dandling a naked baby with golden curls, who is holding a small cross in his right hand.

---

[5] See Cigoli (1998–2000) *Quadri di famiglia. Dalla pittura romana alla pittura del Novecento*, privately produced educational CD. By "family painting" we mean a representation of the family in its totality, not the married couple or the mother–child couple.

[6] To see the family paintings cited in this chapter, see:
 1. "Family portrait": http://www.artunframed.com/heemskerck.htm
 2. "George Clive and his Family with an Indian Maid": http://www.artrenewal.org/asp/database/art.asp?aid=406
 3. "The Acrobat family": http://www.konstmuseum.goteborg.se/
 4. "The Bellelli Family": http://www.musee-orsay.fr/ORSAY/orsayNews/Collec.nsf/0/0189f3699e905a39c1256c320036e770?OpenDocument
 5. "Pine tree on the seashore ": http://www.artonline.it/xx_opera.asp?IDOpera=1149
 6. "Family scene": http://www.arts-studio.com/cgi-bin/shop/botero.cgi?page=3
 7. "Madonna and Child with St John": http://www.louvre.fr/louvrea.htm
 8. "Madonna and Child": http://www.abcgallery.com/M/murillo/murillo.html
 9. "The Great Picture": http://www.open.ac.uk/Arts/a220/greatpic.htm

The first thing one notes is that family fertility is one of the major themes of the painting—the children occupy the center of the canvas, although it is the father, as the true originator of the family, who holds the viewer's attention. However, there is something more important, namely the shift of sacredness from the divine (the Holy Family) to the human. The child with golden curls is the Infant Jesus transported from the crib to the family, and the sentiment of sacrifice (the goblet of wine and the bread on the table recall the sacrifice of Christ) has also been transferred to the family relationship.

As the cult of the Infant Jesus took hold in mid-15th-century Florence, the male child became the object of special reverence and sentimental devotion. This is not to say that the Infant Jesus had attracted no special attention in earlier centuries; rather, the sentiment became deeply rooted and acquired the central role in perceptions of the family.

In the following century, Peter Paul Rubens, Jacob Jordaens, Frans Hals, and Anthony van Dyck would introduce the notion of family value. Their portraits are either snapshots of family life or celebrations of family life based on the lives of the artists' own families. However, the striking thing about these portraits is the fact that, for the first time, the eyes of both father and children are focused on the woman-mother. Direction of gaze and gesture, and the positioning of figures inside rooms, are crucially important pictorial codes indicating how the work of art should be interpreted. Here, it might be appropriate to speak of a shift from the "holy family" and the father of the family to the "woman-mother of the family" who is the recipient of both religious devotion and affective attention.

In Joshua Reynolds's *George Clive and His Family With an Indian Maid* (1773), the setting is a typically middle-class interior—note the brocade chair that Clive, in meditative mood despite his full-dress uniform, is leaning on—and the landscape in the background shows that Clive possesses a large estate. The mother and daughter are looking out of the painting at the viewer, while the husband-father is looking at his wife. The mother is gently fondling her daughter's chin, and the daughter is dressed as a princess, as if she is being displayed as a precious object. We have a clear shift of focus here. The family's possessions are certainly important—the family and its estate form a single entity—and the furnishings point to the well-to-do life its members lead, but all this is subordinated or complementary to the beauty of the mother–daughter relationship. And this is what we need to look at because it constitutes the heart of the family relationship. Unfortunately, Clive's daughter died at any early age, making this portrait a painted epitaph of her.

Pablo Picasso's *The Acrobat Family* (1905) centers attention on the mother-son relationship. The son—the true subject of the painting—looks knowingly at the viewer. The acrobat on the edge of the group looks sadly on, grieving at the mother–child relationship, and the monkey—the animal natural element in the painting—is also attracted to and entranced by the mother–child relationship because he knows he will never be the recipient of such a look, such an embrace, such tenderness. So there is a dual lack, that of the acrobat-male and that of the "animal" presence. However, we must look below the surface because its visual message is deceptive.

There is a process of operant identification at work in the painting. Picasso is the acrobat, alienated and alone, like a clown. At the same time, he is a creator of art, and so is in position (as a genius) to vie with the creative power of the female. This sense of envy and competitiveness is present in most of his work, and it is not surprising that depictions of the family are a constant, even obsessive realization of this idea. The monkey is also Picasso: It represents the sexual drive that certainly has little use for the tenderness that characterizes the looks exchanged between mother and child.

Thus, *felt life* (here, a challenge to the creative power of the female), and the belief that genius is "visited" by creative power and merely translates what it receives into a work of art, become the center of attention. The same experience of affection is central to Edgar Degas's celebrated *The Bellelli Family* (1859), a family portrait that explores the theme of marital conflict. In the center of the painting, one of the artist's two daughters seems caught up in the tension between her father and mother. She is looking at her father, who has his back to the viewer, while her mother, standing behind her, is looking out from the painting but not directly at the viewer, like a Renaissance noblewoman. Degas successfully conveys both the crisis of the married couple (the impossibility of looking at the same thing at the same time) and the blameless suffering of children who find themselves caught up in marital–parental conflict.

The turn of the 20th century saw a veritable upsurge in family painting in which the experiences of the artist—his feelings and emotions—were increasingly the center of attention. In one extreme case, Carlo Carrà's *Pine Tree on the Seashore* (1921), we have a family portrait in which the family itself does not even appear. The painting's geometrical and expressive values are those of Giotto. At first glance, one is aware of normal places (a house) and normal actions (hanging out the washing), but there is something disturbing about the scene. The pine tree is missing a branch, and the mouth of a cave yawns between a dark mountainside and an equally dark sea. The painter's family was mourning the death of a son (the broken-off branch), so the landscape puts forth its feelings of emptiness and grief.

Family painting went out of fashion around the mid-20th century. Having lost its power and representational appeal, the family quitted the stage, although not without one or two last curtain calls. Individualism and mentalism in all their various forms (abstract art, material art, pop art, avant-grade art) now held center stage. Here is one of those last curtain calls.

Botero's *Family Scene* (1969) shows the father seated in the center with his little boy on his knee. Standing behind, towering over him, is the mother. On the father's left there is a huge cat, and on his right, a baby girl in a pushchair.

Irony makes its presence felt through exaggerated size (everyone and every-thing in the painting has the right to be represented, and is therefore *big*) and the reversal of normal seating and standing arrangements. The father is now in charge of nurture and affection, whereas the mother, in the dominant standing position, is authoritative and watchful. Another change is that fidelity is no longer a part of the family relationship: Cats are notoriously independent, self-centered, and unfaithful. Finally, there is a difference between the son and the daughter: The son is weaker and needs care and protection, whereas the daughter seems to have been able to manage on her own right from the start.

Our brief survey of family painting, and what constitutes the central fea-ture of each painting we cited, has touched on some of the crucial relational changes in the modern family from its beginnings through to (almost) the present day. At first, father, mother, and children basked in an aura of holiness emanating from the male child especially (the image of the Infant Jesus). Later, the woman-mother was idealized (conceptualized) as the member of the holy family who served as the center of gravity for both her husband and children. Later still, the father-husband was gradually ousted by the affective dyad of mother and son, a situation already anticipated in representations of the Holy Family in which Joseph is always placed a step behind the holy couple of mother and child. The importance of human affection increased even as the holiness of the family relationship was relegated to the background. Irony was also used to demythicize the family relationship and record unforeseen changes such as reversals of roles, resulting in a dominant woman and a father devoted to the heart's affections.

The matrifocal family, the centrality of the (male) child, and the predomi-nance of the female axis led to the modern situation in which the family has lost its representational and symbolic importance in painting. To be sure, families still appear in paintings, but they have less symbolic weight and no ritual valence. The portrayal is more story-based, more consumerist, suggest-ing a new form of exchange between the family and consumer products rather than between the family and society. Today the family is as much a ubiquitous player on the mass-media stage (especially TV and advertising) as it is the prime marketing target for an infinite range of products. However, there is another art form—cinema—in which family relationships are presented and explored, and we have to take account of its insights if we are to understand the truths and falsehoods, dramas and resources, of the modern family.[7]

We end our brief historical excursus with two observations. The first con-cerns the family subject as a Western social structure. Portrayed as it is today, as a social entity with clearly defined borders, the family is the outcome of a

---

[7]See Centro Studi e Ricerche sulla Famiglia (2000), *La famiglia tra le generazioni*, a privately produced educational video. Regarding the use of movies in clinical practice, see Dermer and Hutchings, 2000.

long process of differentiation from the society in which it is immersed. For centuries it could not be portrayed as a distinct, separate object because, rather than a figure on a ground, it constituted the actual fabric of the ground itself.

The second is that, from the *household*—the paternally led domestic and social unit, variously composed of relatives and servants in which the modern idea of privacy was totally unknown—we see a gradual and wholly nonlinear shift to the *house*—a domestic and economic unit consisting of a father, a mother (with an unequal role and position), their children, and the father's family of origin. In time, the father's family of origin would gradually be excluded from the picture, to the obvious benefit of the married couple and its special relationship with its children. The modern family was born, and with it the child-centered home whose borders are determined by affective inclusion and exclusion.

As Ariès (1960/1962) has clearly shown, modern family sentiment was and is bound up with a new idea of childhood as a specific stage in life calling for affective as well as economic investment. Children have become "special" in some way, whereas before they were miniature adults or (as they were portrayed in art) miniature human beings lacking male/female differentiation.

Let us return to the concept of the child for a moment. Looking at 14th- and 15th-century paintings, one notices that otherwise highly competent painters, perfectly capable of painting adults and old people, have problems in representing the Infant Jesus, who seems awkward, out of proportion, and even ugly. Inasmuch as technique is not at issue, this must obviously have been a mental problem of representation. On one hand, this can be referred to the reduced mental space reserved to the child. On the other hand, this can be referred to the taking shape of the divine by the human beings. The solution to the problem will be found afterwards, so that the child, pictorially speaking, becomes more and more beautiful—in a word, perfect, as in Raphael's *Madonna and Child with St. John* (1516) and Murillo's *Madonna and Child* (1650).[8]

It is impossible not to be aware of the crucial representational and relational importance of the Holy Family—the adoration of the Infant Jesus and the Mother-Madonna—in Western culture. In other cultures, however, the mother–child couple simply does not have the same importance. In African cultures and the Inuit culture of North America, when a child (*not* a baby!) is born, its soul-name has to be *sought,* sometimes with the aid of a shaman. Certain questions are asked. Which ancestor inhabits the child's body? What does it expect? Is this ancestor male or female (Héritier, 1996)? In these and other cultures, one might well ask if anything like a theory of attachment, for

---

[8] In Florence, the Uffizi and Palazzo Pitti (Europe's most magnificent court in the 16th and 17th centuries) house a remarkable series of masterpieces illustrating the progression from awkwardness to perfection in representing the Infant Jesus. Dutch and Flemish painters would later bestow pictorial dignity on lower- and middle-class children.

example, could ever be produced. Although attachment theory is said to have a sound biological–evolutionary foundation, that is, a natural foundation shared by the entire species of *homo sapiens* to whom the concept of mind applies, it is in fact a product of Western culture and its need for a secure base founded on the mother–child relationship. In short, the secure base of the family relationship is founded in other countries on equal exchange between families, or on the beneficial presence of an ancestor whose soul has come to dwell in the newly born child.

In Western culture, as we saw in our readings of what the people in family portraits are looking at, affective centering occurred gradually and increasingly involved the mother and child. By contrast, the father's importance waned, and he was increasingly depicted as a man who either admires or envies the exclusive and all-excluding mother–child relationship.

There was also a radical change in the couple relationship, in the sense that feelings became increasingly important even as the authority and protection provided by the man-husband-father decreased in importance. Mitchell (2002) observes that the spread of romantic married love based on sexual passion and a sense of uniqueness was linked to the idea that one's own children were special, giving rise to the conjecture that the pathologies of adult love reenact the vicissitudes of the original romantic love that bound parents and children to each other. As we shall see, the modern family carries this affective tendency to its logical extreme.

However, the family may be viewed not only as a social structure, with all of its particular forms and boundaries, but also as a cultural–symbolic entity. It is artistic and cultural tradition (mythological and pictorial), and language and etymology, that help us most in the search for the symbolic core of the family down the ages. Unlike the social perspective, which highlights changes in the form of the family, the cultural–symbolic perspective, which is complementary to it, reveals key themes and invariants common to different kinds of family, even those far removed from each other in time. We believe that this perspective helps us to understand not only Western culture, but also other cultures that globalization is increasingly bringing into contact with ours.

These invariants are related to the concepts of the male–female function (*gender*) and ancestry (*ghenos*). We find it in the bustling life of the Greek Pantheon, the mythical progenitors of the Roman world, the holy family of the Middle Ages, and the Renaissance family's search for genealogical authentication. Gender and generation are etymologically related, so that, semantically, the family includes both differentiation (male / female gender) and belonging/ dependence (offspring and genealogy).

We have already noted the importance of the *hereditary line* and patrimonial transmission that bind and span the generations on which not only male-paternal but also female-maternal identity are founded. Once again, etymology (semantic rooting) is extremely important: matrimony (*matri-munus*, i.e., the bride's dowry) is the alter-ego of patrimony (*patris-munus,* i.e., the goods handed down from father to son). It could well be said that the family is based on exchanges of maternal and paternal gifts and duties (*munus* refers both to gifts and to the duty to defend).

One especially fine example of the passion for lineage and inheritance is the triptych commissioned from the Flemish artist Jan van Belcamp by Lady Anne Clifford, depicting nothing less than a family feud over legal recognition of hereditary rights. In the center panel of the *Great Picture,* we see the noble couple and, on the wall behind them, pictures of their ancestors. The mother is gesturing toward her elder son and heir, who is standing in front of his younger brother. The elder son is holding up to view a shield bearing the family tree. Because they are still in their infancy, both sons are wearing girls' clothes, as was then the custom. The right to assert one's gender by, among other ways, wearing male or female clothes, was granted only later in life. As we have seen, it is as if young children lived in a sort of *undifferentiated* state. At the time the picture was painted, all the people in it were already dead, but they live on in the cross-generational story it tells.

In the left-hand panel, we see Lady Anne at the age of 15, dressed as a noblewoman like her mother in the center panel. Near her there is a lute, and behind her, on the wall, there are pictures of her tutors and teachers, together with books whose titles can be read on their spines. Also behind her is the shield bearing the family tree. The message of the picture is now clear: Not only is this woman an aristocrat, she is also well educated and more than a match for any man!

Lady Anne also appears in the right-hand panel, dressed in mourning and pointing to a legal document. A small dog is scrabbling at her skirt. Behind her are two pictures of the husbands she has had. One is dead; the other she has already left after a deeply disappointing relationship. Lady Anne commissioned the triptych to mark the successful outcome of a long legal battle to be recognized as the faithful and legitimate heir of her family, which on the death of its male children bequeathed its goods to a male cousin. Nothing was able to shake her resolve, not even a civil war (the Thirty Years' War).

However, gender distinctions in the exercise of hereditary rights are a feature of many cultures. For example, the Koran gives precedence to certain women in the family nucleus (widows, mothers, grandmothers), but when they find themselves competing with men of the same degree of kinship they are held to the rule that men must inherit twice the amount that is allowed to women.

We have seen how, in more recent times, these themes carry over into the structure of the modern family, in which the figure of the woman-mother, closely bonded to her child, became increasingly important despite her socially disadvantaged role. This mother–child dyad created more room for affection, compared with the older dominance of the paternal line based on genealogy and inheritance.

Finally, we saw that, in our own time, a new way of portraying the family has ousted older forms of pictorial–symbolic representation. The family is now most often represented as a focus of consumer culture, and its internal life is more likely to be narrated in films than in paintings. In short, the descriptive–emotive code has won out over the ritual–symbolic code, and it is certainly no accident that narrative approaches are becoming increasingly prevalent in family psychotherapy.

So what has become of the symbolic aspects of the family? Later in this book we see that they have not died out; they now lead a *latent existence* within the lifestyles of our own times, and it is there that we shall have to track them down.

MODERN TIMES: NEW REPRESENTATIONS OF THE FAMILY

Changes in the form and function of families can be studied with the benefit of hindsight and distance, but it is more difficult to see what the important trends are in the families of today. What one notices most is that the family exists in a wide variety of forms, and that the Western family is both rarefied, and poorly defined in the sense that its boundaries seem to be shifting all the time (Rossi, 2003). It is becoming increasingly difficult to say who belongs to the family, who is inside, and who is outside. In particular, it is easy to see today's family as a private, affective–communicative entity, a structure based entirely on communication and insecurely anchored in society, as Luhmann (1982) maintains.

Doherthy, Boss, LaRossa, Schumm, and Steinmetz's (1993) interesting survey of changes in the American family over the last century adopts a contextual perspective, which is fine as far as it goes. The problem is that unless such surveys are in turn contextualized within a framework that draws attention to the cultural matrices and meanings of the family relationship, the inevitable outcome is merely an increasingly detailed and idiosyncratic description of the family itself. Thus, although the features that characterize each form of family, or at worst, each individual family, are clear enough, the danger, as the authors themselves acknowledge, is that the similarities and commonalities of families are lost.

The theoretical and methodological approach we describe in the next chapter enables us to relate changes in the family relationship to large-scale shifts in meaning that we see as occurring—and here lies the difference—along a shared tripartite axis: the relations between genders, generations, and lineages, and between trust, hope, and justice. We attempt to interpret the present—despite the difficulties inherent in belonging to the present ourselves—through a survey of contemporary cultural trends that entail redefinitions of female-maternal and male-paternal function, and the meaning of genealogy in relation to descendants (children) and families of origin. We focus on new features of marital and parental relationships and how these relationships link back to previous generations.

The modern Western couple is feeling the effects of major demographic changes, including a fall in the number of marriages,[9] a rise in the frequency of cohabitation, and an increase in the number of separations. These phenomena, which are more common in the West than in other parts of the world, with especially high percentages in Northern Europe and the United States, testify to a general weakening of the marital bond that has a variety of causes and ultimately derives from a radical long-term change in the concept of the marital bond itself.

In the past, marriage was the outcome of an alliance between families, who played an active part in choosing the partners to the marriage. Later, especially in middle-class society, it became a pathway to social success and higher social status. Today, marriage is basically a question of emotional self-fulfillment. Families based on blood ties, and therefore the solidarity of shared kinship, have been ousted by families based on the sentimental/affective bond that originates in and with the partners who form the couple. The influence of families of origin no longer occupies the foreground, although in our view this does not mean that these families are any less important, merely less visible.

In short, the couple now takes precedence over the married state. The social aspect of the marital bond is less important within the couple relationship, and the partners tend to inhabit a totally private space free of kinship and sociocultural ties. Getting married today often means living with another person—a he or she who satisfies one's sentimental and affective needs—rather than constructing a "we" through a relationship based on the realization of a shared project. This mentality is an expression of a cultural climate that emphasizes individual rights and self-fulfillment at the expense of the obligations inherent in the marital bond (Doherthy, 1995).

Thus, on one hand, there is massive investment in the couple relationship, in the expectation that the forms of sharing and understanding the partners enter into will affect all aspects of their life together. On the other, the social and institutional aspect of the bond is weakening, with the result that the couple is becoming self-referential. The modern married couple is so fragile because it is based on high hopes that are all too easily dashed, and because it tips the scales in favor of affective self-fulfillment rather than the ethical aspects of marriage and commitment to the marriage vows.

The price the couple pays for this weakening of ties is an ever-present feeling of precariousness, and the fact that the partners are always able to choose

---

[9] It should be remembered that today's plummeting marriage rate marks the end of a relatively brief cycle in Western society, lasting around a century (1870–1970), that could be described as the golden age of marriage. Until the second half of the 19th century, marriage was by no means the most common choice because for both the man and the woman (in the form of her dowry) it called for a minimum of money and other physical resources that were not available to everyone.

someone else adds an uncertainty to their lives that only increases the fear of commitment. Quite often, marital partners will say right from the start that their commitment to each other will not necessarily be permanent, and when the couple first forms, they are already asking each other how long their relationship will last. Even psychology—as much a part of the cultural climate as it is an influence on it—has come to support the idea of a family life cycle in which divorce is just one of many stages (McGoldrick, Heiman, & Carter, 1993), describing as "long-term" those couples who remain committed to their relationship.

To summarize, the high expectations partners have of each other, plus a relaxation of social control and a general search for personal well-being, mean that today's couples are much more likely to question and reformulate their commitment to each other than in the past. The result is a steady increase in the frequency of divorce and, in most cases, families in which the mother, for cultural reasons, is almost always awarded custody of the children. Separation results either in single-parent families (usually a woman and her children), especially in Southern European countries like Italy and Spain, or in several different families (stepfamilies), especially in Northern Europe and the United States. Both outcomes, each with its own challenges and problems, end up exalting the female-maternal figure and denigrating male-paternal figure. This situation would seem to be the outcome of a long cultural process that we have tried to reconstruct in our survey of family relationships and family painting.

In stepfamilies, the maternal figure is a stable and ongoing presence, whereas the paternal function is shared by several male figures (the noncohabiting biological father and the cohabiting stepfather) whom the children have to learn to cope with. By contrast, in mother-led single-parent families, where the woman-mother remains the more dominant (and the weariest) of the two original partners, the male figure is weaker and sometimes even absent altogether. Moreover, women are more likely to turn to their families of origin (the maternal line) for support when they find themselves alone and short of money, and living in precarious economic and relational circumstances. As for separated fathers, psychosocial studies have clearly shown that they become increasingly unreliable in providing economic support for their families and in fulfilling their obligations toward their children. That said, it should be remembered that the pain of divorce turns some men into more conscientious fathers.

So, the once all-important father and paternal line now pales in comparison with the dominance of the mother and the maternal line. As many studies have shown, this matrifocal shift in genealogical dominance is a feature not only of broken families, but of modern families in general, and is linked to the massive importance of the sentimental/affective dimension within the modern family.[10]

---

[10] Matrifocal families are also common among the poor in many countries, especially in Latin America. The matrifocal family has its "rich" and "poor" forms, so to speak.

In Western culture, emotions and feelings have been regarded as the normal, if not exclusive, preserve of the female-maternal figure. We could say, then, that family culture has gradually placed a greater value on affects even as it has correspondingly downgraded the value of commitment and ties. Establishing a harmony between values remains the abiding challenge.

However, within this social panorama where couples are increasingly fragile and ever more likely to succumb to the trend toward self-fulfillment, it should also be noted that, paradoxically enough, the couple is now much more of a social yardstick than it ever was in the past. In line with the significant increase in the average age of the population, the lifetime of the couple has also been extended, especially into the period of senior citizenship that few couples ever reached in the past. Moreover, the couple has inevitably become the clearinghouse for tasks that were once allocated to and distributed throughout extended families. In particular, the couple is now entrusted with transmitting fundamental life values to the next generation, a task for which society at large no longer feels responsible. Finally, despite the increased frequency of separation and divorce in all Western countries, numerous studies have shown that, for young people especially, marriage remains a highly desirable ideal and adult life is usually envisaged within a couple relationship.

Today's social trends also reveal contradictory attitudes to parenting. Demographic statistics show that there has been a significant population decrease since the middle of the last century, so much so that some countries, especially in Southern Europe (with Italy in the lead), have fallen far below the population replacement rate. This is causing not a few problems in terms of social cohesion and the transfer of wealth from one generation to the next, as the West's looming pension problem more than demonstrates. All this points to the inevitable effects that family relationships have on society and the short-sightedness of an approach that limits them to the purely private sphere. The limitations of interactive–contextual and narrative (script-based) models of family relationships are also revealed. Genealogy and its issues—relations between generations and genealogical lines—are proof that family relationships run very deep. They can never be concealed and should never be overlooked.

The falling birth rate might initially be interpreted as a sign that children are now seen as less important, but as many studies have shown, the opposite is the case. In fact, Europeans attach great importance to their children and see the bond they establish with them as the closest and longest lasting of any they are likely to experience in their lives. At a time when the marital bond is weakening, and in a society where guidelines for conduct are becoming increasingly blurred and uncertain, the filial bond is the only one that still represents a reliable ongoing investment (Théry, 1998). Thus, the reliability of the filial bond seems to have made up for the weakness of the couple bond.

This is an authentic cultural and mental reversal. The couple's strength and stability no longer lead as a matter of course to the generation of children;

instead, they have been transferred to the relationship that each parent individually establishes with the child. The extreme and most symptomatic stage in this trend is reached when couples deliberately wait for a child to be born before legalizing their union. When this happens, it is the child that institutes the couple bond, in the sense that the couple arranges and activates itself around the child, to which it is subordinate. Freud (1914) spoke of "her majesty the baby," borrowing the title of a famous painting showing a nanny pushing a pram and two policemen making a way for her through a busy London street. He saw the adored child as representative "here, on earth" of its parents' narcissism. Children, he saw, were unaffected by social rules; they are fondled and protected. Later, as psychoanalysis would make abundantly clear, he saw that there was another side to the coin—children who are raped, abused, corrupted, and incited to commit evil by adults (Miller, 1991). And yet, the generational hierarchy was never at issue. For better or for worse, the child was desired and expected. But when an adult sees the child as the founder and not a product of the couple, the generational hierarchy is inverted.

Thus, "the logic of the child" is becoming increasingly more important than couple and family logic. In this view, the newborn baby is more likely to represent the parents' desire for paternity and maternity respectively (the experience each must have) than the production of a new generation that will have its own place in history—the issue of a couple that feels a link with preceding generations and a clear responsibility for the future of the family and society.

So there has been a remarkable change in the representation of the child, basically due to the decreasing importance of family genealogy, with the attendant loss of the generational implications of having children, and the partners' insistence on self-fulfillment as the most important aspect of procreation. This is certainly amplified by the crucial fact that procreation can now be chosen and controlled. As a result, the child is as much an eagerly awaited event, offering its parents the experience of a unique relationship, as it is the mother's competitor and a threat to her eventual self-fulfillment (as is shown not only by current abortion rates, but also by numerous studies of the time and opportunity women need to have children).

For centuries, the birth of a child was experienced as a natural event that was little understood and therefore could not be controlled. Moreover, infant mortality and the mother's death in childbirth had always been a tragic aspect of the family relationship. Today's possibility of being able to choose not only to have children, but also to program them and monitor the development of the fetus, seems a new and significant social development. Also, the limits and range of procreative choice seem to be extending at an increasing rate, as is shown by ever more frequent recourse to assisted conception in order to have a child "at any cost" and thereby satisfy the parents' desires. Not surprisingly, people envisage—and films actually depict—a future in which parents can choose the sex, physical features, and mental characteristics of their children (see, e.g.,

Andrew Niccol's film *Gattaca* [1997], which explores end-of-millennium genetic angst).

Through genetic engineering, the biological aspect of birth has become the predominant one; meanwhile, on the relational plane, the doctor who possesses information about the birth, and is in a position to unveil its mysteries, has assumed a quite remarkable prominence. Thus do new possibilities, new mythologies, and new family dramas develop and feed off one another.

With regard to procreation, then, we have moved from a situation of impotence (infertility) on one hand and destiny (the woman who does not marry fails to achieve her destiny) on the other, to a situation in which destiny itself may be challenged and controlled. The falling birth rate, and the fact that the birth of a child can be deliberately chosen and therefore strongly desired, means that a child is like a highly concentrated emotional distillate. Parents end up investing too much in the few children they bring into the world, and this may become a problem for the children themselves because they feel they have to live up to their parents' high expectations of them and the extremely self-critical image they, the children, have of themselves. Their self-image unwittingly incorporates their parents' yearning for self-fulfillment, which they find rather more difficult to extricate themselves from. It may also affect the kind of upbringing they receive.

One symptomatic example of the child's importance within the family is the "ongoing family"—the fact that children go on living with their families for much longer than they did in the past. The phenomenon is widespread in Europe, especially in the South, but is also becoming increasingly widespread in the United States (Cherlin, Scabini, & Rossi, 1997), where an increasing percentage of children return to live with their parents after finishing university in some distant city. A new kind of family is emerging, based on the cohabitation of two adult generations within the same family.

This phenomenon could be seen as a prolonged form of *neoteny*,[11] in the sense that the period of time children are looked after by their parents until they are considered able to fend for themselves is growing longer and longer. Thus, despite society's current emphasis on independence and self-fulfillment, young people are defined, paradoxically enough, by the fact of being children, a condition that they and their parents actively choose and experience as being beneficial to all concerned. Young people see their families of origin as oases of security and reliability within the wider context of problem-fraught social relationships and uncertain couple relationships. Parents are, in turn, gratified by this prolongation of the parental function through which their need for affective self-fulfillment finds expression, despite the insecurity they feel as a

---

[11] Here *neoteny* means the slowing down of species development typical of *homo sapiens*. It is because of this slowing down that human beings attach so much importance to the physical, intellectual, and spiritual care of their young.

couple. It also helps them keep at bay the danger of finding themselves living in an "empty nest" and having to hand over responsibility to the next generation.

The child–parent bond is also crucially important to the way adult generations relate to each other. With today's increase in the average age of the population, middle-aged couples are now responsible for their aging parents for a significant period of their lives and, as their children, are directly involved in taking care of them. Today's adult generations are now sandwiched between their young-adult children and their elderly parents.

Thus, we can see emerging what could be described as an adult multigenerational family, which is in turn a reflection of the multigenerational society we live in. Such families may consist of up to four generations, of which three are fully or almost adult. In this adult-dominated family context, it is easy to see that children—circumscribed as they are by the couple that produced them—are in fact burdened with the weight of several adult generations who have invested in them both effectively and symbolically and perceive them as an element of stability in their lives. Society perceives childhood as a category apart, and children as autonomous subjects with their own rights, whereas the reality of human relationships tells us that they are, in every sense, "children of the family." We have here the typically Western process in which the logic of exchange between families—marriage as the creation of kinship, in which the families of origin have an important say in choosing partners and, more generally, in the life of the new family—has given way to the logic of pairing—marriage as the creation of a couple, in which the two partners accept full responsibility for choosing each other and determining their destiny. This in turn is giving way to the logic of the *child* (marriage as dependence on the birth of a child and commitment to looking after it).

At the present time, the fragility of the couple relationship and massive investment in the child–parent bond make it especially difficult for a new couple and family to create a space–time continuum that enables them to hold simultaneously in their minds the awareness that they belong to previous generations, and the experience of detachment and emancipation that leads to the adventure of being generative in their turn. It has become very difficult to forge a satisfactory link between being generated and generating, between being a husband and a wife, a father and a mother.

Thus, family ties and their significance within the larger community urgently need rethinking in a society of individuals ruled by the myth of independence. Ethnic families cannot be understood without also understanding the symbolic meanings that their mother cultures attribute to gender identity and generational role. However, this does not mean adopting some mistakenly evolutionist perspective—a typical shortcoming of 19th-century cultural anthropology—which sees other peoples' solutions to these problems as less evolved, more "primitive" than our more evolved responses. Theirs, like ours, are an attempt to express the primary family bond and its dramas.

We in the West are inclined to locate other cultures' dramas in the subor-dination of women-mothers to men-fathers and the way children are treated, whereas other cultures tends to see the dramas of our culture in the social separateness of the couple and the lack of support for older generations that comes of our marked individualism. In this sense, trying to understand cultures different from our own may help us to rediscover and rethink the symbolic val-ues that made Western society what it is, but have now assumed new cultural forms that can be difficult to recognize.

The aim, for all concerned, goes far beyond simply trying to find nonviolent ways of living with each other. What really counts is that the symbolic lifeblood that unites genders and generations within the family, and constitutes the humus of civilization itself, is made to flow again.

In Spike Lee's film *The Straight Story,* aging Alvin is on his way to visit his brother Lyle and make peace with him after years of silence, when he meets a young girl who has run away from home. After expressing the hope that her family will find a way of coping with her rather minor problem, he tells her a story. When his children were young, he told them to snap a twig in half, and they all managed to do it. But when he told them to snap a bunch of twigs in half, they could not do it. "And that," he tells her, "is what a family is."

CHAPTER TWO

The Relational–Symbolic Model and Its Principles

CASTING THE NET

The purpose of the previous chapter's journey through time was to show two things. The first is to appreciate the multiple forms and modes of which the family is composed; the second is to appreciate that the family is also a unity that can be distinguished from other forms of social organization. Now that we know something about the water in which the family swims, it is time to cast our net and see what we can find.

Thinking requires an epistemological and methodological foundation. The movement of family therapy developed from fundamental concepts of systemic theory (Cigoli & Galimberti, 1983; Scabini & Cigoli, 1998). Our approach is based on those concepts but, in particular, refers to the thought and method of Morin (1986, 2001). In common with Angyal (1941) and von Bertalanffy (1968), Morin sees the system not as a *deus ex machina* but as a *unitas multiplex* in which system, relationship, and organization are three facets of the same phenomenon. For this system concept to work, interaction is needed, and Morin has devised a tripartite concept of method (i.e., way of producing knowledge) based on the relationship–organization–system triangle that comes into operation during interaction.

We use this tripartite concept to develop our relational–symbolic model of the family. To begin, let us briefly consider the notion that a system is a complex unity. Obviously, there is a paradox here. On one hand, a system is original and unique, in the sense that it has its own irreducible features and qualities; on the other, it is a product that comes into being when its components interact with each other. This means that the whole and the parts have to be simultaneously imagined. Koestler (1978) tried to define this kind of paradox as a *holon,* a sort of two-faced Janus (the Roman god of doorways) that simultaneously displays both its wholeness or unity (*holos*) and its constituent parts (*on*).

This idea of the whole and its parts has a long philosophical pedigree. In his *Poetics*, for example, Aristotle tries to define dramatic action as an entity that he calls *mythos*, citing the dramas of family histories and the way they unfold in tragedy (Dolezel, 1988). In more recent times, Hegel (1821 / 1978) reinstated the concept of an all-embracing unity and located it in both the state and the family, which he called "ethical places."

It is to Gestalt psychology that we owe the concept of the "field theory" that organizes and regulates the processes of action. Köhler and Lewin, two of the pioneers of Gestalt psychology, were well aware that interaction is a form of organization that shapes our perceptions of reality. It is not enough to think of the whole just as a complex unity; we must also be aware of the organizational features that constitute both opportunities for action and constraints on it. For example, the ways in which families are organized can either encourage the individuation of family members, or stifle and suppress it. Family relationships are, in turn, subject to the opportunities and constraints imposed by social relationships. There are numerous examples of political ideologies that have tried to weaken and even destroy the basic ties that bind genders and generations together. The result is not just the stifling of family relationships, but also the social degradation and fragmentation generated by the climate of terror, and incitement to inform on fellow citizens, that is a feature of totalitarian systems.

To summarize, we believe that the net that the tripartite method enables us to cast helps us to think more clearly about family relationships. Now it is time to say exactly what that net consists of. Applying a method to reality requires a conceptual and imaginative leap: It is in the gap between epistemic concept and research object that the researcher's creativity comes into operation. In our view, the epistemic and methodological aspects of a theory should be a source of creative thinking, not a peg to hang concepts and constructs on.

PITCHING THE TENT: THE THREE PRINCIPLES

Now that we have cast our net—the tripartite concept of method that will tell us what we want to know about the family relationship—we can return to shore, pitch our tent, and ask ourselves a number of basic questions. Does the family relationship have an organizational principle? How do "interaction and relationship" relate to each other? Can we pierce the surface of interaction to get at "the pattern which connects" the family relationship (Bateson, 1979)? What is the underlying dynamic that determines whether the family relationship prospers or dies? By answering these questions, we hope to arrive at a definition of *family identity* based on three principles: organizational, symbolic, and dynamic.

The Organizational Principle

As good a starting place as any is Lévi-Strauss's (1967/1969) definition of the family as the more or less lasting, socially sanctioned union of a man, a woman, and their children. The family is a primary social form—primary because it is one of the bases of civilization itself, and because it is a biological, psychological, social, and cultural guarantee that procreation will take place. Lévi-Strauss says that the cultural order enters the natural order through the incest taboo—sexuality becomes part of a social order based on obligatory exchanges of goods with other people, in this case the transfer of women (mothers, sisters, daughters) from one group to another.

The structural–functionalist approach (Parsons & Shils, 1959) also sees the family as a living social system that performs such essential functions as the primary socialization of children and the stabilization of adult life, whereas Sroufe and Fleeson (1988) see the family's basic functions as the raising of children and the satisfaction of such adult needs as intimacy and mutual support.

Broadening this perspective, we see the family as an organization of primary relationships based on three differences: between genders, between generations, and between family lineages. Its aim is generativity. Generating minds and generating ties is what the family function is all about, but this can only happen within the conflict inherent in exchange, which can also spill over into violence.

Attempts are sometimes made to downplay the violence implicit in family relationships by separating the quality of the relationship from its concrete historical actualization in exchanges between generations (Walsh, 1982). But this is wrong. The quality of the relationship that expresses itself through empathy, open communication, coping well with problems, and so on, is not in itself a principle, but merely the outcome of intergenerational exchange, which, with its burden of injustice and violence, can be generative *and* nongenerative, as we have seen. Girard (1972, 2003) says that the origin of violence lies the imitative–mimetic nature of human beings themselves, who contend with each other for possession of various types of goods. Freud (1912) maintained that it began with the killing of the father, the primal act of culture. Both cognitive psychologists and dynamic psychologists see violence as the outcome of frustrated basic needs. Whatever its origin, violence has always been fundamental to exchanges between human beings.

Identifying and interpreting cultural change in the family relationship is another matter entirely, because the relationship itself is Protean. The modern Western family is an organization of kinship ties that prioritizes the marital relationship between two equal partners, and between them and their children, on an affective, matrifocal basis, and with their families of origin on an elective basis. As we have already seen, just a few generations ago the family was based on gender inequality, a rigid sex–marriage–fertility equation, and the father's power over his children. Young children were regarded as undeveloped adults and, therefore, incomplete, imperfect, defective.

Let us now comment briefly on the terms we have used to define the family and its identity. The term *organization* is preferable to "group with a history," or the much more general "system," because, as Buckley (1976) and Morin (1986) have shown, the ability to organize is a fundamental feature of sociocultural systems. The family is an organized system with a hierarchy and an internal structure that interacts purposively with the sociocultural context.

What does the family organize? Relationships, naturally, although not of a general kind. Families organize the primary relationships that connect and bind the crucial differences inherent in human nature — differences of gender, generation, and lineage (on the father's or the mother's side). Such relationships produce a relational commodity — the next generation — that is essential to the human community.

At this stage, it is important to note that the family relationship is also a primary relationship because family members are bonded together as *people*, that is, in the totality and uniqueness of their being and existence, irrespective of the roles and tasks they have to perform. In other words, the person, as a relational being, has an intrinsic value that is not determined by utility value and cannot truly be negotiated, even though this has happened and still happens with striking frequency. But when it does happen, the relationship has assumed a degenerative (or perverse) form.

The two cardinal family relationships are those between the married couple and between parents and children. The marital relationship is based on gender difference, and the term *gender* refers to the sociocultural identity of the male and female sex. Every culture translates sex in the biological sense into a male or female identity, each with its own social and cultural functions and roles. Gender identity is rooted in the family.

Kernberg (1995) maintains that human beings create their male or female identities from the moment of birth onward, when they come to acknowledge gender difference in themselves and others. By contrast, other researchers maintain that, in terms of identity, human beings are originally bisexual, as much male as they are female. According to Aron (1995) and Benjamin (1995), the purpose of original bisexual completeness (an assumed form of mental hyperinclusivity) is to enable children to identify with both genders, male and female, and make them aspects of themselves. This could perhaps be described as a form of omnipotence that the family relationship itself turns into a form of humanization: Gender definition implies the recognition of one's own limits and the needs of others. Gender attributions and behaviors may vary considerably between cultures, but this does not constitute a psychological problem of personal identity. What *does* create a problem, however, is rigid attribution of roles, as happened in the past, and excessive similarity of roles, as happens now.[1]

The marital relationship is structured by and develops through marriage, or matrimony. "Matrimony" derives from the Latin *matri-munus,* that is, the gift (dowry) the woman brings with her when she marries, and also the gift of life she carries. "Matrimony" is a calque of "patrimony," the father's gift. Thus, matrimony (dowry; gift of life) and patrimony (the gift of belonging; the inheritance of goods) are the cornerstones of the family relationship. In our culture, matrimony (marriage) treads the borderline between *pact* and *contract.* The marriage pact–contract is legally sanctioned, that is, witnessed by the community, and while it recognizes the rights of the partners to the marriage, it also imposes a series of obligations. In both cases (rights and obligations), the aim is to lay down constraints that are beneficial to both parties, although the act of doing so can often take on a quite different meaning. We return to this later on.

In Western culture, the family relationship is becoming more of a couple relationship and less of a marital one. In other words, the relationship is increasingly seen as an affective pact between two individuals, and less as the form of transgenerational commitment and constraint that has been a feature of European culture from Judaic and Greco-Roman times and is still a feature of many other cultures. One obvious result of this is that the need for a marriage to be witnessed by the community is less strongly felt. Whereas once the individual counted for very little and lineage counted for very much (procreation was essential for the continuation of lineage), now it is the individual who counts for very much and belonging to the family group that counts for very little.

The kindred–child relationship implies intergenerational difference and the attendant responsibility that earlier generations have toward later ones. Obviously, this means that the kindred–child relationship *has* to be hierarchical because the term "kindred" includes not only the child's biological parents but also the kinship network formed by their relationships with their families of origin. So intergenerational difference includes differences between parents and children *and* differences between the parents' respective family lines that gradually dissipate in time.

Parent–child and kindred–child relationships tend to be perceived in affective rather than ethical terms nowadays. As we have seen, children often find themselves saddled with the task of satisfying adult-parental needs of intimacy. But this does not alter the fact that the incest taboo is the fundamental rule underlying the family relationship. The rule may be stated differently according to which degrees of kinship fall within the prohibition, but the imperative

---

[1] Héritier (1996) cites an interesting example of problematic identity in Inuit culture: sex and gender are opposing poles, as in the case of a male inhabited by the soul of a female ancestor, or vice versa.

remains the same: Unless intergenerational difference is respected, transgenerational renewal collapses, a tragic mess ensues, and personal identity crumbles. However, the incest taboo alone cannot supply the organizing principle of the family relationship. The *caring principle*, that is, accepting responsibility for one's own offspring, is also needed—children have to be acknowledged by the couple-family that generated them so that an intelligible, family-specific relationship of ancestry and descent is created. Adults may also acknowledge children who are not their own, as in adoption, which realizes but also transcends the hitherto thwarted hope, and need, of having children that are one's own flesh and blood.

Thus, acknowledgement and recognition are key aspects of family relationships. They define who belongs to the family and who does not, and give rise to any number of dramas (e.g., unacknowledged or abandoned children, the exclusion or disownment of an heir). Even today, abandoning female children is tragically commonplace in countries like China, where Confucianism states that only the male child has the task of remaining loyal to his family's ancestors by generating offspring.

The danger inherent in today's increasing use of heterologous assisted reproduction is that it will create new forms of disownment because these techniques make it difficult, if not impossible, for a child and at least one of its parents to know what the true family lineage is. Reproduction of this sort is creating an upheaval in family relationships whose consequences are difficult to predict. In our view, assisted reproduction gives voice to the recurring fantasy within families of being able to breed in isolation, independently of previous generations and even of the opposite sex.

In today's society, it is mixed (multiethnic) marriages that demonstrate the crucial importance of genealogical difference, the third of the differences the family relationship has to cope with. Although it has been masked in Europe by centuries of common cultural and religious practice, this difference is one of the constants in families. Renewed migration has made visible once again those differences of tradition, custom, and belief we could collectively describe as "transgenerational baggage," or cultural inheritance. The cultural and anthropological concept expressed by the "transgenerational" construct is what distinguishes our approach from evolutionist concepts of family relationships based on the "adaptation" construct. For example, we do not believe that there are new evolutionary forms of the family, but rather a specific core of family-ness that undergoes change and transformation. However, lineage difference is also a feature of culturally homogeneous families because each member of the couple is sustained by, and brings to the family relationship, the "nourishment" of their respective family trees.

So, the family relationship has to cope with three kinds of difference, while the procreation that lies at the heart of the relationship assumes the status of a *generative principle*. Over the years, researchers have expanded the psychosocial concept of "generativity" to include not only the desire to create and raise a new generation, but also the idea of personal productivity and creativity (Erikson, 1968, 1982; Kotre, 1984; Kotre & Kotre, 1998; Snarey, 1998). These authors have also drawn attention to the circular link between generativity and desire for immortality. It is the knowledge that they must die that urges people to be generative. Conversely, generativity makes death easier to accept by instilling in people a greater love of life.

We owe to de St. Aubin and McAdams (1995) a model of generativity that integrates power and love, agency and communion. Co-present within the act of generation are aspects of self-expansion (creating something in one's own image) and caregiving as a gift to the new generation to help it become autonomous and responsible (implying self-sacrifice in favor of the other).

The same authors also show that culture influences how generativity reveals itself. For example, it may influence how children are raised and educated. Japanese mothers, for example, enjoy prolonged, almost exclusive physical contact with their offspring in an indulgent, almost symbiotic relationship that stresses the interdependence of the group's members. By contrast, Western mothers encourage their children to explore the environment, drawing their attention to objects and maintaining remote visual contact. They also seek advice from child-guidance experts and read child-guidance handbooks, whereas Japanese mothers try to help other mothers, as was the case in Western culture until a century or so ago. Finally, the Western society sees the generativity in artistic spheres as a remodeling of tradition and the creation of new values, whereas Japanese society sees it as way of ensuring that the existing tradition and its values are never allowed to die. The learning of artistic skills in Japan's "Lineage Schools" brings to mind the Western tradition of workshops and corporations in the Late Middle Ages and the Renaissance. By observing, imitating, and internalizing skills, the pupil "seizes" his master's secret. The crucial difference is that in Western culture a pupil is expected to surpass his master, whereas in Japanese culture he is expected to reproduce his master's secret.

However, it should be stressed that whereas these studies take the individual's interaction with the environment—be it the mother or the mother culture—as their starting point, we are more concerned with generativity as the outcome of interaction between generations and within the married couple. The construct is the same, but the way of defining and mapping it is different.

We are now in a position to answer our first question—What is the principle that crosses the different kinds of family organization?—by saying that, although the forms families take may differ from culture to culture, they share a common organizational principle based on three types of difference (between genders, between generations, and between family lineages). What we term *family-ness* is the way(s) in which these differences are dealt with and "nurtured." The common aim of all family relationships is generativity ("generativity" and "gender" both derive from the Indo-European *gen:* birth, offspring),

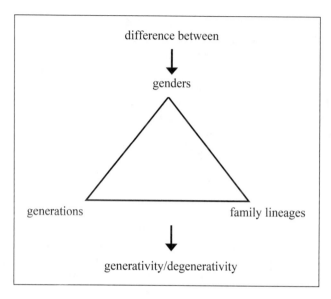

FIG. 2.1.   The organizational principle.

which binds the two genders indissolubly together. Neither gender can quit the parental relationship (one cannot become an ex-parent or ex-grandparent), and together they bind their respective families of origin by producing both a difference between generations and a link between their family lineages that dissipates in time as successive generations are produced.

Figure 2.1 shows the organizational principle of the family relationship. It starts with *difference,* which immediately gives rise to conflict and the need of conflict management, and achieves its final aim in *generativity,* whether of individual minds or of the bonds between them. The converse of this is deficient, defective, or perverted generativity, so that families can also be characterized by their degree of nongenerativity or degenerativity.

Relationship and Interaction: Difference and Connection

We have used the term "family relationship" many times. But how do "relationship" and "interaction" relate to each other? To decide this, we need to understand how they differ and how they connect. Let us begin with "relationship." We see it as both a *reciprocal bond* that emerges from intergenerational exchange, mainly through role attribution, and a *referral of meaning* (i.e., of the meanings and key values that permeate exchanges between genders, generations, and family lineages) that takes place within the cultural context of origin (Donati, 1989, 1998).

In psychology, the *relational principle* developed not only from a crisis in individualism (the monadic mind enclosed in a self-referential energy system), but also from a crisis in systemic theory (the impersonal holistic structure in which individuals are seen as mechanical components acting in response to input). It is no accident that, over the years, family therapy has come to recognize that individuals also have to be seen as actors and agents who are driven by intentions, affects and aims, and who actively create the "family system." In other words, family therapists came to realize that they needed a new perspective that could take account of both the individual and the family without reverting to the individualist method typical of classical psychology or the holistic method typical of some systemic approaches.

The relational principle also has roots in psychoanalysis, especially in studies of groups (Fornari, 1981; Foulkes, 1957),[2] and in the Philadelphia group's groundbreaking insights into the nature of family relationships (Ackerman, 1958; Boszormenyi-Nagy & Spark, 1973; Framo, 1992). We see our own work very much in this perspective, as separate and distinct from the "communicationalist" systemic thinking that has evolved into constructivist, narrative approaches.

Let us now consider "interaction." The first thing to be said is that interaction can be observed, and that this results in different ways of measuring interaction. When we encounter a family in a clinical or research context, we can observe the interaction of its members and note how the partners influence each other when they are physically with each other or, nowadays, in some form of virtual contact with each other. The fact that family members influence each other means that interaction has a joint outcome. When they assert or deny, express feelings, take decisions, and so forth, we can observe their actions, reactions, and reciprocal influence during interaction and conclude that the outcome of the interaction is a shared product.

Family psychologists made the observation of interaction their principal research tool from the late 1960s on. Not surprisingly, the most widespread definition of the family at that time was a unit of interacting people, first coined by Cooley (1909), and then an interactive system. This definition tied in both with the social psychology of small groups (interaction between leaders and followers) and with developmental psychology (mother–child interaction).

Useful though this was, the later focus on interaction was seen from the start as a new and more satisfactory approach than the previous subjective–representational one. Eisler, Dare, and Szmuckler (1988) observe that, to clinicians and researchers, measuring and classifying interaction seemed the most promising way of rendering objectively verifiable an area of study that had

---

[2] Fornari (1981) says that the mind is first structured by family roles like father, mother, child, brother, and sister, and the relationships between them. These later influence other group relationships like those of work groups, peer groups, couples, and so on.

hitherto been judged too unscientific because it was difficult to treat empirically. But as they also acutely observe, the greater the effort that went into developing accurate categorization of behavioral acts, the less attainable seemed
the objective of developing psychological categories able to describe the family
as a whole, an organized entity.

Clinicians and researchers adopted two main approaches in the 1980s. One
was to identify the basic dimensions of family interaction; the other was to
see recurring patterns of interaction as aspects of the exchange process. In the
former, the focus was, by turns, cohesion, flexibility, agreement–disagreement,
the effectiveness or otherwise of communication, the definition of boundaries, and so on (Beavers, 1982; Olson, Russell, & Sprenkle, 1983). Using these
dimensions, it was possible to construe specific types of families along a scale of
functioning from adequate to dysfunctional.

In the latter, the focus was on patterns (schemes of exchange) relating to
conflict management, problem solving, and modes of communication, and
how they could be linked to psychological data about families. Studies by Markman (Markman, Floyd, Stanley, & Storaalsi, 1988) and Gottman (1994; Gottman
& Levenson, 1992) on the predictability of divorce were especially insightful.
Pattern-based models like these are dynamic—they avoid the "photographic"
fixity of dimensional description—but this does not alter the fact that they give
priority to interaction in the here and now, reducing the notion of time to mere
repetitive sequence. Significantly, Hinde (1979) at first regarded relationships
as nothing more than sequences of interactions, whereas Gottman (1982) saw
them as patterns constructed by people when they are with each other. In the
interactive paradigm, then, a relationship either reduces itself to interaction
because it is just an interaction repeated in time (a sum of interactions), or
coincides with patterns of exchange constructed by the couple.

The prospect of ever being able to classify adequately the types and patterns
of family exchange seemed increasingly unlikely in the 1990s, as constructivism
and postpositivism took hold (Boss, Doherty, LaRossa, Schumm, & Steinmetz,
1993). Descriptions of exchange began to center on the idea of "communication," but in the sense of discourse, conversation, narrative, script, and routine
(Fiese & Kline, 1992, 1993), rather than the effectiveness or otherwise of the
communication itself. Particular attention was focused on the meaning that
family members attributed to everyday behaviors and events. The constructiv-
ists maintained that researchers first had to uncover the meanings that families
attribute to events (Reiss & Oliveri, 1991), just as therapists had to juxtapose
their version of the reasons for the family's dis-ease with the family's own
version (Goolishian & Anderson, 1992). As a result, the narrative or story-based
approach, focusing on the construals that individual family members make of
their family history and how their stories compare with each other's, became
increasingly important. As White and Epston (1990) stress, the narrative approach is different from other approaches in which the family has a rule- and

strategy-based structure and a healthy or pathological organization. The narrative metaphor is based on the assumption that human experience is organized
as stories from which perceptions of oneself and others emerge as a system of
beliefs. In therapy, this means listening to individual stories and helping their
narrators to construct others that will help to regenerate family relationships.

However, the importance of narration eclipsed the importance of action–
exchange and its outcome in the family. The crucial distinction between narration and dialogue (mimetic structure) can already be found in Aristotle. As
Minuchin (1998) points out, the narrative approach places the emphasis on
individual psychology (the narratives of individual family members) and the
family becomes just one context among others. We believe, however, that the
growing popularity of the narrative approach should be linked to a specific
"communicationalist" current in systemic family research and therapy that
has evolved along constructivist lines. Clinicians and researchers who have
adopted this approach are increasingly concerned with individual settings, and
their work, which goes beyond basic encounter with the family, has produced
interesting results (Boscolo & Bertrando, 1996; Ugazio, 1998).

We stress here that, since the very beginning, family therapy and research has
centered on interaction and reciprocal action in its efforts to define the family
pattern, drama, or "game" and the unstated rules and constraints that govern
it. Obviously, this approach is *theatrical,* whereas the narrative approach plays
down this enthusiasm for "family theatre," which is directed as much toward
openly acknowledging the sense of belonging and constraint that binds family
members together, as toward dramatic *praxis* and its features. It is also worth
pointing out that represented action and contemplated action are as much
the basic principles of theatre as they are of the interactional and relational
process.[3] And yet interest in individuals, the accounts they give of their lives in
the family, and their positioning within the family system has only increased.
Curiously, a variety of psychodynamic approaches to the semantics of narrative
are possible.

So, on the interactive plane, attention focuses on communicative exchanges
occurring in the present time between family members and/or with research-
ers/therapists. Interaction concerns events and exchanges taking place in the
here and now between the subjects who produce them. The key concepts
are coconstruction and sequence. As Magnusson and Törestad (1993) say, the
concept of interaction includes interdependence, reciprocity of exchange, nonlinearity, and multifinality, in the sense that one cause can have a number of

---

[3] Mejerchol'd (1962) speaks of a "theatre revolution." He sees the theatre as a place for the
synthesis of the arts, and movement in all its forms is its crucial feature. The aim of theatre is to
involve the "fourth actor" (i.e., the spectator) in the hope that this will help alter his existence.

It is no accident that Russian culture, part Eastern and part Western, is the most interested
of all in social and family drama and how it develops from an event of happening into a plot.
Dostoevsky's entire literary output is an exploration of this idea.

effects and one effect can have a multiplicity of causes. An interactive perspective takes researchers and therapists directly to the heart of the family through careful observation of how family members interact with each other. They are both actors, in the sense that they play roles, and agents, in the sense that they are individuals who have intentions and are able to generate meaning.

On the other hand, an interactive perspective picks up only the opportunities and constraints inherent in the situations and settings in which interaction occurs. It cannot detect the opportunities and constraints of either the cultural and social structure the family interacts with or the family history that resides in individuals and reveals itself in relationships. As a single, self-enclosed horizon, the interactive perspective alone cannot encompass the family as an organization of relationships and matrix of individual identity. It is, however, a useful and indispensable means of accessing the higher, relational level in the family.

In our approach, we try first to identify and then to interconnect the two levels of analysis. That is, we think in terms of multilayering and figure-and-ground. Let us now go back and define what we mean by "relationship." A relationship is what binds subjects to each other even when they are unaware of it; it is a never-ending accumulation and sedimentation of values, myths, rituals, and patterns of exchange generated by, among other things, role attributions. Relationship is an anthropological and psychological matrix; a linkage between past, present, and future; constraint and opportunity operating through ties between spouses, between siblings, and between the family and the community.

Hinde (1997) recently pointed to another difference between interaction and relationship: the fact that relationships contain superordinated focus, that is, meanings transcending those that emerge from interaction. We see these focuses as the ways in which families deal with gender, generation, and lineage difference, and the symbolic nature of family ties.

It is also worth remembering that family members stake their entire personalities in family relationships, not just the role they are performing at any given time. For example, *being* a parent means more than performing the role of parent, even though the former includes the latter. On the other hand, relationship without role would be pure self-expression, a sort of non-tie. It is well known that the roles people perform are influenced by culture, and the same is true of the connection between role and relationship. In the past, for example, the parental relationship was based on role performance rather than expression of emotion. In extreme cases, the parental role (especially for fathers) was almost exclusively an exercise of power. Nowadays, however, expression of emotion is so prevalent a feature of role performance that parents may actually forego the exercise of authority altogether. The confusion of roles engendered by the widespread notion that parents are also friends, and increasing parental waywardness in the raising their children, are clear examples of this tendency. In such cases, exercise of authority is feared because it is confused with mere exercise of power.

It could be said that, in interaction, researchers are interested in what sub-jects jointly construct through their shared action, whereas in relationships they are interested in what binds and constrains the actors, things that the actors themselves are unlikely to be aware of. As we have said, what we are dealing with here are histories of family ties that are part of the mother culture. Such long-lasting, constantly self-renewing ties transcend interactions between fam-ily members. The term "history of ties" is concerned with the influence of pre-vious generations on later ones, as well as the influence of earlier stages in the family life cycle on later ones. It is only at the relational level that we can link up successive generations and connect past, present, and future. Making these con-nections in time reveals how meanings are interwoven with values (freedom of thought, the search for truth, increasing recognition of others) that are the outcomes of relationships experienced within a context of intergenerational exchange. It goes without saying that these outcomes are frequently poisoned by the falsehood, delegitimization, and violent coercion that intergenerational exchange can also leave in its wake.

We agree with McGoldrick et al. (1993) that, for the most part, life is given and we have to accept it. The extent of human freedom and responsibility is determined by what human beings decide to make of this fact. Relationships operate vertically, therefore, although their effect on interaction is horizontal and circular.

How has the relational level in families been dealt with in clinical and psy-chosocial research? Some studies link family psychology to personality struc-ture (L'Abate, 1994, 1997); others use attachment theory as their base (Doane & Diamond, 1994), although it should be remembered that the duality of at-tachment (the mother–child relationship) and the notion of transgenerational relationship as simply a direct link between ancestry and progeny (mother of mother–mother–child) obscures the triangularity (father, mother, child) of family relationships. Moreover, it uses the concept of nurture rather than caretaking. Nurture, with all its affective features, is fundamentally a biological concept, whereas caretaking, as we shall see, suggests that children are also nourished with values.[4]

In therapy studies, clinicians who adopt the psychodynamic-intergenera-tional approach (Andolfi, 1988; Boszormenyi-Nagy & Spark, 1973; Framo, 1992; Paul, 1980)[5] describe relationships as the "underground forces" and "invisible loyalties" that bind children (young or adult) to their families of origin. The

---

[4] For these reasons, which we have only summarized here, we believe that attachment theory, although concerned with bonds (secure, ambivalent, avoidant, disorganized), cannot convey the full complexity of "family-ness."

[5] Starting from an interactive-behaviorist position (behavior, communication, use of paradox), Selvini Palazzoli (1986) eventually came to interpret intergenerational relationships and their effects as instances of the "game" concept-metaphor.

TABLE 2.1
Characteristics of Analysis Levels

	Interactive Level	Relational Level
Characteristics	Exchange between partners, between siblings, and between parents and children, as revealed by their interactions	Ties as a product of family history and intergenerational relationships
Observational setting	Daily routines, typical sequences of situations in various contexts	Family crises and transitions (in which ties are revealed)
Space/time predominance	Horizontality and circularity (forms and modes of communication, sequences)	Verticality (connection between past, present and future)
Aim	Analysis of types of exchange, knowledge of transactional rules and patterns	Analysis of the values and symbolic qualities of ties; management of crises and transitions
Model	Descriptive-evaluative	Evaluative-inclusive*

*We use this term to mean giving and having an overview of the family relationship. Cigoli (1992, 1997) uses the term *weave* borrowed from Victor Sklovskij (1976), who has done major studies of the structure of novels. The family weave is an attempt to give the family relationship an overall meaning.

problem here is that a psychodynamic-intergenerational approach makes it difficult to connect the intergenerational relationship to the couple relationship as the fulcrum of the family's affairs. As we have said, we believe that the couple relationship is crucial in redefining intergenerational exchange within the family and exchange between the family and society. Although it does have some psychodynamic-intergenerational features, our approach attributes great importance to the generational and generative complexity of the couple relationship and takes full account of the relationship between sociocultural context and family context.

To summarize, analyzing interaction tells us about family exchange in terms of boundaries, alliances, coalitions and exclusions, communication styles, prevalent affects, and negotiation processes. Analyzing relationships tells us about family ties (resources, traumas and loss) and the values (meanings) that permeate them. It should be remembered, however, that it is through interaction in the here and now that certain family ties and their meanings may be revisited and modified, and it is this that gives us a comprehensive sense of both the difference between and the complementary functioning of interactions and relationships. Complementarity and difference share in helping us to understand the family as a generational context. The characteristics of the two analysis levels are summarized and compared in Table 2.1.

The Symbolic Principle

Etymologically, a symbol is what binds and connects different parts together and, as a result, enables them to be recognized.[6] We employ the term "symbolic" as it is used in cultural anthropology and, more recently, cultural psychology (Cole, 1996; Mantovani, 2000) to mean the family relationship's latent structure of meaning. Symbols are also species specific, that is, typical of the species homo sapiens.

The symbolic matrix of gender, generational, and genealogical ties has to be defined because it gives family life its substance and enables us to determine the meaning of individual family events. It constitutes the family's affective and ethical base. The family is an affective setting par excellence, but it also generates personal responsibility and the ethos of the family relationship. We believe that ethical and affective qualities form the backbone of both the couple (marital) relationship, the parent–child (parental) relationship, and the genealogical relationship.

We identify these qualities as trust, hope, and justice, and maintain that they should be understood in the dialectical sense, that is, they coexist with their opposites mistrust, despair, and injustice. As Jurkovic (1998) says, justice and trust are essential ingredients of healthy family relationships, whereas mistrust and injustice threaten the health of family relationships. It could be said that diabolic is the opposite of symbolic, in that it indicates something that splits, divides, or breaks ties. Significantly, we have already described the family as a dramatic space that can generate serious pathologies in individual people and the relationships between people. The symbolic qualities have both a factual nature and an ideal tension; furthermore, as recalled by the book cover, they show a *spiral structure* emerging from generation to generation.

Trust and loyalty are closely interconnected. Being worthy of trust is as important as trusting others, just as keeping one's word is as important as expecting others to do so. There have been very few empirical studies of trust, even though it is acknowledged to be the crucial factor in "close relationships" (Kerr, Stattin, & Trost, 1999; Rempel, Holmes, & Zanna, 1985). Two states characterize the trusting relationship: the state of uncertainty, and therefore risk, in which trust operates; and the state of interdependence, which is its relational foundation. Its code is affective and ethical: Someone who is trusted enjoys a certain independence and decision-making power, but is always committed to not betraying the other person's trust. Pelligra (2002) uses the term "trust responsiveness" to describe this exchange in which the trusted person feels pressed to act in ways that confirm the other's trust.

---

[6] The term drives from the Greek *symbolon*, in turn derived from the verb *syn-ballo*, literally "to throw together." More specifically, it conveys the idea of a sign of recognition formed by bringing the two halves of a single object together (Sini, 1989).

Hope is the search for something beyond the self, so it expresses relational intent. Moreover, it is hope that enables us to deal with the crises that inevitably arise in the relationship with the other. It produces a forward shift in encounter and dialogue with the other. Without hope, life would be an uninspiring, anxiety-fraught present. There is no new deal, and no solid rock to stand on when things are bad. Hope fights on the side of trust and justice in relationships between human beings.

Finally, justice is one of the principles of exchange with other people. It translates into laws and cultural rules, but it is much more than a rule because it is connected to the ethical principle (Amerio, 2004). It may sometimes happen that rule and law are opposed to the ethical principle.

The importance of trust and hope has been explored by Erikson (1968, 1982), who sees trust and hope as properties of the ego within the dynamic of psychosocial development. By contrast, Meltzer and Harris (1983) list instilling hope and engendering trust as two of the basic emotional functions the family performs in its fostering of personal growth. It is only in a climate of hope and trust that a person can develop the desire to know and learn. In a climate of mistrust, however, a person learns how to threaten and persuade, and feels that destructive forces are outdoing constructive ones. Attachment theory also emphasizes how important the primary trust-based relationships are for child development.

So, trust plays a decisive role in the construction of social and personal ties. Trust and hope are key expressions not only of the affective and aspirational properties of the family relationship, but also of its ethical power: trust and hope are virtues, after all.

Major insights into the nature of *justice* have come from the work of Boszormenyi-Nagy & Spark (1973), who base their approach on the "dialogic principle" of Martin Buber, that is, the need of the Other in forming and developing the Self. Justice is, they say, a human order: Every act of justice or injustice has a psychological effect on not only the subject who is the recipient of it, but also on posterity and the transgenerational chain. They distinguish between distributive, predefined justice based on destiny and the inheritance of previous generations, and retributive, bottom-line justice determined by how much is given and how much is taken in intergenerational exchange—in accounting terms, the balance of expenditure and income that runs between generations. Every action that seals obligations contracted at the generational level raises the level of loyalty in the relationship. Loyalty is a relational quality that weaves itself like an invisible thread between generations, forming the connective tissue of families.

According to Boszormenyi-Nagy and Spark (1986), it is justice that engenders trust and hope, and commitment (loyal) rather than affect is the cornerstone of contextual therapy, where "contextual" means consideration of the amount of care and attention lavished on ties. Their approach is, therefore, a reaction to the almost ubiquitous tendency in clinical and research practice to define the quality of a relationship as the degree of personal satisfaction it makes possible, without taking into account that the family tie is an irrefutable fact, and that each member of the family is responsible for the effects that their actions and decisions have on all the other members. In this context, trust is a consequence of just and equitable intergenerational exchange, and has to be earned.

Turning now to *loyalty*, it should first be noted that its etymon is *lex*—that which binds—which indicates the existence of law. Loyalty is a preferential attachment toward people one is tied to by a primary bond. It has a triangular configuration: the preferring one, the preferred one, and the one who is not preferred. Thus, interpersonal loyalty is intrinsically conflictual: People can be torn between loyalty to spouses, loyalty to parents, and loyalty to children. This conflict is overcome when the people involved avoid falling into the either/or trap we have called "diabolic principle," which splits them apart. We are asked to be simultaneously loyal to parents, spouses, and children. If we are able to appreciate the absolute, unique value of the person, we can understand that preferential choice excludes no one; rather, each separate person is the recipient of a different preference. This is an example of creative paradox.

To summarize, the symbolic principle present in the family relationship draws life from a three-way, reciprocal relationship between trust, hope, and justice. Another way of putting this would be to say that in relationships, there is an affective pole (trust and hope) and an ethical pole that encounter and influence each other. In this we differ from Boszormenyi-Nagy and Spark (1986), who see family dynamics mainly in terms of the consequences of just/unjust acts within a system of credits–debits and obligations, overlooking the eroticism (loving kindness) that is present in the tie and was instrumental in forming it. Justice is not based on loyalty alone; it also requires the performance of a just act. Aristotle (trans. 2002) stresses that the purpose of a just act is to restore justice to a relationship. It works like a plumb-line, showing where the vertical truly lies in the family relationship. But can a just act be performed without a basis of trust and hope in the relationship with the other person?[7] We think not. In our view, trust and hope are original, not derived qualities: Usually there is certain gratuitousness about them, a willingness to grant unconditional credit to others The tie matrix is *latent:* although hidden, it is what gives the family relationship its meaning.

Figure 2.2 illustrates the tripartite nature of the symbolic principle. The symbolic trinity of hope, trust, and justice is opposed by despair, mistrust, and injustice, and is by no means certain to emerge as the winner in the ensuing conflict.

---

[7] See Zanetti (1993). Book V of the *Nicomachean Ethics* contains the fullest treatment of the theme. Aristotle (2002) says that justice has an immediate, intersubjective basis in the sense that it, of its nature, is concerned with the other, that is, with interaction.

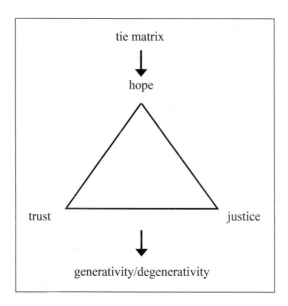

FIG. 2.2.   The symbolic principle.

The Dynamic Principle

To understand the dynamics of exchange in family relationships, we have to take into account another triangle formed by giving, receiving, and reciprocating. Basically, there are three major approaches to the study of exchange dynamics: One is sociological–psychosocial, the other is psychodynamic–transgenerational, and the third is anthropological–ethnological.

The first sees giving and taking in terms of the utility principle. The version of exchange theory most widely used in the social sciences applies to human relationships the logic of commercial exchange and cost–benefit—the logic of equivalent value (this item corresponds to this price).[8] According to the theory, family members are motivated by the search for reward, and family relationships are based on a contract designed to facilitate reciprocal gratification of affective and economic needs. Exchange is governed by short-term reciprocity: Unless the cost–benefit ratio balances out within a given period of time, family members will begin to feel stressed in various ways.

In psychology, the theory is used to explain not only the stability or instability (cost–benefit ratios) of marriages, but also the functionality–dysfunctionality

---

[8] The theory was developed by social psychologists in the 1960s and 1970s and applied to various aspects of interpersonal relationships (Kelley & Thibaut, 1978; Thibaut & Kelley, 1959). In the 1980s it was applied to close relations, and more specifically to their formation, persistence, and dissolution (for a review see Clark & Reis, 1988), as well to family relationships, thanks to Nye (1979).

of the couple relationship. For example, the concept of marital quid pro quo has been used to explain why some relationships are healthy and others are pathological. The theory has undergone extensive revision and development over the years, most notably through the application of "equity theory" to family relationships by Pina and Bengston (1993), Scanzoni (1972), and Sexton and Perlman (1989). Rusbult's (1980) "investment model" is based on the notion that interdependence is an important constituent of intimate relationships (Kelley et al., 2002), whereas Clark and Mills (1993) distinguish between cost–benefit relationships and intimate relationships in which the well-being of the other is an important consideration.

As can be seen, these studies attempt to get beyond the utilitarian concept of exchange, which seems too simplistic and restrictive when investigating something as complex as a family relationship. Not surprisingly, all three approaches (equity, investment, interdependence) stress the ethical aspect of family relationships. The first states that just (balanced) exchanges are more advantageous to both partners than unjust (unbalanced) ones; the second emphasizes the importance of investment and commitment in relationships; and the third says that the well-being of the other partner is paramount. Our view is that one does not get very far in understanding family relationships without recognizing the uniqueness of those who are party to the exchange, and the value of the bond between them.

The second major approach (psychodynamic–transgenerational) derives from Boszormenyi-Nagy and Spark (1986), who see exchange as ethically based. Even when exchange is asymmetrical, as in parent–child relationships (the parent gives care, the child receives it), it is motivated by a sense of justice founded on the child's right to receive care because of its dependent status (neoteny). In other words, exchange is motivated by the need to do one's duty (Rossi & Rossi, 1990) and by a sort of prescriptive altruism (Finch, 1989). This is most evident in parent–child relationships, but it is also a feature of the commitment underlying marital relationships.

It is important to note that the transgenerational perspective typical of this approach extends the timescale of exchange. Exchange between parents and children should be studied across a multigenerational timespan as well as in the present, bearing in mind what has been passed on from previous generations and what the consequences will be for future ones. This perspective makes visible the reciprocity of giving and receiving even where the generational asymmetry of the parent–child relationship is most apparent. Reciprocity is seen as an ethical balance (scales are the classic symbol of justice) that works itself out across generations. By giving care to their children, parents reciprocate, at least in part, the care they received as children from their own parents. The debt is repaid forward rather than backward in time.

According to the authors we cited earlier, bringing a new generation into the world and accepting parental responsibility for it is the true foundation of the ethical code that binds generations together. Even deficient, nonresponsible parenting, with its fatal consequences on present and future, needs to be related to what has happened in the past if it is to be understood. In this sense, deficient parenting is a response to the parental injustices and shortcomings that today's adults-parents suffered as children in the past and have never been able to come to terms with. In this approach, then, reciprocity is seen as a long-term, not a short-term event.

The third approach, which derives from anthropological–ethnological studies (Benveniste, 1969; Godbout, 1992; Levi-Strauss, 1967/1969; Mauss, 1954; Nicolas, 1991) and from cultural–historical psychology (Vernant, 1965/1983), uses the concept of *gift* to explain the creation of social ties and their forms. The anthropological–ethnological approach is fundamentally opposed to the utility principle that forms the basis of the sociological–psychosocial approach. A gift is seen as the expression of an act of trust that gives rise to a tie, which can be interpersonal or social. Exchange begins with an opening gift, a granting of credit. Godbout (1992), in particular, turns the obligation–debt equation on its head and stresses the primacy of the gift in building ties. The essential feature of a gift is that it is unconditional; in other words, family or social ties are fuelled by actions that place trust in the other. There is a certain gratuitouness in giving; there are no strings attached. Trust and hope (see the symbolic principle) are reinstated, therefore, as the foundation of interpersonal and social exchanges. Games theory casts interesting light on the nature of trust. Taking risky decisions (as in "The Prisoner's Dilemma") shows that it is only the trust placed in the other that can break the impasse in a relationship. In other words, cooperative actions are, of course, risky, but they are also actions in which the gift of trust leads to positive outcomes.

Thus, the inability to give, and the perversion of the gift (its purely instrumental use, and its exploitation in defining power relationships) are pathological forms of relationship. One typical example is potlatch, a now-outlawed cultural practice in which the ability to offer lavish gifts is an indication of a person's social prestige and power. The result is that not only the person in question, but also later generations, are burdened with massive debts. Another example is throwing the gift back in someone's face, insisting on returning it; yet another is making the other person feel that she or he is indebted for life.

However, the dynamics of giving are rather more complex than this. A gift, as the unconditional principle (initiation) of exchange, coexists with debt and obligation (duty, task), which are the mirror opposites of giving. Obligation is part of the dynamics of giving—the more a gift is freely given, the greater the sense of obligation it creates. Obligation manifests itself through the duty or task that has to be performed, and through the debt that is created by giving. Here we see the ambiguous nature, the uncertainty, of the dynamic principle. Just as it can create ties, it can also hinder their formation by forcing or negating their value. How can this ambiguity be dealt with?

We believe that the dynamics of gift and obligation can explain how exchange works within the family if the triangle of giving, receiving, and reciprocating (doing for the other in one's turn) is kept alive. Let us see how this triangle works. "Giving" requires unconditional openness toward the other (gift) and the acceptance of species-specific tasks (the duty or obligation to be performed), as in taking care of the next generation, which is both a gift and a task to be performed. In turn, "receiving" requires openness toward the other, acknowledging what the other has done and is doing for me, and how much I owe him or her for this (debt). Finally, "reciprocating" requires knowing how to give and perform tasks in one's turn, which does not necessarily mean giving to the people from whom one has received, but extending the notion of giving to future generations and participating in social and community life. Thus, giving is, of its nature, expansive.

The very delicacy of this triangle means that perversion and deficiency may occur in any field of action. This is as true of the inability to give, which imposes only burdensome duties on the other, as it is of unwillingness to receive so as not to feel beholden to the other, and the inability to reciprocate that leads to retrenchment in relational stagnation and narcissism.

Consider, for example, the dynamics of the intergenerational exchange that occurs when a child is born. The birth of a child sets in motion the mechanism of giving while also revealing its opposite, the systematic creation of debt. Whoever has received life is automatically indebted, but the system does not stop there because parents, like children, received the gift of life in their turn. Thus, the truth of generational exchange is that parents and children are united by gift *and* debt, and this truth can be distorted and betrayed to give precedence to only one of its two aspects. For example, it is by no means rare to see children feeling crushed by and heavily indebted to their parents, living with constant guilt feelings, and parents who see themselves exclusively as givers of life without evaluating what they received from their parents and what they receive from their children.

Let us look more closely at how reciprocity works in the triangle. Reciprocity, too, is ambiguous, in the sense that it has a dual nature. On one hand, there is the duty to clear one's debt with the other person; on the other, there is the desire to reciprocate by identifying with the source of the gift, that is, by giving in one's turn. Thus, identifying with one's origins seems to play a crucial role in the construction of identity. Children can commit themselves fully to a new generational project only when they are motivated by some form of gratitude, and not only by the obligation to reciprocate. It is the gratitude of whoever is doing the reciprocating that makes possible a certain degree of freedom in the obligation–debt equation: The giver does not want reciprocity *tout court;* he wants it to be voluntary and therefore uncertain. Giving encapsulates the freest, least obligatory of all social bonds, which is why it has to be created not only in every moment, but also in each generation (Godbout, 1992). Gouldner (1960) also touches on this idea when, in an example of family restitution, he notes that gratitude and rectitude are both present.

When the dynamics of giving are in operation, people who give feel inversely indebted, or *positively* indebted, in the sense that they feel they owe others something. This explains how important it is, in giving-oriented family therapy, that people are encouraged to search for beneficial sources of giving in previous generations, however partial or deficient. If such sources no longer exist, family members will have to mourn their absence and once again redirect positive action toward new generations.

Thus, the gift-duty dynamic is asymmetrical, in the sense that a difference—a degree of personal freedom—is inserted into the relationship. This is what distinguishes it from the "balance-sheet" model based on equity of exchange and the squaring of intergenerational accounts as an exercise in loyalty.

Thus, the typical form of interchange in family relationships is giving or offering the other what he or she needs, and this activity is backed by trust, the belief that the other will reciprocate with a symbolic equivalent at some opportune moment. To be more precise, reciprocity occurs across a span of generations rather than within the life span of the individuals involved. It should not be forgotten that "family-ness" binds the living and the dead, past and future generations. If there are no ties with ancestors and no faith in generations to come, the family dies. So long-term reciprocity can happen only if it is supported by a component of unconditional trust/hope in the relationship.

To summarize, the dynamic principle in exchange between genders, generations and lineages obeys the logic of giving and indebtedness, and is based on giving, receiving, and reciprocating. Of the various ways of conceptualizing action in families, we prefer a dynamic approach that is consistent with generational exchange and its symbolic cores. As is now clear, the dynamic principle is inseparable from the symbolic principle (hope, trust, justice) already discussed, and all three principles, with their respective trinitarian features, do in fact intersect. We return to this interweaving of the dynamic and the symbolic later in this book. Figure 2.3 illustrates the dual nature (giving and indebtedness) of the dynamic principle.

This duality underlying the generational dynamic and its asymmetrical mode of operation may easily cause the triangular giving–receiving–reciprocating process to seize up and assume various forms of stasis (i.e., repetition of violence and indifference), thereby giving rise to degenerativity in the family relationship.

TRINITARIAN VALUES AND COMPLEXITY:
THE QUESTION OF METHOD

Morin (2001) has developed a trinitarian, interaction-based concept of method that interconnects relationship, organization, and system. He has also developed

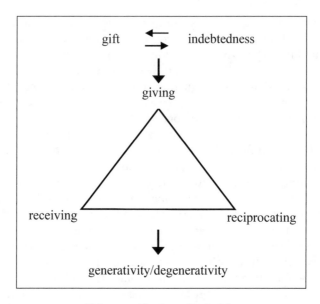

FIG. 2.3.   The dynamic principle.

a trinitarian concept of individual identity based on species-specific, social, and cultural dependence. Morin says that identity is always a play-off between dependence and independence in relation to personal, cultural, and family–social inheritance. As we have seen, non-Western cultures place greater stress on belonging rather than on autonomy: Personal, cultural, and family-social dependencies have different meanings and values in these cultures.

The trinitary attention expressed through reference to triangularity, though, is also specifically derived from earlier research on family relationships. It is sufficient, here, to remember concepts such as Ackerman's (1958) "scapegoating," Haley's (1973) "triangular attention," and Bowen's (1978) "triangulation" in the emotional family field.

Referring to the Oedipal situation, Winnicott (1965) says that the triangle concept epitomizes the complexity and abundance of human experience. By contrast, Kandinsky (1926) says the triangle is yellow because, unlike the tranquil blue of the circle and the fiery red of the square, yellow is a hot, agitated, even irritating color. In short, the triangle is complex both in terms of abundance and in terms of the conceptual and experiential problems it poses (for a discussion of complexity, see Bocchi & Ceruti, 1985; Ceruti, 1995).

One typically interactionist procedure is to see the concept of triangularity in triadic terms. An interesting and instructive example is Fivaz and Corboz's (1999) concept of the "triadic game." But "triangularity" must be distinguished from "triadic." A triad is the copresence of three distinct family members, whereas triangularity is a unity in difference and difference within the unit. Our research points to a unity identity based on three triangular principles.[9]

In our efforts over the years to discover exactly what "family-ness" is, we have tried to map the complexity of family relationships and make this complexity our matrix of research and clinical intervention. We have chosen "relational–symbolic" as the descriptive term for a model that identifies and intersects the three principles we use to explain the family relationship. These principles are different from each other, and should be studied as such, but they are also interwoven. It is certainly no accident that the outcome of all three is the family's generativity or degenerativity. Also, each triangle has its own specific origin: The organizational principle is based on difference, the symbolic principle is based on tie matrix, and the dynamic principle is based on giving and indebtedness. All three principles reveal the dramatic nature of the family relationship that emerges in conflict, whether between genders, generations, and lineages, or between hope, trust, and justice and their opposites, or between giving and indebtedness, whose duality underlies the actions of the family.

We have also tried to illuminate concepts like interaction and relationship, which are often assumed to be the same in research and clinical practice but in fact are significantly different. This is why we have insisted on both the specificity and complementarity of the two concepts.

This brings us to the following question: Which psychosocial research methodology does the relational–symbolic model rely on if it is to work, and which kind of clinical intervention in family relationships does it encourage?

It is well known that no single thread can reveal the full reality of the family relationship. Each of the different methods that are used to access "family-ness" (perceiving, representing, observing, and describing interchange with the other, and with family members) has its own special features, but these are both strengths and limitations. For its part, clinical practice is based on models that differ widely both in conceptualization and in technical procedure.

We try to answer this question in the next chapter, in which we discuss the problem of methodology and the need for coherence between theoretical principles and empirical models.

---

[9] Triangularity is expressed graphically as a triangle, whereas examples of triads expressed graphically include:

CHAPTER THREE

The Cores of the Relationship

Having explored the characteristic principles of the family relationship, we now turn to its core settings. In the last chapter, through an epistemic approach, we showed that the family relationship is a unitas multiplex of interrelated organizational, symbolic, and dynamic principles. In this chapter, we try to define the operational settings of these principles and the basic task they perform.

In this book we have set ourselves the conceptual and methodological task of defining a prototypal model of the family relationship. That is, in attempting to define a model of how families function, we draw on psychology and on anthropological, philosophical, historical, and artistic sources. We have seen that the "family object" can be described in a variety of ways: there are categorical and structural–factorial approaches, as well as the prototypal approach we have adopted. The prototypal model, founded on standard-based comparative procedure, has mainly been used to study personality (Carson, Butcher, & Coleman, 1988; L'Abate, 1997). We use it to study family relationships, which in our view constitute a matrix of personality construction, although not the only one. It should never be forgotten that personality construction involves more than family relationships alone.

The characteristics of the family prototype can be inferred from the three relational principles discernible in family relationships: organizational (gender, generation, family history), symbolic (trust, hope, justice), and dynamic (giving, receiving, reciprocating). Thus, acknowledging multiple differences, activating and maintaining symbolic features of relationships, and continually renewing the dynamics of giving and indebtedness constitute the core of the prototype. But as we have seen, the core problem is generativity, which may either be satisfactorily achieved by taking cultural differences into account, or fall short of adequate realization for a variety of reasons. These may include the inhibition or even perversion of the generativity itself. In reality, widely differing kinds of functioning caused by, for example, family members' lack of interest in generativity, or static overinvolvement with each other, add up to the same thing in the end: inhibition and perversion of the mental space of new generations, who find it hard to say and do something new about intergenerational exchange.

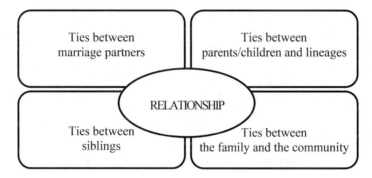

FIG. 3.1.   The settings of the family relationship.

The cores of the family relationship are grouped around a shared focus that we identified earlier in our description of the organizational principles, namely *care*. Following Erikson (1964), care may be defined as "the widening concern for what has been generated by love, necessity or accident; it overcomes the ambivalence adhering to irreversible abligation" (p. 131). Care should not be confused with nurture. The latter is a biologically based adaptive behavior that can assume a wide variety of forms, whereas care is an attitude toward a relationship, a way of nourishing the *values* inherent in relational ties. Its semantics are ethical and affective, but the way it is represented has to be tailored in each case to the specific settings. We examine the role of care in relationships between marital partners, between parents, children, and families of origin, and between the family and the community. We also try to define the symbolic features of each setting (Fig. 3.1).

THE MARITAL BOND AND THE PACT OF TRUST

As the etymology of "conjugal" (*cum-iugo,* with yoke) suggests, the conjugal or marital relationship is both a tie and a constraint. Its downside is that the individual freedom of each partner is reduced; the upside is that both partners experience an enhanced sense of belonging. Conceptually, the constraint may be described as both a contract and a pact. The concept of the (marriage) contract has a long pedigree; in every age, the terms of the contract have been established through negotiations of varying complexity between the families involved in the marriage. The tradition lives on today in the contracts that marriage partners draw up privately between themselves, or publicly in the presence of legal attorneys. The contractual concept has also been used (Dicks, 1967; Pincus & Dare, 1978; Sager et al., 1972) to describe the secret agreement that couples unconsciously underwrite regarding their needs, fears, and expectations.

By contrast, the concept of the pact refers both to the crucial and immutable gender difference between the partners (male, female), and to their wish to establish peace (*pax, paciscor*), which already indicates that a pact is something that has to be worked at all the time, rather than an immutable existential state. Two mental ingredients are necessary for a pact to work properly: acknowledgement of the other's difference (the marriage partner has his or her gender, family history, and personality traits), and, at the same time, acknowledgement of the similarities deriving from participation in a shared human condition (humankind is as much male as it is female). Intergenerational exchange has a powerful influence on the presence or otherwise of these ingredients, which may be either internalized by the partners, or distorted, belittled, and rejected.

The concept of the pact also shows that the formation of the couple is based on a reciprocity rule that includes the symmetry–equality inherent in the couple relationship itself (the partners have the same value and the same right to receive from the other), but also transcends it in the sense that the partners give themselves to, and place trust in, the other. We might say that they make a gift of themselves to each other when they put themselves in the hands—and arms—of the other. The gift of self includes the gift of one's personal limitations, while entrusting oneself to the other also implies a certain fear of the other. Overcoming the challenges of limitation and fear is what establishes the pact. A pact is not something given. On the contrary, it starts with public commitment to the relationship ("to have and to hold from this day forward, for better for worse, for richer for poorer, in sickness and in health, to love and to cherish, till death us do part . . . and thereto I plight thee my troth") and is the outcome of the challenges that the couple has faced and overcome during the course of time.

We are describing here an ideal, prototypal model, yet concrete examples of its successful realization are often to be found in the day-to-day reality of human relationships. Generally speaking, psychosocial and clinical studies have tended to concentrate on the interpersonal skills of the marriage partners—for example, the ability to negotiate and communicate beliefs and feelings effectively. In our view, it is equally important to grasp the true nature of the problem that lies at the heart of all couple relationships, namely the reciprocity rule, according to which the partners not only give themselves to and take care of each other, but also trust in each other. The great challenge of the conjugal relationship lies, therefore, in the ability to open oneself up to the other and to be the first to make the opening gift of trust in the other. Openness and self-disclosure should not be seen in emotional and affective terms alone; it also implies commitment to the relationship. No pact is worthy of its name unless it implies the promise to keep one's word. All cultures are well aware of the difficulties involved in upholding a pact, which is why witnesses have to be present when people enter into pact so that they may attest to the truthfulness and even holiness of what has been promised.[1] In contemporary Western culture, we have a situation in which the pact itself is all too easily broken, together with a marked increase in the degree of intimacy expected of the couple relationship. In effect, the couple is adapting to the social ideal, which dictates that its partners should be emotionally close and share a major portion of each other's lives. As a result, the affective–expressive sphere is tending to obscure the ethical sphere, which is more closely concerned with the partners' commitment to each other and their acknowledgement of the challenges they will have to face. This also means that they are more likely to be disappointed by their relationship, and that future generations will display unusual caution (fear, anxiety) in committing themselves to a couple relationship. It is not just that the divorce rate is rising; we are also seeing, especially in Europe, a decrease in marriage (both civil and religious) and an increase in cohabitation, partly to avoid the risk of disappointment should the marriage fail and the pain that partners would suffer as a result. In the past in the West, and also in contemporary non-Western cultures, there was and is an evident and widespread need, on the part of families of origin and of the community in general, to control and safeguard the couple, as well as a clear domination of one sex over the other.

We might say, then, that the challenge has always been how to find some connection between, on one hand, openness to and trust in the other, and on the other, formal commitment to the relationship, even though the ways that various cultures have chosen to keep the two sides of the relational coin separate may differ widely.

The individualism that has long been a dominant feature of social relationships in the West—the desire of individuals to express themselves at all costs—has been a major influence on how couple relationships are described and the kind of psychological intervention they subsequently receive (Bellah, Madsen, Sullivan, Swidler, & Tipton, 1991). Therapists often evaluate couple relationships in terms of the individual happiness of each of the partners, but are unable to help them commit themselves to and accept responsibility for each other (Doherty, 1995), which is the reverse side of openness to and trust in the other. In any case, personal defects and limitations inevitably lay the couple open to the pain of the wounds that the partners inflict on and receive from each other. In this respect, the ability not only to sympathize with the other (feel that pain is a shared experience), but also to pardon the other, is very important. As the word suggests (*don* = gift), pardon is a trustful act of giving that draws on reserves of hope and derives strength from the unconditional aspects of the relationship. It can break the chain of injustice and restore order

---

[1] The holiness of pacts is what serves to make them binding on those who enter into them. Their word is given not just to the other person, but also to the social group, and the giving of it is witnessed both religiously and socially. It should be remembered that the etymology of "relationship" (as of "religion") includes the notion of bonding ("re-ligo").

in personal exchanges (Scabini & Rossi, 2000). Not surprisingly, one of the tasks of intergenerational family therapy is to create the conditions in which acts of pardon (forgiveness) are possible. Together with reconciliation, which calls for reciprocal decision making, the ability to forgive marks an important stage in the revision of family and couple relationships.

Let us look a little more closely at this idea. As we have said, giving is a reciprocation of value—that is, recognition that the other deserves to be loved to the same extent that I feel that I deserve and am able to receive love from the other—and it is the foundation of the couple relationship (Fletcher & Fincham, 1991; Singer, 1987).[2] But so, too, is forgiving because it says that a mistake is tolerated and accepted in the other to the same extent that I would tolerate and accept it in myself. Without forgiveness and "blessed forgetfulness," all the mistakes and limitations of the other are meticulously catalogued and preserved until the right moment—the day of reckoning—comes along.

Worthington (2001) recently designed a model, called the Pyramid Model to REACH[3] Forgiveness, for the treatment of negative unforgiving emotions (like resentment, bitterness, hostility, anger, fear, ruminating on a hurtful event and the perpetrator) and their replacement with positive, other-oriented emotions (like empathy, sympathy, compassion, love). Worthington shows that, for an act of forgiveness to be real, it needs to be repeated (consolidation of forgiveness, persistence in forgiving) and sincere. In particular, he stresses the crucial role played by empathy and personal humility in bringing the forgiving process to a successful conclusion. Fincham's studies (Fincham, 2000; Fincham & Beach, 2002; Fincham, Beach, & Davila, 2004; Paleari, Regalia, & Fincham, 2005) suggest that forgiveness has a positive impact on marriage, both concurrently and longitudinaly; forgiveness predicts less ineffective arguing in the relationship as well as less psychological aggression and more constructive communication.

We return to these ideas in the chapter on the clinical aspects of couple relationships, divorce, and stepfamilies. In particular, we describe in detail how "encounter and promise" and "secret agreement" are connected to each other in couple relationships.

Figure 3.2 illustrates the role and symbolic features of care in the marital relationship. The affective sphere reveals itself in openness to and trust in the

---

[2] Fletcher & Fincham (1991) described the giving process as reciprocal attribution at work in intimate relationships. We return repeatedly to this fundamental process that simultaneously involves action, cognition, and affect.

[3] The acronym REACH refers to the five steps to forgiveness suggested by the Author: Recall the hurt, Empathy, give an Altruistic gift of forgiveness, Commit aloud to forgiveness, and Hold on to forgiving when you doubt. Worthington (2001) has pointed out the difference existing between forgiveness and reconciliation. The first one is individual: It is a decision or an emotional replacement of negative with positive emotions, so, by definition, it occurs within an individual. Reconciliation, which is the restoration of trust in a relationship where trust is violated, takes place between people: By definition, it is interpersonal.

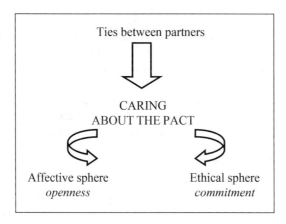

FIG. 3.2.   Symbolic features of the marital relationship.

other; the ethical sphere reveals itself in commitment and the attribution of value to keeping one's word.

THE GENERATIONAL TIE AND ITS DUAL NATURE

The family relationship centers on biological procreation, or procreation through adoption, which, as we have seen, is another form of generativity. To study generational ties, we first have to consider the parents–children relationship and the relationship between parents and their families of origin. In this sense, the generational tie has a dual nature. We look first on responsible caretaking with regard to the symbolic component of the parental relationship (or parent–children bond), and then on caretaking with regard to the notion of inheritance that constitutes the symbolic component of the relationship between family lineages.

The Parental Couple and Responsible Caretaking

Responsible caretaking is a symbolic component of parenting because the parent–child relationship is hierarchical: Earlier generations are responsible for the mental and physical conditions in which later generations are raised. Responsible caretaking is one of the couple's joint tasks, although this does not prevent us from symbolically connecting the affective sphere to the maternal function and the ethical sphere to the paternal function. As we have said, we see the symbolic dimension as that which joins up separate parts to make a whole. In this particular case, it is a matter of joining up spheres (maternal or paternal) and functions to make a whole.

Let us consider the first of these spheres. Hope and trust are the cardinal features of the maternal function, the mental equivalent of giving and transmitting life (where there is life, there is hope). Hope and trust are not merely the affective ingredient in taking care of a newborn baby; they are also an inexhaustible source that we can draw on throughout our lives to combat anxiety.

Hope and trust are clear expressions of the unconditional aspect (giving) of the family relationship that is particularly evident in the mother–child relationship. The child who receives care deserves hope and trust, irrespective of his or her responses and abilities. Anxiety, on the other hand, reveals itself in the desperation and profound mistrust that can, in turn, result in neglect, abuse, humiliation, rejection, and abandonment.

The other sphere of the parental relationship, the ethical one, is the cardinal feature of the paternal function, which is etymologically related to patrimony (*patri-munus*), that is, the transmission of material and moral property, and the entitlement to property. The ethical sphere operates on the principle of justice. Its violation (injustice) occurs when there are unjust laws, or when parental responsibility is not exercised or is inverted (e.g., when a child has to play a parental role at an inopportune time, or act as the partner of one of the parents). Another of the ethical sphere's operative principles is loyalty, in the sense of feeling connected to and part of the family history, with all its resources, joys, and sorrows.

As we have said, the ethical and the moral must be distinguished from each other. Since Aristotle, the former has meant wanting and being able to respect the value of a family tie and, where necessary, restoring order by setting injustice to rights and assuming responsibility. The latter consists of cultural norms that often attack or inhibit personal responsibility and the value of the family tie. Thus, the moral may sometimes work counter to the ethical.

Not only do trust and hope, justice and loyalty, the ethical and affective spheres, operate interdependently, turning paired terms into single entities; they also require that both parents (mother and father) assume responsibility for them. It is precisely because parental functions are invariant, and do not coincide with roles, that it is possible for both males and females, fathers and mothers, to dispense trust, hope, and justice. When intergenerational trust and hope are seriously neglected, as in cases of child abuse, systematic violence, or total lack of care, a negative chain is established that some family scholars call the "recurring cycle of violence." However, the concept of the recurring cycle, which is both linear and mechanistic, overlooks other crucial variables at work in the generational tie, such as relationships outside the family, which can be beneficial sources of new ties and serve as a barrier against deteriorating intergenerational relationships, and even the marital tie itself. In some cases, people can use relationships outside the family (stepfamilies, other adult reference figures, a new couple relationship) to reinstate the ethical–affective core that lies at the heart of the family relationship.

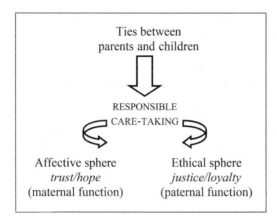

FIG. 3.3.   Symbolic features of the parental relationship.

This can also be achieved through therapy. As a family member, the person concerned may be encouraged to review and reconsider his or her family history. In this connection Kancyper, (1997) refers to the "generational comparison," meaning that the person is asked to recognize what has been left through the generational exchange. But, besides this, the person is also asked to reevaluate his or her own ties. For example, without in any way playing down the emotions that have been experienced, it may be possible to help a person understand that a bad parent is someone who was crushed by life as a child and is therefore incapable of assuming personal responsibility as an adult. This may bring into the relational arena the compassion and forgiveness already discussed with reference to the marital bond. The marital and parental bonds are closely intertwined precisely because, in both cases, the other is always both the goal of commitment—the other as partner; the other as a member of the preceding generation—and the object of commitment—being able to pardon the other both as a partner and as a member of the preceding generation, and being able to reconcile oneself to the other.

The chapter on transition will deal with responsible caretaking of children, included adopted children and children produced by assisted procreation. Figure 3.3 shows how caretaking and the ethical–affective spheres are related to the couple and parental bond.

The Parental Couple and the Custody of Heritage

As we have said, the generational tie is a dual one. On one hand, there is the bond of the parental couple and the effect it has on relationships with children; on the other, the relationship between family lineages (paternal and maternal) and their respective heritages. We have already seen this dual tie in operation in the picture gallery of time, and we cited Levi-Strauss (1967/1969) and Héritier (1996) in particular to show that taking care of the new generation is both a part of, and is fuelled by, a cultural heritage that links children to ancestors through parents. So, in addition to taking responsible care of its children, the parental couple is faced with the task of keeping alive the family memory and its dual paternal–maternal heritage.

Let us look at the idea of family memory in more detail. In a good many cultures, family memory may go back several generations, embracing the founder of the family and successive heirs. In modern Western culture, however, children very often "belong" to the couple, in the sense that the members of the couple make no reference to their respective ancestries and families of origin when giving them names. In choosing fashionable or favorite names, they put family history behind them, but the importance of the maternal and paternal families of origin reasserts itself with a vengeance whenever some serious crisis like divorce overwhelms the couple. What has been pushed into the background flows on like an underground river until it suddenly returns to the surface.

What does the couple inherit from its maternal and paternal lineages? Inheritance includes, first, a person's cultural as well as genetic make-up; human existence cannot be reduced to a matter of biology alone, although people often assume that it can. It also includes property (land, houses, savings, movable property), status (the family's social standing), philosophy of life, and ties with a native region and/or country. The bond between progeny and their native region is an important aspect of the intergenerational relationship. The ceaseless, even convulsive movement typical of postmodern society transforms but does not override the relationship between families and their native regions. Every parental couple feels the need of a "native land" that it can feel at ease in (and with), and that serves as a reservoir of memories, whether painful or pleasant.

To fully understand how different family ancestries relate to each other, we need to think about the crucial importance of the relationship with the other. A family is the outcome of an encounter between strangers—two people belonging to different groups or clans who come together to form a couple—and yet it is precisely because strangers are dangerous that measures are taken to keep them at bay. We could say, then, that families tend to be both endogamic and exogamic, that is, they simultaneously welcome and reject the other. The incest taboo, a cultural constant with a wide variety of very different meanings, should be seen as an exogamic impulse and law.[4] Endogamy was once the exclusive

---

[4] Incest is a recurrent theme in creation myths, symbolizing the return to primordial chaos (the Dogon culture in Mali) and the extinction of the human race (the Kongo culture in Zaire). But it is also a mark of divine descent and signals the founding of a new clan (the myths of eastern central Africa).

prerogative of gods and terrestrial deities like the Pharaohs—as a special form of religiously sanctioned coupling, it expressed the divine nature of the parties to the pact. Much later, Europe's ruling houses used intermarriage to protect their interests and extend their power, giving rise to the idea of "blue blood." Intermarriage was both a distinctive feature of royal houses that set them apart from the rest of humanity (their subjects), and a catastrophic harbinger of fatal illness (hemophilia). Endogamic tendencies have been and still are a feature of economic power groups and unusually tight ethnic–religious groups.

The church has campaigned for centuries against the risks of endogamic marriage, establishing rigid, complicated lines of kinship enabling it to prohibit marriage even between very remote cousins. The prohibition is more than a biological defense of the species (renewal of blood); it is also a way of encouraging broader social ties—awareness of ties and recognition of shared belonging are safeguards against outbreaks of violence between families, districts, and neighboring villages, and between town and country.

So two opposing forces are pitted against each other in the family relationship. One favors and protects internal ties (one's own family and interests), the other urges openness and encounter (with the other and the other family). The endogamic tendency, which may even override the exogamic one, is certainly a force to be reckoned with. Tajfel's (1981) psychosocial study reveals that individuals and groups usually show a preference for the in-group, and anthropological studies demonstrate that almost all ethnic groups consider only themselves as fully human ("we are the world of men") and label other groups as nonhuman. Unfortunately, as we all know, when the other is deprived of recognizably human features, she or he becomes a "thing" against whom any kind of violence is possible.

In families, the endogamic tendency expresses itself in the fantasy of self-generation, a sort of myth of autogenesis. This myth, which has been a feature of many different ages and cultures, suggests that procreation does not require the presence of the other. As we have already seen, the myth of a purely male, paternal heritage never ceased to fascinate the Greeks. As Vernant (1965/1983) says, it was the man who sowed the seed; the mother merely protected and took care of the young plant. In the Roman family, it was the gens that likened newborn sons to the family's male founder. Females carried only the *nomen* (of the gens they belonged to), whereas males received three attributes: an individual praenomen, the family cognomen, and the nomen of the gens.

The myth of autogenesis, which eliminates either the male or female line, can be seen today in the desire of some women to have a child without the presence of a father-husband, and in homosexual couples who assert the right to have and bring up children.

In the end, a widespread family form is the one consisting of those mothers who "alienate" fathers and establish families with only themselves and their children. Such desires and assertions are seen as a way of resolving the conflict

between endogamy and exogamy through a notion of "what is one's own" that
ensures intergenerational continuity.

This makes it easier to understand the difficult situation of the parental couple, both of whose members are both the recipients of their respective family
and cultural heritages, and responsible for passing these heritages on to the next
generation. The process is all the more fruitful if children are allowed access to
both family lines. Thus, custody of heritage consists of keeping alive the memory of one's origins (the affective aspect) and remaining loyal to one's maternal
and paternal families of origin, while also acknowledging their traumas, positive
and negative values, deficiencies, and resources (the ethical aspect).

Moreover, the cultural and symbolic components of the heritage are passed
on unconsciously. Centuries ago, Virgil reminded us that we drink from the
Lethe, the river of forgetfulness, before being born, a way of saying that,
although we forget our ultimate origins, they remain an active force within us,
and that we participate in the passions and endeavors of our *manes* (ancestors)
even though we never knew them. Similarly, most mental events are inacces-
sible to consciousness. Freud conceptualized the transmission of heritage as
transference, in the sense of transplanting prohibitions and death-inducing ties
and constraints.[5] In both *Totem and Taboo* (1913) and *Introduction to Narcissism*
(1914), he proclaimed the right of individuals to free themselves of inherited
taboos, giving rise to a concept widespread in psychoanalytical circles that
intergenerational transference is a repetition and revival of prohibitions and
constraints one must try to free oneself of.

We, too, see transference as a crucial concept,[6] although we regard it as a
vehicle not only of prohibitions but also of resources and myths of origin,
values, and traditions. Moreover, the transmission of heritage is by no means
always linear, that is, through maternal and paternal family lines. Rather, it is
the outcome of the encounter between maternal and paternal ancestries in the
parental couple—an encounter between the beneficial and harmful aspects of
intergenerational transference that mixes up and reshuffles the cards of inheritance. Our current research shows that generations come together in couples
in a variety of ways, creating different kinds of space in which to manage the
roles, tasks, and functions of parenting (Cigoli, Marta, Gozzoli, & Tamanza,
2003, in press).

---

[5] Freud (1953/1974) said of the Id: "(Wishful impulses) can only be recognized as belonging to
the past, can only lose their importance and be deprived of their cathexis of energy, when they have
been made conscious by the work of analysis (. . .)" (Vol. 22, p. 74).

[6] Transference is a relational principle that can be used both clinically and in research. For
example, Gill (1982) says that transference is a constant feature of the analyst's relationship with
the patient, from the beginning to the end. We make use of transference in our research when
we explore the relationship between researchers and family members. Our assertion here is that
transference is omnipresent in all human relationships, from the interpersonal to the generational.

Finally, it should be remembered that intergenerational transference takes place in specific situations, not in a vacuum. A parental couple may be well off or living on the breadline, at peace or at war with its neighbors, unable to have children or blessed with numerous offspring, coping with the expected rather than unexpected death of a family member, and so on. Our point is that intergenerational transference is itself subject to ties and constraints, and that it mobilizes certain relational themes rather than others.

Awareness of the influence that families of origin have on their children and the couples they subsequently form lies at the heart of the intergenerational approaches to family studies that have achieved great prominence in recent decades (Andolfi, 1988; Boszormenyi-Nagy & Spark, 1973; Framo, 1992; McGoldrick et al., 1993; Paul, 1980; Pontalti, 1993, 1994). According to these authors, at least three generations have to be taken into account if we are to understand the full range of emotions in the family and how gifts and obligations are exchanged. We are of the same view, although we also insist on the parental couple's crucial role not only as responsible caretakers, but also as custodians of heritage.

As we have seen, intergenerational transference is neither linear nor conscious. Like Hermes, it operates at crossroads, dovetailing family lines together. And like an underground river, it waits for the right moment (an event or transition) to resurface in the form of beliefs, fantasies, and actions. It is here, where it breaks the surface of life, that intergenerational transference has to be caught unawares, challenged, acknowledged, revised, and sent on its way.

Figure 3.4 illustrates the role of custody of heritage in relationships between family lines, and their symbolic features.

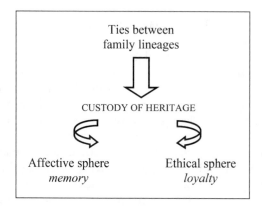

FIG. 3.4. Symbolic features of the relationship between family lineages.

The Parental Couple as an Intergenerational Mediator:
The Process of Correlated Distinction

The couple is a intergenerational meetingplace and mediator of family histories and cultures. There is an element of unpredictability in the way this happens. The principle of nonsummativity is the operative one here. Partners certainly bring to the newly formed couple the relational deficiencies and resources of their respective families of origin, but it is also true that the new couple bond's features are not simply the sum of those deficiencies and resources, the "baggage" each partner brings to the relationship. In other words, the new parental couple may or may not succeed in exploiting the resources and making good the deficiencies in caretaking that the partners inevitably bring with them, and that can be traced back to their respective family histories. Intergenerational exchange takes place through different kinds of marital–parental encounter.

There is some empirical confirmation of this theory. A study comparing nonclinical parental couples with parental couples with a non-HIV positive heroin-addicted child (Cigoli, 1994) has shown that a critical family history, bereavement, and parental deficiency are not enough in themselves to produce serious mental pathology in children. Bereavement and serious parental deficiency are also features of nonclinical parental couples. What makes the difference is the marital–parental couple's ability to cope with intergenerational difficulties and distress by drawing on the resources of its members and their relational network.

In short, when the couple fails to function as an intergenerational mediation device, it becomes either chaotic or indifferent and unseeing. In such cases, as we have said, intergenerational transmission is a hindrance to generativity. It is important to remember that social mediation also breaks down in these situations. Either social contact is seen as the root of all evil, or it is placed on the same footing as the family itself: The family and social relationships are both governed by evil.

In terms of the family, the crucial generational transition the couple has to make depends on the fact that the newly formed couple has acquired parental power and is able to exercise it. The couple's identity is at stake here, the critical questions being: How can the marital pact and the parental function be conceived in relation to what has been learned and assimilated from families of origin?

The process at work here—the counterpart in families of individuation in personal development—is a related distinction. Just as children and, later, adolescents achieve individuation by constructing an identity that distinguishes them from their parents while maintaining ties with them at a higher level (Noack, Hofer, & Youniss, 1998), so the parental couple constructs its identity by distinguishing itself from its respective families of origin.

Obviously, there are cultural factors at work here that, depending on historical period and ethnic origin, define the degree of autonomy a couple enjoys in comparison with couples of previous generations. In a good many cultures, couples have very little room to maneuver when it comes to saying and doing something new about the upbringing of their children. This is certainly the case in Hindu, Confucian, and Islamic cultures. Husband–wife roles, and the parental couple's duty to previous generations (i.e., to generate in turn), seem to absorb the regenerative potential of the couple, which becomes no more than a link in the chain of intergenerational transmission. However, it is the newly formed couple that interprets the generational mandate (legacy), and this can be done in either a constructive, a conflictive, or a destructive way. Thus, the parental couple's room for maneuver as a mediator between generations is culture-specific.

Let us look at the concept of related distinction in more detail. As we have said, it applies not so much to individuals as to the parental couple itself. There have been many studies of concepts like regulation of distance and family boundaries (Anderson & Sabatelli, 1992; Cooper, Grotevant, & Condon, 1983). Their merit is that they have shifted attention away from a narrowly individual perspective toward a wider group perspective. In particular, the couple's interactive patterns are studied in relation to how it handles conflict with its families of origin, and the degree of parental intrusiveness on the part of the families of origin. However, the inter- and transgenerational nature of the family relationship must be taken fully into account.[7] Our approach insists on the crucial importance of the intergenerational perspective, and links the spatial nature of interaction to verticality of relationship. The concept of related distinction stresses both the intergenerational reciprocity of the process, and generational difference.

The term *distinction* is used in social psychology to describe the construction of identity. Of particular interest is Brewer's (1991) Optimal Distinctiveness Theory, which shows that social identity is a play-off between the need for recognition by and similarity to others, and the need for individuation and uniqueness. Studies have also emphasized the cultural aspect of these needs. More individualistic cultures like those of Europe and North America attribute greater value to autonomy, whereas more collectivistic ones stress the importance of close family relationships (McAdoo, 1993). Unlike in individualistic cultures, the prevalent need in collectivistic cultures is to belong, and being able to satisfy this need is widely associated with well-being and self-esteem (Chun & MacDermid, 1997), whereas emotional autonomy is taken as a sign of problematic behavior (Fuhrman & Holmbeck, 1995).

Be all this as it may, the need for autonomy and the need for belonging are, to varying degrees, essential components of identity construction and must be

---

[7] Helm Stierling (1974) applies this perspective to relationships between adolescents and their parents. He uses the term *related individuation* to emphasize the reciprocity of the relationship between the parents' ability to tolerate the pain of their children's detachment from them, and their children's ability to achieve the autonomy and sense of responsibility typical of adults.

taken into consideration. In family studies this is done empirically, analyzing the "cohesion" variable. Cohesion is defined as "the emotional bonding that family members have towards one another," which includes variables such as "emotional bonding, boundaries, coalitions, time space, friends, decision-making, and interest and recreation" (Olson, 1993, p. 105). According to Olson, optimum family functioning lies in the midrange levels, in bonds that are neither too close (enmeshed) nor too distant (disengaged). This conceptualization has been called the *curvilinear hypothesis*. By contrast, Green and Werner (1996) maintain that we should distinguish between cohesion and enmeshment. The former, they say, is concerned with the power of the family bond, the latter with clear definition of boundaries. The two variables are orthogonal and move in a linear way, so that high differentiation is, they say, typical of strongly bonded families with clearly defined boundaries, whereas low differentiation is typical of families with weak emotional bonds and poorly defined boundaries. All this shows how difficult it is not only to conceptualize about constructs and relational processes, but also to render them in empirical terms. However, both models do operate within the confines of a horizontal–spatial metaphor.

In our view, intergenerational connection and differentiation can only be adequately understood by joining up the horizontal–spatial and temporal–vertical axes, and the generational mediation construct helps us to do just this. The parental couple must be able to process what it has received and still is receiving from the previous generation with regard to parental functions. Disregard or denial of this "historical" belonging are both a sign that some past family relationships are too painful to be endured, and an abortive attempt to establish a new distinctive identity. Similarly, parental intrusiveness or indifference toward the new couple are signs of mistrust or an inability to give care.

The process of distinctive identity construction is fuelled by reciprocity and results in the ability to be autonomous: The partners are able to respond as a couple to the need to perform parental duties. Awareness of the couple's boundaries, taking decisions, and accepting responsibilities, are outcomes of the kind of cross-generational negotiation needed to generate new ties and give fresh meaning to existing ones.

The process by which the couple establishes its identity goes through several stages. For many years after it has been formed, the couple compares itself to its respective families of origin. Each partner identifies with or rejects the kind of couple relationship he or she experienced and internalized within his or her own family. Other significant groups to which they belong (including religious groups) may also have offered ideal representations of family function against which young couples measure themselves. Thus, the internalized couple relationship, with all its cultural and family associations, serves as a yardstick for the couple's ongoing marital and parental experience.

It is usually said that earlier experience of parental conflict in families of origin is a problem for young couples, but this is not to say that highly successful parental relationships do not also have their problems. For example, when their parents got on well, children are likely to take it for granted that any couple relationship will be successful, and are likely to feel inadequate and have difficulty in accepting that their own couple relationships have problems, especially when conflict surfaces in violent ways.

As the years go by, the couple will feel less need to compare itself to others, provided that the couple bond remains strong and they manage to cope with the crises that come along. A couple is held together by many experiences: The husband and wife are party to a unique and specific life story. In a manner of speaking, the couple "appropriates" its own uniqueness: The partners "know" that this, and not another, is the life that has been given to them, and that they have constructed together. Nostalgic journeys into the past are ruled out. Instead—humorously and with a degree of emotional aloofness—they come to terms with themselves, their partners, and life's events. It is as if they have sifted out what really counts in life, the things that usually affect the nature and strength of the bond that joins them together.

So, when related distinction works properly, it brings about a new kind of transformation that enables similarities and differences between generations to be preserved. The danger in all this is the couple's counterdependence or passivity. In the former case, the couple feels it has to assert its distance and difference from its families of origin, as if making a totally fresh start that owes nothing to origins and roots. In the latter case, the parental couple allows itself to be engulfed by the possessiveness of one or the other of the families of origin, and makes no attempt to act as a mediator between generations. Thus, children experience either isolation and vindictiveness in their relationships, or confusion and blurring of roles.

THE SIBLING BOND: DIFFERENCE AND SHARING

The sibling relationship merits careful conceptual, empirical, and historical study. In its present-day form, it displays a number of new and in some ways contradictory features. In Southern Europe especially, sibling relationships are increasingly rare because of the high percentage of only children, whereas in Northern Europe and the United States, the relationship is a composite one because of the widespread presence of stepchildren in stepfamilies.

It is easy to think of sibling relationships in terms of polarity: on one hand, cooperation, solidarity, and mutual support; on the other, the competiveness, conflict, and brinkmanship that can trigger violence, mutual rejection, and hatred. And yet, a whole set of differences has to be taken into account if we are to arrive at a full understanding of the sibling relationship. As we have seen, siblings are already genetically different at birth; each child draws on the gene pool of four generations. Moreover, each child, although it shares the same family of origin, has a distinct sexual identity, is older or younger than its siblings (first child, second child, etc.), was born during a certain period in the life cycle of the family, and has the responsibility of living up to the expectations of its parents and relatives—what clinical studies call *family legacies*.

One or two examples will serve to illustrate the complexity of the sibling relationship. For centuries, in the West, a clear hierarchical distinction between brothers and sisters was enforced in order to keep families together—cohesion was intimately bound up with the inheritance of property. Gender and order of birth had specific consequences, as in the case of cadet sons, who were denied inheritance, or daughters, who could either marry or become nuns. Nowadays we might think more in terms of the difference between a child born after the serious illness or even death of a sibling, a child who is much older or younger than its siblings, or a daughter born later than a son and vice versa. On one hand we see that chance, which can be favorable or unfavorable, is at work; on the other, we see that culture, with all its traditions and laws, is the operative force.

So the fundamental questions are: What value and meaning is attributed to the children by previous generations? What mandates do they receive? Where do they stand in relation to the values and meaning attributed to other siblings? What part does chance play? In short, we need to think of the sibling relationship first as a constraint that manifests itself through a tie of dependence on previous generations, and second as the acceptance of unpredictability.

Dunn and Plomin (1991) and Hetherington, Reiss, and Plomin (1992) have studied sibling differences in terms of shared and unshared environments. Although interesting, this distinction is too general when applied to family relationships because one of the features of the family is its well defined generational ties. In our view, it is more productive to think in terms of the family's potential for differentiation and the children-siblings' sensitivity to belonging. The antecedent and interactive variables at work here result in a complex relationship, that is, a relationship with very different alignments, alliances and outcomes.

Let us begin with the family's potential for differentiation—the ability of the parents and their families of origin to create unique ties with, and therefore different and distinctive identities for, each child that is born. This involves the kind of genuine relational competence that enables siblings to feel they are part of a family, both in terms of what they share with the other siblings and in terms of what makes them unique. We might say that parents' and relatives' attribution of value to each child constitutes the ideal matrix for the kind of positive bond that enables siblings to give each other mental as well as physical support. Attribution of value to each individual child does not deny the different feelings the child may elicit in parents and relatives, or the different kinds of commitment and involvement parents and relatives must give as it grows up. For example, it is well known that first children cause more anxiety, and that their parents tend to control their lives more closely than those of second children, whose relationship with their parents can be less anxiety-inducing provided that certain events do not occur. By contrast, strictly imposed differences between siblings can lead to rivalry, injustice, and persecution. It is also true that parents' indifference to the unique qualities of their children can make it very difficult for siblings to share a sense of belonging. In such cases, what is handed down from one generation to the next is the rule of life that says that people must fend for themselves.

The family's potential for differentiation is most evident when crises occur. Things like divorces or the splitting of an inheritance are likely to create opposing factions within the family. Such situations make clear whether children are totally drawn into the dispute or are spared involvement, and in what way.

In addition to the family's potential for differentiation, we must also take account of children's awareness of belonging, that is, how siblings manage relationships with each other and their family, although it should always be remembered that potential for differentiation is the frame for sensitivity to belonging. Taking account of the latter enables us to discern positive sibling relationships even in families where the family bond instills very little hope and trust. This is what happens in "sibling families" where, despite the neglect and/or abandonment they have suffered, it is the siblings who succeed in constructing and sharing a family bond, especially through the agency of sisters (Cigoli, 1992). This does not happen when siblings are rigidly differentiated, or when they become involved in the split between their parents. Shared experience of bad parenting is needed if siblings are to make their "own" family in this way.

Another important consideration is how sibling relationships develop in time. Sibling relationships last longer than any other family relationship, sometimes 20 or 30 years longer than relationships with parents. This means that siblings are the true witnesses to the viability or otherwise of the family bond, which is often put to the test in a whole variety of ways. Nowadays, for example, it is the frequency of divorce and the growing number of stepfamilies that test the strength of sibling relationships, whereas in the past it was the early death of one or both parents.

In psychosocial research, it was only in the mid-1980s that sibling relationships came to be studied across the entire span of the family life cycle (Goetting, 1986). Looking at adult sibling relationships reveals that, despite the influence of family history and ties, such relationships allow more room for personal choices and decisions, and that relationships between siblings are less "obligatory" than those with parents, spouses and children (Rossi & Rossi, 1990; Scabini & Cigoli, 1998). In other words, adult siblings are free to bond with each other if they want to.

The distancing that occurs between siblings when they get married or choose to live separate lives is "reversible," in the sense that long periods of infrequent contact (apart from ritual family occasions and events) may be followed by others in which siblings are extremely close, especially when they need each other's help. Bedford (1989) coined the term *hour-glass effect* to describe how involvement with siblings decreases as children grow older, and increases when children leave home and parents feel at a loss. Such cases lay bare the essential nature of the relationship because the family legacy is channeled through siblings' choices and decisions (sensitivity to belonging).

Psychosocial studies in particular have shown that, when critical events like divorce, the death of a spouse, and financial or schooling problems occur, there is a significant increase in emotional closeness and frequency of contact between siblings, as well as in the practical help they give each other (Bank & Kahn, 1982). These studies also show that gender difference is a factor in sibling relationships. Adult women are more aware than men of the feelings present in relationships (i.e., they handle ambivalence better) and are more likely to keep relationships alive.

According to Cicirelli (1995), merely knowing that one's siblings are still alive can be a potential source of security in old age. Many studies have shown that sibling bonding is very strong at this age, although this is mainly true when family experiences have been positive or when siblings have, in any case, made some sort of emotional investment in the relationship. Old age does not have the power to transform indifference or deeply felt hostility in past relationships, but it does offer an opportunity to put to rights a relationship that may have suffered from low levels of emotional involvement. In any case, elderly sisters are better at offering help than their brothers. This is an outcome of women's greater willingness to help each other throughout their lives, but as we have seen, women are also more aware and more tolerant of ambivalence in relationships. Men are more reluctant to say how they feel about their siblings, and when they do agree to talk about their feelings, there is a marked discrepancy between the feelings they are conscious of and the ones they actually communicate in their relationships.

Gold (1989; Gold, Woodbury, & George, 1990) has built up an interesting typology of the sibling relationships, extending from intimate ties, and ties based on obligations and rewards prescribed by family mandates, to ties of envy/hostility and mutual indifference lacking all psychological engagement. The latter two pathologies both result from dysfunctional family situations, confirming what we said earlier.

Another important area of research is the care given by siblings to their aged parents. It has long been known that women are caregivers par excellence, but the problem in terms of the family is to understand why other potential caregivers are excluded or sidetracked, and how the sibling relationship may serve as either a resource or a hindrance in caring for sick, aged parents, which can often extend over many years. First of all, it should be noted that the burden of care is not equally apportioned, even when there is an extended network of siblings. Rather, there is an "unspoken agreement" that care should be delegated to someone in particular, and that whoever that person is should carry out his or her appointed task. Examples of this are the child earmarked as the caregiver from birth; the only daughter in the family; the youngest child; and the person who tries to persuade an aged parent to satisfy his or her lifelong need of being the favorite child (Cigoli, 1992; Tamanza, 1998). As can be seen when crises occur, ancient bonds and constraints are likely to win out over personal choices.

To summarize, the sibling bond is based on the family's potential for differentiation, that is, its ability to construct a special bond with each individual child. This also includes "mandates," which should not be seen as pathological in the first instance because they can differ widely. If the family's potential for differentiation results in rigidly imposed differences based on gender, order of birth, and family legacy, or in systematic indifference to the differences between children-siblings, the sibling bond may be seriously weakened. We know that generational variables have to be linked to what we call "awareness of belonging," but it should also be remembered that these variables form a hierarchy. The nature of the relationship created between parents and siblings in the family's past does appear to influence sibling relationships much later on in life. Kancyper (1997) refers to the "sibling complex" underlining the value of the sibling relationship for the personal identity formation. This tie takes in both resources and limits from the generational exchange. Speaking of limits, we are used to talking about the "fratricidal struggle."

Studies of sibling relationships in adulthood and old age suggest that the ability to choose how parents and children relate to each other becomes more important and more widespread as people grow older. That said, the importance of the family's potential for differentiation, and of the ups and downs in sibling relationships, is clearly revealed in the kind of care given to aged parents, especially when they are sick. The family relationship reveals its true colors in moments of crisis and transition, and the same is true of the sibling relationship.

Figure 3.5 illustrates the role and symbolic features of care in sibling relationships.

If it is the duty of previous generations to foster difference in each individual child, it is the task of children-siblings is to safeguard their awareness of belonging to a family. Sharing means being able to "split" resources and suffering, while fairness means that each sibling has equal value, and that the relationship can be set to rights should any unfair attribution of role, feeling, or task occur. Fornari (1981) speaks about a sibling code regarding not only the family relation but also the social relation. This code allow the person to create and nourish the social tie. The following section is devoted to this topic.

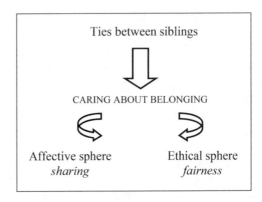

FIG. 3.5.   Symbolic features of the sibling relationships.

BONDING WITH THE COMMUNITY: MEDIATION
OR RECIPROCAL INFLUENCE?

The family's bonding with the community has often been backgrounded, or dealt with only in general terms, in psychological and sociological studies. Proof of this comes from the fact that the term *community* is used only rarely in these studies; researchers prefer to use the behaviorist term *environment*.

Our procedure is as follows: We concentrate mainly on studies that link the functioning of the family to the kind of relationship it has with the environment (social context). Turning things round, we then show that some family dynamics are closely linked to specific historical and cultural situations, and therefore that personal pathology cannot be accounted for in family terms alone. This will bring us to our crucial question: Does the family mediate individuals and their sociocultural context, or do family and society share the generative–degenerative dimension of the relationship? If the latter is true, both the family and society are responsible for what happens, and both are in a position to influence each other. In short, both play a part in how individuals and generations develop and grow, and both should be held responsible.

Some studies have reported a close connection between the family's functioning and its relationship with society. For example, Oliveri and Reiss (1982) say that families' views ("paradigms") of social environment are associated with specific styles of interacting between family members. Using the results of problem-solving exercises administered to family triads, they narrow their focus to three dimensions—configuration, coordination, and closure—that together make up the paradigm, that is, the family's set of shared assumptions about the social world. The coordination refers to families' level of beliefs that the environment has a uniform impact on all family members: Families high on coordination adopt a unitary stance toward the world, whereas families low on this dimension deal with environmental events as separate individuals. Finally, the closure refers to variation in families' perception of events in the social world as readily interpretable on the basis of past experience versus fresh and new.

Beavers (1982) shows that enmeshed families, who find it difficult to encourage the differentiation of their members, have a centripetal relationship with environment, whereas disengaged families, who find it difficult to establish and preserve trust between their members, have a centrifugal relationship with society. Both types of engagement lead to suffering: in the former, mental illness in a family member (anorexia, drug dependence, schizophrenia); in the latter, suffering that is directed outward to society (delinquency, sociopathic behaviors). By contrast, connected family functioning promotes well-balanced interaction with the outside world.

Olson (1993) contextualizes family functioning styles within the phases of the life cycle by considering the influence of the "cohesion" and "adaptability" variables. A critical event like a parent's illness or the birth of a child may temporarily result in an extreme rather than a balanced type of functioning, both within the family and between the family and the environment. So the disorganization brought on by a critical event has consequences not only inside the family, but also in how it relates to society at large. The underlying assumption here is that the family works as a system with variable, semipermeable boundaries, that is, not so open as to compromise identity and autonomy as a system, and not so closed that interaction with the outside world is prevented.

As we have said, all these models, although interesting, treat the community only in a general way. It is not considered in its social and cultural features but, more generally, as everything that it is outside the family. Consequently, the pathology of family members cannot be described or accounted for in social and anthropological terms.

Take, for example, such Italian criminal organizations as the Mafia, the 'ndrangheta, and the camorra. Their members' antisocial pathology is clearly connected to a certain type of family organization (cosa nostra) that is, in turn, the product of a specific culture. In these organizations, the person as such has no value; the family, with its code of honor and secrecy, comes before everything. It offers its members total protection in exchange for total obedience to its rules, while society at large is regarded as nonfamily (Lo Verso, 1998).

This kind of family culture is linked to specific historical and social phenomena. Feudal organization and mentality were an active force in Southern Italy until the early 19th century, and latifundism existed until the 1950s. Obviously, and unlike in Northern Italy, this hindered investment in that which is "common and public," and the architecture of Italy's southern cities bears spectacular witness to this fact. In Naples, for example, the first piazza (i.e., the public place equivalent to the agorà in Ancient Greece) was created only after the Congress of Vienna (1814). So the inward-looking, self-referentiality of Mafia families should be seen as a form of social pathology and not just as a pathology intrinsic to their internal relationships.

In recent years, some researchers have begun studying families from the sociocultural point of view. Most notably, McGoldrick et al. (1993) have openly described the social environment as *cultural history*. As such, it has a marked impact on family life and should therefore be studied alongside family history and genetic influence. Examples here might include the tragic experiences of Jews and Armenians across so many generations or, in more recent times, the ethnic conflicts in former Yugoslavia, Palestine, and Africa, and even the seemingly less dramatic but certainly more widespread phenomenon of mass immigration. There is no ethnic group that has not at some time experienced traumatic events, and has sought—and is still seeking—ways to regenerate itself.

McGoldrick et al. (1993) locate the family in an intermediate space between individuals and the sociocultural context: The family mediates interaction between people and the sociocultural context. We prefer to think in terms of mutual influence—the sociocultural and community context on one hand, and the family on the other. We also attach great importance to family culture—anthropological features of the family such as traditions, myths of origin, attitudes to outsiders, and so on—and our interpretation of it is both generational and generative. We have already advanced the view that the generative dimension is a specifically family code that keeps alive the connection between generations, both past and future, and can be seen at work in the responsible care given by parents and relatives to younger generations. Dollahite, Slife, and Hawkins (1998) also maintain that generativity is a ethical–affective generational construct: "the moral responsibility to connect with and care for the next generation that resides in the family and extended family systems and in adult family members" (p. 452).

McAdams (2001) has explored the concept of generativity and its extension to the social dimension.[8] Following Erikson (1982), he defines generativity as "the concern for and commitment to promoting the next generation, through parenting, teaching, mentoring and generating products and outcomes that aim to benefit youth and foster the development and well-being of individuals and social systems that outlive the self" (p. 396). From the psychological point of view, generativity is driven by "an inner desire for a genetic immortality and communal nurturance" (p. 396). In social terms, it is a crucial resource "that may encourage citizenship's commitment to the public good, motivate efforts to sustain continuity, and initiate social change" (p. 396).

Snarey (1993, 1998) has drawn attention to the fact that there is a transfer of generativity from the family to the social context. In a study of four generations, he has shown that people who have experienced parenthood to the full

---

[8] Essentially, generativity is "the intergenerational transmission of which is valued" (de St. Aubin, McAdams, & Kim, 2003, p. 266).

tend to redirect their generative urges into social activity when their children have grown up. Their commitment to caring for a new generation is mostly transferred to work and the professions, and they take active steps to help younger people make the transition to full adult life. It is crucial that adults make the effort to transmit their inheritance of values to younger generations. We might say, then, that success in transferring generational responsibility into the social sphere depends on already having tried to do it in the family, in those intimate relationships that may also prove more risky in the end. As L'Abate (1997) well says, the most painful wounds are those inflicted on us by those closest to us, and that we inflict on them.

Facing the challenge of generational responsibility, with all the doubts, fears, and crises it entails, seems to help people to avoid basing their interpersonal and social relationships on the lure of power, success, and possessions. A similar approach is adopted by Pratt, Danso, Arnold, Norris, and Filyer (2001), who show that generative parents are able to transmit moral values and social confidence to their adolescent children and encourage them to behave responsibly.

To summarize, a generative shift from the family to the community occurs when the experience of intergenerational relationships within the family is redirected toward a caring interest in the future of society. By contrast, pathological intergenerational family relationships have an effect on social pathology; in such cases, the shift from the family to the community is degenerative.

So far we have looked at the transfer and transmission of generativity from the family to society and the community. Now we must turn our attention to the similar process we find at work in the social context. Society, with its institutions and various forms of community organization, is not an undifferentiated quid but an organized entity that develops out of interaction between the various generations present in society. The family perceives it as a set of "places," some distant, others closer to home, with which it can interact. However, it should not be forgotten that relational networks like the school, the neighborhood, associations, and psychosocial organizations may be generative or degenerative.

So if it is true that a transfer of generativity from the family to the community occurs when the family has a certain degree of trust and openness toward it, it is equally true that there is transfer from the community to the family. This happens when adults in society behave in a supportive, responsible way toward the young, and act cooperatively rather than competitively. It goes without saying that if the "social plurality" (school neighborhood, community organizations) acts on behalf of totalitarian states or warring clans, the family relationship will be seriously damaged.

Sampson (1992, 1999), developing on an idea of Coleman's (1990), describes generativity in terms of family and social capital. In particular, he stresses the part played by boundaries in safeguarding this capital, in the sense that total openness does not promote productive exchange between the family and the community. A certain degree of "closure" is required if the generative capital of the family and community is to be used to best effect and made available to whoever needs it most. In neighborhood relations, for example, adults can form networks to help each other raise children and adolescents. As Small and Supple (2001) point out, it is no accident that resilient children are partly the way they are because they have been able to use the human capital generated by other families, even when the care they received from their own families has been less than adequate.

So in society, as in the family, there are generative and/or degenerative processes at work. The former produce relational well-being and add to family and social history; the latter lead to discomfort, undermine family history, and result in the attenuation and disappearance of social traditions, and even civilization itself. The two processes are interdependent: What happens between generations within the family influences what happens between generations in society, and vice versa. However, it should be emphasized that social generativity can easily be repressed, as happens, for example, when adults drive a wedge between how they behave in the family and how they behave in society. This is true in Southern Europe, and in Italy especially, where adults adopt a twin-track form of behavior. In social life they maintain a due distance from young people by making it difficult for them to find work (current youth unemployment rates are symptomatic of this) and take on responsibility, whereas in their family lives these same adults support and protect their young people for years on end. So young people's dependence on their families is much prolonged, while adults remain permanent fixtures in the social sphere for much longer.

As our studies have shown (Scabini & Cigoli, 1997; Scabini & Donati, 1988), this kind of "prolonged protection" is not only a specific type of intergenerational relationship within the family, but also a way of compensating for an obvious intergenerational imbalance in society. Such a solution is inherently risky because it is fuelled by schism and does not encourage interdependence and generational exchange between the family and society. It may work as a short-term tactical and adaptive solution, but in the long term it causes the family and social fabric to unravel and heralds serious social conflict.[9]

To summarize, when we look at relationships from the family's point of view, we see that there is a transference of generativity–degenerativity to the social sphere. The extent of this transference correlates with the willingness of previous generations to invest meaning and positive action in the environment (social sphere), starting with the immediate community. Similarly, when we look at relationships from the social point of view, we see that the "generative capital" deriving from community relationships may be transferred to the family. Supporting and fuelling a generative society means seeing the future of

---

[9] We shall return to this theme in the chapter on young adults.

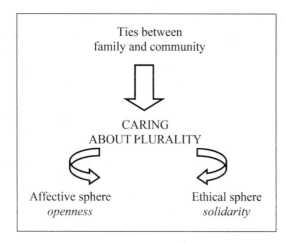

FIG. 3.6. Symbolic features of the relationship between family and community.

society and new generations not just as a family matter of relations between parents and children, but also as a matter for society (Sasaki, 2003).

Figure 3.6 shows the symbolic aspects of care in the relationship between family and community. Society and the family's shared responsibility for generativity in relation to new generations should not be overlooked. We use *care of plurality* to indicate that family members feel they are involved in ties that transcend those of biology (blood) and family history. This involves openness both to the community and to species itself, that is, the shared feeling of belonging to the human race. The affective sphere of the tie represents openness to the other (other families, the surrounding community), whereas the ethical sphere represents solidarity, that is, sharing with others the experience of living a life on Mother Earth.

THE CORES OF THE RELATIONSHIP

In this chapter, we have focused on the "cores" of the family relationship. These cores are both separate and intertwined, so "family-ness" can never be defined in its entirety, once and for all. We can only access and understand it by investigating the bonds and ties through which it reveals itself. The affective and ethical nature of these bonds becomes especially clear when there are crises or major transitions in the family. We return to this theme when we examine the idea of the epiphany of the relationship.

The cores of the family relationship share the fundamental task of giving and receiving care. Within the epistemic prototype we have chosen as our

model, care assumes a variety of forms, each with its own symbolic, affective, and ethical features—caring about the pact, responsible care-taking, the
family's heritage, belonging, and plurality.

In particular, we have shown that to understand generational exchange, we
first have to consider its distinctive dual nature—the fact that the couple bond
between parents has the dual function of mediating between generations and
caring for the family heritage. The couple relationship is the crucial junction
between one generation and another; it both articulates and connects marriage
(de facto marriages also have ties), parenthood, and care of family heritage.
Awareness of the dual nature of generational exchange also helps us to distinguish between intergenerational (what generations exchange) and transgenerational (what runs through generations) from one to the next (unconscious
fantasies, myths of origin, hereditary rules, values).

As we have seen, the dynamics of generational exchange are governed by
the dual register of giving and indebtedness. Finally, we noted that, in the
symbolic dimension, the basic features of relationships that we have already
investigated—trust and hope on one hand; justice on the other—acquire new
values. Thus, trust and hope are enriched by memory, sharing, and openness
(the affective sphere), whereas justice is allied to commitment, loyalty, fairness,
and solidarity (the ethical sphere).

Values, and the transmission of values, are a preferred domain of psychosocial research. In particular, Goodnow (1997) has studied the transmission
of values through such standard family routines as home management and
participation in rituals (anniversaries, celebrations, shared meals). Goodnow,
whose approach is ecological rather than relational–historical, emphasizes the
dynamic nature of the value transmission that reveals itself in the dialectic
between the continuity and renewal of values, and between the production and
reproduction of values that may vanish and be replaced by others.

Our approach is concerned not so much with the values that are continually
negotiated and redefined between generations, as with the basic values underlying whatever the family does—the family relationship's anchoring in the
symbolic dimension, that is, the affective and ethical values of trust–hope and
justice we spoke of earlier. These basic values are not so much what family
members say they are, as what they do and experience as a result of being part
of the family relationship. A value is a value because it's "worth doing," because the expectation of something beneficial to the relationship in the future
involves a cost or sacrifice (commitment) in the here and now.

Finally, we believe that the family relationship itself has value, in the sense
that it performs the essential task of mediating the generativity of individual
minds. The "value" of a family, which runs across periods and cultures, reveals
itself in family members' actions. However, this does not alter the fact that
many of these actions may strip the family relationship of its values—our
insistence on the dramatic nature of the family relationship is fully intentional.

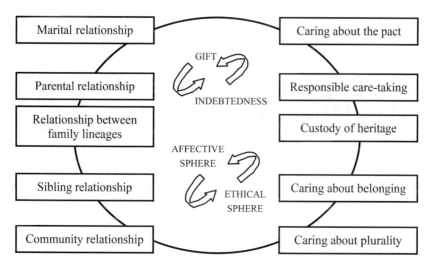

FIG. 3.7. The cores of the family relationship.

Figure 3.7 shows the cores of the family relationship and illustrates the functioning of their dynamics and symbolic principles.

CHAPTER FOUR

The Epiphany of Relationships and Its Methodology

CRITICAL EVENTS, TRANSITIONS, AND AIMS

Transitions have long been a central concern in family studies. Several decades ago, Haley (1973) remarked that some of the symptoms observable in a family member—usually a child—could be linked to crises brought on by transitions in the family. Such crises point to a family's difficulty in coping with change, but they are also valuable opportunities to transform relationships. Hadley, Jacob, Milliones, Caplan, and Spitz (1974) in their turn showed that family crises brought on by the loss or acquisition of family members are linked to the appearance of symptoms in one or more family members.

Over the last decade, transition became a leitmotiv in psychology literature (Bengston & Allen, 1993; Ruble & Seidman, 1996; Wapner & Craig-Bray, 1992), partly thanks to Family Stress Theory, which has shifted the focus from analysis of individual stages in the family life cycle to the coping processes that enable families to pass from one stage to the next (Falicov, 1988). As we argue later, however, "stress" and "crisis" are not homologous concepts.

Transition is a key concept in the relational–symbolic approach. As we have said, the relational–symbolic tissue that actually constitutes the family, and that family members engage with in their day-to-day interaction with each other, is difficult to see at first. It is precisely when transitions occur that this tissue is laid bare because transitions put relationships to the test, highlighting their strengths and weaknesses.

In this sense, a transition may be seen as an epiphany of family relationships because transitions bring to light the types of bonds that connect family members and determine how they try to cope with the challenges life brings.

Transitions are triggered by specific events, that is, events that expose family members to crisis. Unlike the more general concept of stress, crisis indicates important, symbolically charged events that mark transitions involving the entire family. Critical events are points of no return: One chapter of the family's story ends and another begins. So a "critical" event is one that potentially demands change in family relationships, given that the family's earlier mode of functioning is no longer suited to its present aims and purpose.

The finality (purposiveness) of the family's responses to critical events should certainly not be overlooked, although "purpose" in this sense is nothing like the kind of role labeling used, for example, when the birth of a child results in a transition from being a spouse to being a parent. It would be better defined as task and an aim that requires a response, as we said in our discussion of relationship cores. A critical event calls for action but does not determine what the action will be: It urges the achievement of an aim but waits for family members to decide to take action and then decide what the action will be. To do this, the family group needs to draw on its internal or external resources in order to restructure its own functioning. Significantly enough, the etymology of "crisis" contains the ideas of separation and choice, that is, a process of distancing and disjunction from someone or something, and a decision regarding how best to perform the relationship task.

The key transitions in the family life cycle are brought on by gaining new members (marriages, births, adoptions) and by loss (deaths, divorces, marriages). As can be seen, marriage is an especially critical event because it is both a loss and a gain to the family. Some family transitions are connected to the family's relationship with society, things like sending children off to school or work. Others are brought on by setbacks like economic problems, job loss, natural disasters, wars, and so forth, or are less focused and more difficult to pinpoint in time, like the transition to adulthood.

There can be no doubt that this "blurring" of critical events has, to an extent, resulted from the loss of the rituality that attended life's various transitions until very recently. In premodern society, transitions were major community events, indicating that powerful relationships of social role and membership were in operation, whereas in postmodern society, transitions are increasingly portrayed and experienced as individual, poorly defined (in terms of how and where), almost entirely nonritualistic, negotiable, and offering plenty of room for personal choice. One example is the couple that is able to decide when to make the transition to parenthood. What looks like "free choice" is actually a result of cultural influence and the need to feel attuned the current cultural climate, and therefore "normal."

In Western culture, a transition was once a prescribed, ritual moment ("the right time"), but now it is a transitional process in which individual expectations and rights loom rather large. As a result, the concerted approval and response typical of ritual events has been lessened or even nullified. It is no accident that social psychologists are especially interested in "micro-transitions" (Breunlin, 1988).

In studying transitions, we now have to be more focused in our consideration of the linkage between the interactional and relational levels because the "here and now" of interaction between family members lays bare the deep and long time that connects generations to each other. Moreover, it has become clearer that the meanings of actions are part and parcel of relationships that were in operation previous to the performance of those same actions. One example is the transition to parenthood—a key one in families—and interaction between families when a child is born. Obviously, day-to-day caring for the child is an integral part of the relationships (largely outside of conscious awareness although operative nonetheless) that connect the newborn child to the family's previous history. Who does the child look like? Which side of the family does the resemblance come from? What expectations will the child have to live up to? How does the mother get on with her mother-in-law? Are the newly formed relational triangles (father–mother–father's mother; mother–her mother–child; etc.) constructive, or problem-fraught and even potentially destructive?

Also, our evaluation of the outcome of a transition changes depending on whether we adopt a short- or long-term perspective. One classic example is the transition brought on by divorce. If, for example, we take the social adaptation of the children involved as an indicator of success in weathering the transition, it seems that this is achieved when relational conditions are favorable, within a shortish period of time (from 1½ to 2 years). But if we consider the children's ability to invest in and maintain trustworthy relationships over time—as in a couple bond, for example—it seems that the earlier adaptive outcome may turn into an ongoing, long-term problem. As Hawley and Dehaan (1996) remark, short-term adaptive responses may lead to long-term risks.

So we might say that the short-term effects of transitions are observable at the interactional level, whereas their long-term effects are observable at the relational level. The latter are, in fact, generational effects because family transitions in the strict sense always include them. They may be revealed using cross-sectional as well as longitudinal research procedures, or through the study of individual cases, provided that the research focus and resulting methodology enable intergenerational relationships to be observed.

It is precisely because transitions reveal and challenge relationships that they should be seen, as Lewin noted (1951), as an outcome of group dynamic. In our view, family grouping is inter- and transgenerational. The fact that they challenge and provoke the entire family organization, casting doubt on existing relational balances, can certainly result in transition and transformation, but it can also lead to blockage and collapse in the relationships themselves. Transition goes through a number of stages. In his study of the impact of war on family relationships, for example, Hill (1949) identifies threes stages following the soldier's return to his homeland: a period of disorganization, a period actively spent searching for solutions, and a period of reorganization.

Turner (1982) and Van Gennep (1909) identified definite stages in the social transitions of the various cultures they studied. The first is *crisis* (interruption of social relationships, isolation, the possibility that conflict may spread, formation of factions), followed by *compensation* (various kinds of active reparation and setting to rights), and then by *reintegration* (reconciliatory ceremonies and rituals, as well as acknowledgement and negotiation of detachment) or *schism* (the outbreak of violence). We use Turner's anthropological research to illuminate how families deal with crisis.

Finally, in his studies of rituals in two widely contrasting cultures (Iatmul and Bali), Bateson (1936, 1972) showed that these rituals are founded on different ethical principles. By "ethical principle," Bateson means a cultural group's customary way of expressing and organizing relationships. Thus, Iatmul culture is based on the opposition between male and female, whereas Bali culture is based on the search for harmony.[1] In our approach, ethical principles are an aspect of the "symbolic," that is, the latent structure of the relationship concerned with justice, hope, trust, and their opposites.

In short, crisis may result either in a constructive transformation of family relationships, or in their attack and destruction. Rituals play a crucial role in this: No relationship can be reconstructed without a rite of passage, and this rite of passage must include ethical principles, or if you prefer, action guidelines.

The typical timing of each transition also has be taken into account. Our view is that the best moment for intervention and research is the phase in which family members are looking for solutions. This is the *borderline* phase between the onset of crisis and the search for ways and means of compensating for it. Families have two options here: either to reorganize their relationships, or to remain in a situation of stalemate. Stalemate is a static situation because family members are unable to break it and start making a transition; they are in a state of constriction. Stalemate can take the form of emotional blockage, violence, perversion, or lack of interest in generativity, all of which attack family relationships and create fault lines in them, but it is an essentially constrictive situation that leads to a worsening of the relationship. Eroticism is stifled; everything becomes obligatory. The family finds itself in thrall to a system of prohibitions, restrictions, and paradoxical injunctions that always run counter to independent thought and feeling.

So the family finds itself at a crossroads: Either it reorganizes its relationships or it must see them degenerate. Obviously, how the family deals with this situation depends a good deal on its previous experiences of crisis management and what "transition memories" have been handed down from generation to generation.

---

[1] In *Naven,* Bateson (1936) gives a detailed description of the young male's rite of initiation into manhood. His maternal uncle becomes of little value like a female, while the females adopt the aggressive, histrionic attitudes of males. Bateson sees this as a form of self-correction that serves to loosen the grip of schismogenesis (the difference between males and females). However, his interest in interaction blinds him to the essential meaning of the ritual, that it is the men who give birth socially! It is they who admit young males into the clan, not the females, whose role is biological, not social. This ritual is widespread across cultures (see chapter 1).

Let us look for a moment at the various forms of degeneration–stalemate. Some are already well known from literature. Frye (1967, 1983), who sees literary fiction as a form of human relationship, employs the Aristotelian concept of "drama"[2] in his analysis of three forms of relational degeneration–stalemate. The first is tragedy of order, characterized by plots involving murder, vendetta, and blind faith in the settled order of things; the second is tragedy of passion, characterized by family feuds and sibling conflict in which the main characters are torn between what they owe to themselves and what they owe to others, insofar as they belong to the same group; and the third is tragedy of isolation, in which the main characters find themselves isolated after committing some crime or other (betrayal, abandonment, violence, abuse). Here the recurring theme is dislocated time, time out of joint.

These tragic forms are also found in family relationships, but the forms of tragedy are offset by equal and opposite forms of comedy, that is, constructive, "beneficial" solutions to family problems. As we said in chapter 2, the family relationship is, of its nature, dramatic in the sense that it is bound up with the tripartite difference between genders, generations, and lineages, but the drama can also end up benefiting family relationships. For this to happen, certain actions need to be performed—recognition and legitimization of the other, reparation of damage inflicted, acceptance of life's events, intergenerational reconciliation, forgiveness of oneself and others. In other terms, this could be called the turning point in the action both because family members are able to think about what has happened and because they perform acts of atonement or reconciliation. When thinking about what has happened does not result in some action directed at others and relationships with them, it merely upholds "the order of things," that is, it is an insidious form of stalemate.

Why is transition difficult? Because it is, of its nature, hazardous, painful, and of uncertain outcome. It is no accident that clinical studies of the family have been so concerned with unresolved mourning handed down from generation to generation like some family tomb or ghost. However, we should guard against too narrow a definition of mourning and loss; they are not necessarily the same thing as the death of a family member. As Freud said (1914), some losses are bound up with ideals and values, others with economic failure, or with existential transitions such as no longer feeling young or no longer being able to have children. In short, the death of a family member, although important, is just one of the typical events that fuel transition within the family.

The other risk to be avoided is seeing critical events as things that happen at a specified time. Rather than dwelling on the present or past, people may well be thinking ahead to a critical event that has not yet happened. For example,

---

[2] "Drama" comes from the Greek *drama, dramatos* meaning "action," and its prime mover is the pathos of generational relationships. Dramas are always about group relationships and membership in or exclusion from the group.

a young mother, Maria, had been having dreams about death for some time. More specifically, she was unable to enter the cemetery in her dreams because she would either lose consciousness or wake up with a start. She had also had feelings of panic and several fainting fits, one of which required hospitalization. The truth of the situation was that the person most likely to die was Maria's aged grandmother, who had been a second mother to her. Maria's mother, Giovanna, had devoted herself to caring for her mother (Maria's grandmother) for quite some time. In the past the family had suffered a tragic loss, the death of Giovanna's 18-year-old brother in a motorcycle accident.

In this stage in her life, Maria was happy to be useful to her mother at last; for her it was a time of atonement (her words) for her lengthy dependence on her mother and a relationship that had been marked by frequent arguments, lack of understanding, and mutual disappointment. Maria, like her mother before her, was now the only remaining sibling in the family because by a tragic twist of fate, her brother, who had the same name as her dead uncle Luigi, had been killed at exactly the same age in an "ordinary" motorcycle accident! Thus, both her mother's family of origin and the present family had had to cope with grievous loss. Maria had always been jealous of her brother Luigi, who was younger than she, and his death had caused her terrible guilt feelings. It was for this reason that she had gone to a psychotherapist quite some time earlier.

During therapy, Maria revealed that what she feared was not her grandmother's death, which would be painful but bearable. What she did find unbearable, however, was the idea that she might no longer enjoy the excellent relationship she had with her mother, especially now that she had a 2-year-old daughter, Leda. This female trio was the life force of the family—the males had "abandoned" the surviving family members to their paralyzing, petrifying grief, but it was the females who ensured that life would win out over death. In other words, the grandmother's approaching death was a "pretext" for the fear and grief of losing what was there now, the bond between the grandmother (Giovanna), the mother (Maria herself), and the daughter-granddaughter (Leda) that generated so much giving.

The family had already been severely tried by death; if the excellent relationship that had recently formed between the women were also to die, it really would be the end. This was the explanation of Maria's anguish over her grandmother's death.

The transition ritual brought about by the clinical encounter involved acknowledging the value of the reciprocity that bonded together the women in the family. This ritual also includes the mother, who was more than willing to be involved. As we have said, transitions are always group-based, meaning that fathers must not be excluded from them. To do so would be to rob the generative enterprise of a vital resource. In the case in question, the fathers belong to the gender that had brought so much grief to the family in the past (two tragic deaths). After the encounter with the women, another was organized that included the husbands of both Maria and Giovanna.

What could the husbands do for the women? Could they be relied on to be resourceful in the face of grief? Giovanna, Maria's mother, acknowledged how much her husband had contributed to the couple bond, and how their bond had been the "rock" that had helped them to cope with the grievous loss of their son. Maria and her husband listened to this and then mused aloud on their thought/desire to have another child. If it was a boy, it would fill a void and rekindle life, however fearful that prospect might be, in the sense that when the boy reached adolescence the family would be terrified that the same tragic destiny would repeat itself. But the thought/desire of having another child had remained alive, and on this occasion it was the elderly couple that listened, overwhelmed by emotion.

There is no way of knowing in advance what will happen if Maria's mother falls dangerously ill and in turn finds herself close to death. But we do know, as St. Albertus Magnus said, that goodness begets goodness, and that goodness helps us to face the loss of those who are nearest and dearest to us, as well as rekindling life when such losses occur.

To summarize, transition should not be thought of in merely factual terms, in relation to some critical event. We prefer to say that a critical event mobilizes people, gets them thinking, shakes up minds as well as relationships, prefiguring future scenarios and revisiting past ones. One is never dealing with a single event, but with a *plot* in which a major event has occurred.

Figure 4.1 shows the various stages of transition and the crossroads the family is faced with.

As we have said, the family relationship most clearly reveals its characteristic features (resources, ongoing problems, sometimes serious symbolic shortcomings) during critical transitions that require that the generations involved detach themselves from the affective and cognitive procedures of earlier relational patterns and regenerate the ethos on which their relationships are founded.

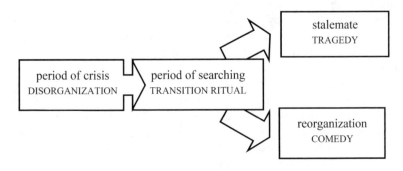

FIG. 4.1.   Transition in the family.

This process connects, in turn, with the way family members have handled crucial transitions between and across generations. Which pattern of giving and obligation (giving–receiving–reciprocating) has been established? How much time and attention have been given to the symbolic principles of trust, hope, and justice, and what damage have these principles suffered? What has been learned? What is there to hope for? What must be done? This "heritage" of knowledge and action is transmitted culturally, not genetically, and forms a sedimentary deposit for future generations.

This has important consequences from the clinical point of view because it means that certain care practices have to be activated in order to help family members to:

- think about how they interact with and relate to each other,[3]
- identify with similarity and acknowledge difference,
- go back through the generations,
- acknowledge their involvement in transition rituals.

Western culture's almost exclusive emphasis on the mother, or parents, has obscured the fact that many people and many generations have played a part in generating and consolidating how individuals relate to the other, and to each other. It is in the family relationship that respect, concern, dedication, and sacrifice toward the other are mutually exchanged, and also their opposites—hate, envy, hostility, coldness, cunning, calculation, and contempt. And finally, it is in the family relationship that schism, denial, projection, withdrawal, and idealization occur, together with the realization that there are problems that have to be faced, as well as acknowledgement of the relationship and its value, reconciliation with the other, and so on.

Transitions of various kinds highlight these themes and "presences" circulating within the relationship. It is not so much a question of obscuring individual responsibility, as of willingness to accept the idea of joint responsibility—several people, several generations—in managing family transitions. These instill fear of the new and feelings of loss, but also embody aims and purposes, the expectation that the relationship will be renewed. We explore these ideas in later chapters.

THE THREADS OF METHODOLOGY

Our approach to the study of the family is based on what we have called a relational–symbolic point of view. Now we must see how it relates to research methodology and intervention procedures.

---

[3] In family therapy, time "slows down" in the sense that the family members involved in therapy postpone action in order to make sense of things before deciding to expose themselves once again to the risks of interaction, that is, interchange with the other.

The need to establish a clear link between theory and research on one hand, and psychosocial and clinical applications on the other, was postulated by Olson as far back as the mid-1970s in a review noting the marked separation of the two fields at that time (Olson, 1976). Later (Olson & Larsen, 1990), he returned to the methodological implications of his observations, emphasizing the need for methodological consistency and the creation of a virtuous circle that could link theory to research method and results. Identifying constructs, choosing and defining methods, and defining data analytic strategies constitute a process that enables researchers to achieve results that, in turn, can help refine theoretical concepts, and so on.

In methodological terms, how may we define the research procedure that best enables us to understand the relational structure of the family and its affective and ethical features? A method is a way of getting at whatever it is that is being studied, in our case the family defined as a relational organization different from the sum of its parts, and the interaction between them. In this sense, the family is a unitas multiplex that can never be encompassed and understood. Our approach is far removed from relativist philosophies, which say that one point of view is as good as another. It is more "approximative," in the sense that we set up research procedures as close as possible to the object of study, seen from our rather special relational–symbolic point of view.

Bray, Maxwell, and Cole (1995) maintain that family studies are intrinsically complex because family relationships themselves are complex, and this is why there are so many different methodological approaches. However, this does not alter the fact that researchers have to ensure that the choices they make are consistent with what it is they are studying. The main options are: definition of the research design (observational study, correlational study, experimental study); choice of the best approach (quantitative, qualitative, integrative); definition of the research context (field research, laboratory research); definition of the unit of analysis (dyad, triad, group); choice of assessment instruments (self-report, observational, graphic/symbolic); and data analytic strategies (dyadic scores, discrepancy scores, typologies).

The first problem we pose could be formulated in this way: How can the idea of the family as a unitas multiplex be rendered in empirical terms? Deal (1995), analyzing research on families, proposes two different perspectives, one convergent, the other divergent. Studies that use a divergent perspective assume that the reality of the family is to be found in the disparate, or nonoverlapping, reports of its members. Each member expresses his or her own point of view that matches with a part of the family, and the "family object" that emerges from all these points of view. Researchers who adopt the convergent perspective assume that the reality of the family lies in what its members hold in common, and that this commonality influences individual perceptions.

We believe that one way of understanding the family's unitas multiplex is to compare and then integrate the divergent and convergent perspectives. We need to gather information about what family members share, what unites them, and what the product of their history is, as well as about what each of them thinks and feels individually, that is, their disparate individual perspectives.

Another way might be to connect and compare different methods using a multimethodological approach. In this case, the research design investigates the same constructs using a variety of instruments (self-report, interaction observational coding schemes, joint tasks). In other words, points of view are multiplied in order to construct a network of meanings. Many attempts have been made to do this, especially in the 1980s and 1990s (Kog, Vertommen, & Vandereycken, 1987; Kolevzon, Green, Fortune, & Vosler, 1988; Wilkinson, 1987), and they have largely confirmed how difficult it is to connect different points of view. The information produced by a variety of different informants (family members, researchers) is unlikely to match up because the differences are greater than the similarities. This problem had already been raised by Olson (1972), who noted the discrepancy between a subject's self-report and the researcher's assessment of the interaction, and by Sigafoss, Reiss, Rich, and Douglas (1985), who showed that there are no significant correlations between conceptually similar dimensions.

So the relational perspective urges us to *compare* multiple points of view. How are we to deal with the methodological problem this raises? We believe that the differences resulting from comparisons of this sort should be seen as sources of useful information rather than as obstacles. They are an obstacle if the researcher uses just one point of view in considering them. But if she or he assesses the internal coherence of each single study (the relationship between hypothesis, constructs, type of analysis, and results) and thinks about the metameaning of the differences she or he has found, it becomes clear that they are in fact useful sources of information. For example, the researcher may wonder why the way family members describe their relationships differs from what he or she sees in their interaction or what they do during the performance of a joint task.

In a multiple perspective (of comparison), every item of information says something about the relationship. It is as if the researcher is able to *triangulate* the information coming from perception-representation and interaction respectively. As an example, consider the answers of a group of family members to Olson's question, "Who has power in the family?" Their self-report responses should be seen as statements not of what is actually happening, but of what they assume is happening (e.g., they think the father should have power). On the other hand, direct observation reveals the discreet yet active role of the person (e.g., the mother or son) behind the actual decision making, even if that person has no apparent power. In this example, the information only seems to be contradictory; self-report instruments tell us who is believed to have power, whereas observation tells who really makes the decisions.

Every approach has its specific features, and it is not always easy to account for the differences in the results they produce. This is especially true of the relationship between qualitative and quantitative research (Sells, Smith, & Sprenkle, 1995; Tashakkori & Teddlie, 1998), although to a lesser extent it is also true of studies that use different research instruments. However, we believe that meta-analytic comparison is a good way not only of holding on to what makes each individual study different and special, but also of establishing a multiperspective point of view. We call this point of view *the researcher's triangular position.*

This brings us to another aspect of method of interest to researchers who adopt the relational perspective—the researcher's role in the production of data. The researcher is neither a foreign body nor a neutral presence, but an integral part of the research design; he or she is involved in a *relationship.* As Reiss and Oliveri (1984) shrewdly observe, different instruments structure different types of relationship between research subjects and researchers. The researcher's chosen instrument is placed between the subject and the researcher and creates specific relational configurations. Reiss and Oliveri (1984) say that researchers already reveal to subjects much of what they want to find out from the self-report instruments they give them, so the real task facing family members is to decide what and how much they should tell the researcher. Self-report data should be seen as the result of two factors. One is the representation that each individual family member has of the family relationships under investigation; the other is what degree of closeness with the researcher each individual considers desirable. Social desirability response bias is an unavoidable element of self-report instruments, even though it is possible to measure and control that desirability.

By contrast, researchers reveal much less of what they want to find out when they use observational instruments. So the research setting distances researchers from subjects while bringing subjects closer to each other. Subjects have to respond as a group and by interacting with each other, so the data they produce help us to identify not only interaction styles between family members, but also interaction styles between the family group and the researcher.

In short, the data produced are dependent on the method employed, and the researcher is always a part of the method, so differences in results present researchers with a variety of questions, inviting reflection on the type of setting, the influence of setting on the production of results, and the nature and comparability of the constructs under investigation. Finally, they may encourage the researcher to fine-tune the inferential and interpretative framework of the study. Divergent results are also a useful antidote to reductionism, that is, the lurking temptation to find just one or two factors (causes) to explain a whole set of phenomena. This is especially true of clinical interpretations of data.

This brings us to our third point about methodology: how the information gathered using one or more methods should be managed and analyzed. Here, too, the complexity and uniqueness of the family is very evident. The essentially relational nature of the family means that researchers are dealing with nonindependent data and are denied the use of many standard analysis techniques that require independent data if they are to work.[4] Kenny and Judd (1986) point to three factors that lead to the production of nonindependent data: compositional effect, common destiny, and mutual influence. The compositional effect means that groups or families are not composed randomly: We know that roles in families are neither randomly assigned nor interchangeable. Moreover, family members share a common fate recognizable in their common life context and common future expectations. Finally, family relationships are characterized by lasting mutual influence that extends even beyond death.

Statistical models like Cole and Jordan's (1989), and the Social Relational Model used by Cook and Dreyer (1984) are interesting attempts to consider nonindependence as a source of information and not as a statistical obstacle to be overcome.

Nonindependence of family data forces researchers to think in terms of families rather than individual family members. In this way, it is possible to consider and analyze the different levels (individual, dyadic, group) that are sources of the family data variability. These approaches, together with recently developed structural equation models, are an interesting step toward a "relational conception" that takes account of the group aspect without losing sight of the information provided by individuals and subsets (Bray et al., 1995; Deal, 1995; Gonzales & Griffin, 1997).

We often use a multimethodological design that combines large-sample quantitative research, and qualitative research based on a specific subsample. In quantitative research, we always collect data from several family members. We agree with Feetham (1988) that considering individual perceptions of family relationships, which is very common in research practice, leads to *family-related studies* and not to *family research*. We normally use questionnaires with ad hoc and widely used standard scales, and we ensure that they include constructs calculated to produce both cognitive–affective information (attribution, support, relationship quality) and ethical information (commitment, values) about the relationship. In analyzing data, we have switched from dyadic or family scores that approximate as closely as possible the "relational concept" (discrepancy scores, congruence scores), to statistical models that allow different levels of family analysis (individual/dyadic, family) to be simultaneously present in the study. Using second order scores gives a synthetic score for the dyad and the family group, but leaves out individual peculiarities, whereas complex statistical models enable us to infer latent constructs from measured variables, so that the specific contribution of each family member can be disentangled into its common and specific components. It also enables us to analyze the influence

---

[4] The assumption is that people belonging to the same group are more alike than those belonging to different groups.

of latent variables and assess the fit of the model; that is, it tells us how much variance in family members' score the model can explain.

In qualitative studies, we also try to develop research designs that match the complexity and uniqueness of the family as a unitas multiplex, that is, an organization of relationships between genders, generations, and lineages. In our view, there are two crucial elements here: choosing the right units of analysis and choosing the right measurement units. The unit of analysis is closely bound up with the interpersonal and group aspects of the family relationship, and is mainly concerned with intergenerational relationships, family space and time, and values. The timing of the meeting with the family is important here, that is, deciding which moment/stage in the family's evolution to concentrate on. Our timing is never accidental; it is chosen to coincide with a specific transition or critical event because we believe that the family's latent organizational structure (the relationship and its symbolic core) is more likely to be visible during evolutionary transitions.

In keeping with the theoretical assumptions of our model and the unit of analysis we have chosen, we believe that a joint meeting with the entire family group and the most significant family subsystems (married couple, phratry, parents–child triad) is the most effective measurement unit for qualitative research. Joint interaction analysis enables us to access what Fisher, Kokes, Ransom, Philips, and Rudd (1985), in their major study, call the transactional level in family relationships. Fisher et al. (1985) say that this level of analysis enables us to assess the family as "interchange among system members that indicates the transactional unification of the system's elements into a whole that is significantly different from the sum of its parts" (p. 215).

As we said, we see interaction as the medium that gives access to the relational level. "Transactional" and "relational" are not the same: It is one thing to look for interchange patterns and rules, quite another to look for relational typologies and find plausible meanings for them. Patterns define recurring features of interchange (i.e., they are descriptive), whereas typologies are designed to answer questions about generational interchange and give it some plausible meaning. However, this does not alter the fact that the two approaches see interaction as the basis of our knowledge of the family.

The meeting with the family group usually employs a range of techniques involving dialogue production (targeted interviews) and joint activities and tasks (graphic–symbolic tests). The information this yields is of varying kinds but it always originates in interaction and has the same objective. It applies to two registers. The first is the verbal register, which includes the semantic–representational dimension and the pragmatic–performative dimension (aims and intentions). The second is the joint action of family members who "reveal" themselves through their actions and communicate with the researcher as they perform them. It is well known that doing something together is a much less controlled activity than saying something. The joint production of verbal and graphic–symbolic elements thus provides an extremely abundant and well integrated information base that simultaneously illuminates the overall dimensions of the family group and each family member's representational and action modes.

To illustrate more fully the logic and usefulness of this procedure, and how well it enables us "capture" the latent organization of family relationships, we now discuss in some detail two of the qualitative research tools we often use: the Generational Interview and the Family Life Space.

The Generational Interview (Cigoli, 1992, 2000), which we use for married and parental couples, is based on the fundamental conceptual constructs of our relational–symbolic model. These include *awareness of time* (how families connect past, present, and future); *bonds* (the kinds of relationships that unite family members); and the *values* (spiritual, ethical, material) that govern how family members behave. The interview has three parts: an origins axis (relationships with each partner's family of origin), a marital pact axis (relationships between partners), and a parenting axis (relationship with the next generation). The theme areas, which are submitted to both members of the couple, consist of individual narrative, dialogue, and graphic–symbolic tasks.[5] Analysis of the couple's verbal production based on a transcript codified using a standard procedure, enables the couple relationship to be located on a three-level ordinal scale for each of the three axes (fecund–positive, critical–problematic, failing–negative). This combined assessment makes possible a synthetic measurement of family functioning and, more exactly, enables the couple under investigation to be fitted into a typology of generativity transmission within the family.

The second of the qualitative research tools we use, the Family Life Space, is a graphic–symbolic instrument that is easy to administer but provides a very wide spread of information. The technique was first illustrated by Mostwin (1981), whose use of it was essentially clinical. After using it extensively and conducting a metrical analysis of it, the staff at our research center provided researchers with software based on geometric and statistical algorithms (quantification of the elements; indicators of occupation in space; overall form of the design; contribution of the individual participants; Gozzoli & Tamanza, 1998).

Each family member is given a sheet of white paper with a circle indicating the family space, and is asked to position him- or herself, other family members, and people and events he or she finds important. When all family members have performed this initial task, each is asked to join up the people in the drawing to indicate whether, and to what extent, relationships between them are positive, negative, or problematic.

---

[5] Two sets of images are shown during the interview. The first consists of twelve landscape paintings, second of twelve paintings of couple scenes. The aim is to elicit comment on and comparison of the paintings in terms of families of origin (landscapes) and the origin and evolution of the marital relationship (couple scenes; Cigoli et al., 2003, in press).

This instrument is useful because in the end it produces a graphic–symbolic representation of the family group that provides much valuable information (family members may produce a single well-connected grid, several disconnected grids, and so on). Because it represents each family member's individual contribution to the group product, it also enables us to determine his or her positioning within the family (central or peripheral, close or distant from whom, good and bad relationships with whom, the absence of some important member). It can also sometimes be used to build a temporal perspective on the family, or administered to individual members and then to the whole family to observe how the positioning changes.

We end this chapter with an example of multimethodological design, in this case a study of foster families (Greco & Iafrate, 2001) comprising a quantitative research based on self-report instruments to a representative sample of foster families, and a qualitative research based on clinical interview and a graphic–symbolic instrument to a smaller sample of families.

The aim of the quantitative research was to draw a correlational map of relationships between foster families and foster children, focusing on their perceptions of family boundaries. A questionnaire was administered to 117 family triads consisting of a mother, a father, and a foster child aged 9 to 17 years. There were two versions of the questionnaire, one for parents and another for foster children. In addition to structural data, it included Barnes and Olson's (1982) Parent–Child Communication Scale, Family Boundaries Scale (Greco & Iafrate, 2001), and Foster Child Adjustment Scale rated by foster parents (Greco & Iafrate, 2001).

The aim of the qualitative section, which was explicative and interpretative in design, was to verify the hypothesis that, in situations of "dual family membership" such as foster care, individual and family relationships work well when they attempt to integrate the child's dual sense of belonging. The instruments were individual and couple interviews (for the foster child and the foster parents respectively) with symmetrical questions designed to elicit a mutual representation of the foster care situation and relationship quality, and a graphic–symbolic instrument called the Double Moon Test (Greco, 1999). This is very close to FLS and specifically focused on the theme of boundaries and the feelings of belonging within the family, always including reference to "missing element." The qualitative study involved 27 families from the previously used sample. In 10 cases the researchers were also able to meet the foster children's biological families, which is notoriously difficult to do.

These two procedures make possible a comparison of some of the central constructs used in the study of foster family relationships. For example, in family relationships it has been possible to compare information from the Parent–Child Communication Scale, the clinical interview, and observation of interaction management during performance of the joint task, whereas in perceptions of family boundaries it has been possible to compare information from the Family Boundaries Scale with graphic production from the Double Moon Test and interview responses.

As the authors point out, in some cases the various information sources give a uniform picture of the foster situation, although in others they do not. The Scale for Perception of Family Boundaries definitely shows that foster children want to be members of their foster families, whereas clinical interviews and the Double Moon Test show that foster children feel they belong to their biological families, although in quite a few cases they also try to build a link with their foster families.

As regards foster parents, the self-report scale shows that they do not want to make the foster child a member of the family, whereas the graphic–symbolic instrument reveals that they consistently locate the foster child within their family boundaries. When these seemingly contradictory results are compared and interpreted, it appears that foster children want to belong to both their biological and their foster families. The questionnaire shows that foster parents want to respect the child's ties with its biological family, and the drawing exercise, which is less subject to rational control and verbal defense, shows that they want to see the child as a member of their own family. So only the joint use of several instruments is able to reveal the ambivalence of both foster parents and foster children regarding which family the children do and should feel they belong to. It is worth remembering here that ambivalence is a sign of relational complexity, certainly not of pathology.

Results like these bring clinical consultancy and practice closer to empirical research because both are ambivalent in their accounts of over ethical-affective factors.

In the following chapters we often make comparisons, whether between our own results and those of influential researchers, or between our own quantitative and qualitative studies. The common thread running through these comparisons is the search for what constitutes the risk and resource factors in family relationships.

CHAPTER FIVE

The Destinies of the Couple's Pact

In this chapter we explore the couple relationship and its vicissitudes. We do so by examining the part that destiny plays in the couple relationship, where cultural changes and the partners' respective family histories are crucial influences. We also examine the effect of the "new birth" the couple relationship represents, before considering the factors and "ingredients" of the relationship with the other, basing our ideas on the more significant results of clinical and psychosocial studies. Our focus then shifts from the interpersonal (how each partner relates to the other) to our central theme: the couple pact and its crucial variables, the promise, and the secret agreement.

Our discussion of the couple relationship also leads to the issue of divorce: We show that in reality there are different types of divorce, each with its own cluster of features. These include the various ways of accepting rather than denying that the relationship has ended; making or refusing to make new pacts; and deciding to nurture pacts rather than seeking to attack and destroy them. Finally, we look at stepfamilies, using case studies to illustrate the relational challenges they face.

ENCOUNTERING DESTINY: FAMILIES OF ORIGIN AND CULTURAL CHANGE

In our discussion of "relationship cores," we touched on the theme of the couple relationship and its destiny. To speak of destiny in this way means acknowledging that the couple relationship has antecedents and aims, that it is an adventure in the sense that not only things that are desired or feared, but also things that are unknown, will eventually have to be dealt with—for example, an unforeseen event that may bewilder or traumatize the couple, or a moment when fortune suddenly smiles on them.

The antecedents of the relationship are fuelled by generational exchange. As far back as the 19th century, Freud (1895) showed that the presumed ability of the other to satisfy one's own needs and desires—a presumption typical of being in love—draws on the image of the mother who succors and protects. Much more recently, analyzing romantic love, Mitchell (2002) shows that the illusory security of the couple relationship is a throwback to the protected space the mother provides for her child to grow up in. Mitchell also says that the feeling of uniqueness typical of romantic love harks back to the uniqueness of the parents' love of their child. In our view, this feeling of uniqueness originates in the fact that each of the partners is offered exactly what he or she needs. This sense of the other's uniqueness is undervalued nowadays, either because people have become cynical about couple relationships, or because the partners' respective rights are of paramount concern. In the former case, lack of confidence in the relationship is voiced in a variety of ways; in the latter, partners assert their right to seek happiness through unique, intense emotional experience. Here it is the emotion that is "unique," not the relationship with the other.

Family therapy and research has gradually taken a more inclusive view of the couple relationship's antecedents. Analysis now extends to such predictors of the quality of the couple relationship as children's internalization of their parents' relationship style, and the generational transmission of marital relationship models. It is here that transgenerational transmission comes into play, especially in relation to sexuality and fecundity, beliefs about male–female relationships and gender specifics, and the value of the relationship with the other as such. For example, is proven affection worth more than social honor?

We have already looked at the sometimes profound changes that can occur in the family relationship, and the myths that are one of its distinctive features. One of the more recent of these myths is the notion that a child has the power to "make" a family. However, modern ideas about sexuality and fecundity constitute a new kind of division within the couple relationship. For many centuries, sexual pleasure and desire had to be kept clearly separate from marital love, which was a matter of mutual respect and ensuring that lots of children were produced. In today's world, sexual pleasure is unconnected with generativity, which advances in medicine (the new master of the human body) have turned into an objective to be desired and achieved "in due time." Procreation that runs counter to male and female self-fulfillment needs is now regarded as culturally improper. Women, long considered unworthy of mention in their own right because they were "merely" the emotional core of the man's household, have now become the official repositories of family memory. One of the gifts they bring to the relationship is this peculiar ability to remember, that is, feel sincere concern for the history of the family's relationships and what the couple has lived through.

Finally, another important cultural change has been the devaluation of marriage and the increase in the number of couples who live together without being married. It is no accident that the term *marital therapy* has disappeared from clinical use, to be replaced by *couple therapy*. The cultural benchmark is now the individual, whose expectations, feelings (desires, fears), and choices are what really count. These are all signs that emotional individualism is at work in society.

Let us now turn to romantic love, and the process of falling in love. Although present in all cultures, romantic love is most widespread in Western culture where, as we have argued, it has taken on some of the features of divine love, including unity and eternity. In *Anthony and Cleopatra,* Shakespeare (1597/2001) says that eternity and the grandeur of love are brothers. To measure love requires the "new heaven, new earth" (I, 1, 14–17) that forms part of the Christian eschatological tradition—love does not die when the physical body dies. This comes as no surprise to anyone who takes a transgenerational view of human relationships. Love spreads of its own accord and its traces carry over into future generations, as does hate, the opposite side of the coin.

As for the eternity of love, suffice it to say that falling in love is a union of souls and a vehicle of ideal intents. In an important study, Alberoni (1968) describes falling in love as a collective phenomenon (in the sense that the couple is a group) epitomizing the desire to change social relationships. Romantic love, which rebelliously opposes social norms and traditions, suddenly broke out like an epidemic around the turn of the 19th century, provoking disorder and even tragedy in clans, families, and society at large. Today we might say that romantic love has become endemic and has lost much of its ideal intents and sense of adventure into the infinite. To counteract its force, culture employs not only violently repressive measures, but also more subtle weapons like sarcasm, cynicism, and the false wisdom of those who have experienced love.

Several decades ago, De Rougemont (1963) said that romantic love feeds on its own impracticability and inhabits a world of illusion, and a whole phalanx of psychologists, psychoanalysts, and sociologists (the new *maîtres à penser*) followed suit by siding with the individual and his or her state of health. They did so by warning them of the dangers of falling in love and advising them in various ways to keep their feet firmly on the ground. At the other extreme, the world of fashion and entertainment are striving to turn falling in love into a seemingly imperishable staple commodity. So there are ways and ways of debasing romantic love, but the fact remains that it is only by loving that people can "overhaul" themselves and enhance their ways of relating to others.

From a research viewpoint, therefore, we need to look not only at how one individual relates to another, but also at what the relationship is in itself, and the extent of its influence. It is this "third entity" that we must concentrate on, although without denying the existence of individual differences that are connected in turn to lifestyles, histories of family ties, and idiosyncratic ways of representing them.

As regards family antecedents of the couple bond, we think it is important to bear in mind the relationships that emerge between the newly forming couple and their respective families of origin. It is significant that family therapists see one or both partners' failure to detach themselves from their families of origin as one of the commonest causes of crisis in the couple relationship. Haws and Mallinckrodt (1998) found a significant curvilinear relationship between the level of individuation of both husbands and wives from their parents and the husbands' marital satisfaction. This means that men experienced problems with marital adjustment both at low levels of dependence and at protractedly high levels of dependence on the couple's families of origin. In our view, the root of these problems lies in the difficulty of making a pact with the other.

The woman's relationship with her family of origin is equally crucial. Even today, and in many cultures to a very noticeable extent, parents exercise great influence over their daughter's affective choices. Moreover, bitter conflict between parents and a daughter has more serious repercussions on the couple relationship than in the case of a son (Sprecher & Felmlee, 1992). Literary fiction clearly shows the importance of this theme. Whereas 19th-century novels ably testify to male conflict in families (sons against fathers), late 20th-century novels deal with conflict between females (daughters against mothers), confirming that the cultural importance of gender is changing. Once the couple has taken radical decisions, they defend them to the hilt, but there always comes a moment in which criticisms made by the families of origin resurface in the partners as personal doubts and even as genuine personal beliefs.

From our intergenerational perspective, the notion of cross-lineage acceptance—how the man and woman are accepted by each other's families of origin—is also important. In a female-oriented culture, the relationship between daughter-in-law and mother-in-law, and the woman's family's representation of the man she has married, are especially important. Obviously, mutual acceptance should be correlated with the partners' expectations. Some may be looking for a "family next door" where people are loving and communicative, whereas others may be looking for someone who will not take them away from their family.

ENCOUNTERING THE OTHER: FACTORS AND INGREDIENTS IN THE RELATIONSHIP

As we said, our methodology is based on developing and testing prototypal models. The model focuses on a "family object" (in this case, the couple relationship), looks for its symbolic matrices, and identifies its aims. To speak of the "aims" of a relationship, which are quite different from the conscious intentions of family members, means accepting that couples not only have unavoidable tasks to perform (challenges to be faced) but also a dynamic sense of purpose and therefore of perilous adventure. It is no accident that pathological family relationships are characterized by denial on the part of family members that there are tasks to be faced and/or by perverse uses of the relationship with the other that grow like cysts and set the relationship on a tragic course.

Over the years we have developed a model of the couple relationship that defines its features and aims as a question of making and nurturing a pact. However, we know that there can be no pact without people to make it and keep it alive. We have already said that the antecedents of the couple relationship immediately bring individual differences into play. Now we would like to look at some aspects of this that we think have important implications for psychosocial research, and then some aspects of clinical research in order to assess the weight and value of individual variables. However, the perspective on these variables is interpersonal. We have already said that human existence is predicated on relationships, that people are relational beings. The interpersonal perspective brings us into contact with the pact that partners make between themselves, and we look at this more closely in the next section.

Social psychology, especially in the field of close relations, has long been concerned with key factors that influence and codetermine how individuals relate to the other. These factors may be affective–cognitive (intimacy, attributions, beliefs, attachment styles), ethical (forgiveness, commitment, and support) and interactive (conflict, communication, and coping styles). We believe that the most important of these are, in the affective–cognitive sphere, intimacy and attributions; in the ethical sphere, forgiveness and commitment; and in the interactive sphere, coping style.

Closeness and "satisfaction" form a construct that is widely used in studies of couples. Closeness has many components, including a generalized sense of closeness to another; mutual interaction; in-depth awareness–expressiveness from and to the other in emotional, cognitive, and physical terms; and the ability to communicate and disclose (Moss & Schwebel, 1993)

Studies of attribution are also important to us because they reveal how the other is present in the self in cognitive terms. Of particular interest are Fincham and Bradbury's studies (Bradbury & Fincham, 1990; Fincham & Bradbury, 1987, 1993; Fincham, Harold, & Gano-Phillips, 2000; Karney & Bradbury, 2000) of attributive processes in couples. In their longitudinal studies, they have drawn attention to what might be called the "positive preconception" of the relationship with the other. The empirical evidence for this is that spouses who evaluate their relationship positively tend to boost the number of positive behaviors they see in their partners and play down negative behaviors. This prorelationship attribution can also predict future satisfaction with the couple relationship. By contrast, dissatisfied spouses tend to explain relational problems and their partners' negative behaviors by attributing negative internal motives to them: It is all the other's fault; they are the cause of what has happened.

So, the attributive process typically undergoes a distortion that may plausibly be connected to the long-term internalization of the relationship with the other. Positive "bias" is typically revealed as a safeguarding of the couple's "we-ness" and the value of the other.

Let us turn now to the other factor: the process of forgiveness (Fincham, 2000; Fincham & Beach, 2002; Fincham et al., 2004; Fincham, Paleari, & Regalia, 2002). In marital relationships, the partners usually hurt, offend, or betray the other, undermining trust in the bond. Those members of the couple affected by this suffer emotional and cognitive disorientation that reveals itself as anger, pain, and detachment. In a relationship's inevitable moments of crisis, being able to forgive plays a crucial role in healing wounds and revitalizing the relationship. As Fincham and colleagues say, forgiveness helps to encourage more constructive communication between partners, handle conflict more effectively, and strengthen the partners' involvement in the relationship.

In particular, a recent study shows that, when a spouse's response to some offense from the partner includes the possibility of forgiveness, rather than just revenge or avoidance, satisfaction with the couple relationship increases 6 months afterwards (Paleari et al., in press). However, if there has been no empathy with or positive attribution to the other when the offense occurs, there is no real chance of forgiveness. Negative attribution and rumination on the hurtful event make forgiveness a remote possibility.

Another of the ethical factors we regard as especially important is commitment. Hinde (1995) defines commitment as endeavoring to ensure continuity in, and improve the quality of, the relationship, and links it to closeness. It could be said that there is a virtuous triangle in the couple relationship, composed of commitment, closeness, and trust–hope. There can be no closeness without sufficient faith in being understood, or the hope that wounds can eventually be healed. Rusbult, Bissonnette, Arriaga, and Cox (1998) see commitment as a relational factor, drawing attention to the process of "accommodation," that is, an individual's willingness, when the partner's behavior has been potentially destructive, to curb the urge to react destructively in turn and instead behave in a constructive manner. Rusbult and colleagues suggest that transformation of motivation lies at the heart of the process by which individuals come to forgo self-interest for bond-interest. The partners take account of broader considerations such as long-term goals and knowledge of and concern for the partner's outcome.

In our perspective, stifling destructive aggressiveness, and forgiving and making up with the other, are indeed factors that prevent a build-up of injustice and mistrust in the relationship, notwithstanding the wrongs that have been suffered and the wounds that have been inflicted. Moreover, there is basically one reason behind this behavior: the desire to safeguard and nurture the relationship. We could say, then, that the factors we have listed are the converse of negative attribution, impulsive overreaction, and feeling that one's self-interest must be defended at all costs. Instead of connecting up, self-interest and bond-interest end up opposed and ready to do battle with each other.

Finally, one of the interactive factors we see as especially important is the way in which partners go about coping with stressful situations. If the measures they take are inadequate, they may turn out to be risk factors for the couple. Especially noteworthy is Bodenmann's (1995; Revenson, Kayser, & Bodenmann, 2005) recent attempt to develop a dyadic coping concept based on the couple's communication styles, and marital enhancement programs that utilize it (1997). We look at conflict in greater detail in the section on divorce.

Let us turn now to some clinical research issues. The needs that the couple bond exists to satisfy have been widely studied. They include healing old wounds, transcending bodily limitations and merging with the other, and improving the self-definition, that is, having clearer personal boundaries and relating more effectively to oneself and others. The fundamental process that clinical research has been able to identify in couple relationships is idealization and how it is managed over time. The tragi-romantic perspective of some psychoanalytic methods has painted a rather black picture of idealization that fails to appreciate its dual (i.e., uncertain) nature. On one hand, idealization is seen as a basic ingredient of romantic love that helps to build the couple relationship and "challenge" time; on the other, it may well be subject to disappointment and disenchantment. Equally, idealization may help partners to reach out to and find new value in each other, but it may also be motivated by self-interest alone. So idealization has, at one and the same time, a kernel of ideality that is necessary to the relationship in the sense that it urges commitment and care, and a kernel of negativity that urges denial of the sometimes profound differences between partners and of negative feelings like anger and envy. Kernberg (1995) uses the term *mature idealization* in discussing the need for commitment in the relationship, and Kaes (1989) uses the term *denial pact* to describe the components of denial in the idealization process that are there to keep aggressiveness and fear of the other at bay. We prefer to say that idealization is *ambiguous*, that is, of uncertain outcome and subject to numerous trials that may lead either to maturity and creativity, or to defensiveness and impoverishment.

Clinical research, both psychoanalytic and cognitive, has attempted to identify the mental ingredients on which the relationship with the other is founded. Kernberg (1995), for example, lists erotic desire, tenderness, being able to identify with the other (empathy), and being able to feel gratitude and guilt. On the other hand, Jones, Christensen, and Jacobson (2000) list empathetic sharing, being able to stand back and think about the relationship, and building and maintaining tolerance, that is, accepting one's own and one's partner's limitations, and identify cognitive distortion, prejudice, and idiosyncratic interpretations of facts as the ingredients that undermine the relationship.

Finally some researchers believe not so much in ingredients of this type, as in the existence of conflicting mental states. J. Fisher (1999), for example, advances the neo-Kleinian concept of the mind as an arena where a narcissistic state and a matrimonial state collide. In the former, the psychic independence and otherness of the partner is unacceptable, so the other is absorbed into the self, that is, redrawn in the image of the other that the self has created, and is used to satisfy the self's needs. In the latter, the psychic otherness of the partner is accepted and the stance is one of interdependence, that is, acknowledgement of each other's needs, each other's weaknesses, and each other's value. As can be seen, the couple is conceived as a mental phenomenon in individuals that may be beneficial or detrimental to the couple relationship proper.

To summarize, cognitive–interactive psychosocial research and cognitive–psychoanalytic clinical research have identified factors and ingredients specific to the relationship with the other. But as we have said, it is important to focus on the couple relationship in and of itself. This is a difficult task because the thing itself is difficult to see and even more difficult to analyze. Few have attempted it in the past, and few are inclined to attempt it now.

MAKING THE PACT: THE PROMISE AND THE SECRET AGREEMENT

Two major points have emerged from the discussion so far: the fact that male and female destiny is the same, and the importance of gender difference. Shared male–female destiny in "making" the couple is concerned with how partners relate to their families of origin, and cultural changes in society, but it also involves shared mental functions such as attribution and projective and introjective identification, the need for closeness, support, acknowledgement, et cetera, and processes such as commitment to the relationship, forgiveness, and reconciliation.

Gender difference is concerned with male and female awareness of the bond and how it is handled. As we have said, the gender difference embodied in sexual difference[1] is connected to the more radical difference between the self and the other. In other words, the other as such cannot be reduced to, assimilated into the self; it is not just a "container" or merely some object of attribution. Becoming aware of otherness is a long and difficult business, and the couple relationship is an ideal arena for acknowledgement or disavowal of otherness. As Meltzer and Harris (1983) say, to acknowledge otherness is to acknowledge the other's freedom from control, intrusiveness, and manipulation.

Similarity and difference both come into play when the bond with the other is being forged. But what is this bond in and of itself? As we have

---

[1] "Family-ness" has its tasks and limitations: It interlocks differences of gender, generation, and lineage. In this sense, a homosexual couple is a form of adult relationship that can be as supportive and beneficial or as damaging and pathological as any other couple relationship. Such couples come under "family-ness" because they have relations with their families of origin and family lineages, but are excluded from "family-ness" on grounds of gender difference. When the partners of a homosexual couple have children from heterosexual relationships, they become fully involved in "family-ness" and how it develops.

already argued, there is a difference between the interactive and relational levels. Interaction is located in the here and now, and in sequences of events; researchers study it in order to discover the patterns that define the couple in terms of boundaries, coalitions, communication styles, conflict management, and so on. Relationships are located in the history of the partners' relationships and what binds partners to each other. To describe this, we use the theatrical term *drama* because it enables us to connect partners' expectations (needs and desires) to their memories (past experience, things remembered and forgotten) and the critical events of life in the present, which include the decision to live as a couple and start a family.[2]

The interactive and relational levels share the concepts of interdependence, mutuality, nonlinearity and multifinality, but differ in their aims and the "depth" of their historical antecedents.

It is now time to ask how the couple relationship as such may be defined. Psychoanalysis offers one kind of answer. Dicks (1967), for example, says that two inner worlds create a shared boundary and thus a new unit (unity). This is made possible by the process of collusion in which partners unconsciously exchange needs, feelings, and fears. In addition, the partners idealize their relationship. The purpose of this idealization is not only to deny the destructive–sadistic aspects of the relationship, but also to maintain the system's equilibrium. According to Dicks, collusion is possible because the mind is not sufficient unto itself and actively seeks the other; it is constantly extending its boundaries, so to speak. It does so, for example, by exporting and depositing aspects of the self in the other, be they constructive or destructive, and by persuading the other to adopt certain attitudes during interaction, be they critical or supportive.

By contrast, Whitaker and Bumberry (1987) and Framo (1992) see the couple as a therapeutic system, in the sense that the couple relationship is able not only to heal wounds but also to enrich the personalities of the two partners. A person in love "expands" and sees the world with new eyes, as the poet Ezra Pound says. However, the "system" may fail in its aim and therefore degrade and pervert the relationship itself.

Another perspective on the couple as a *unit* (i.e., focusing on what actually makes the couple tick) came from the cognitivist–interactionists, who as early as the 1970s had already made a number of significant contributions to the de-

---

[2] In *Confessions*, St. Augustine (397) defines a new kind of time that is not cyclical, as in the Ancient World, but an arrow. Time's arrow connects *expectation* (desire), *attention* (the present moment), and *memory* (what has been deposited). Although connected to the past, time's arrow is oriented toward the future. The origin of this idea is the Hebrew tradition of a purposive link between the exodus from Egypt and the entry into the Promised Land. Critical event and transition, or *passage*, are central to time, therefore. Our view of *transitions* utilizes this concept of time's arrow, which has been the subject of several of major philosophical and scientific studies (see Cigoli, 1992).

bate. The construct they used was that of the schema borrowed from Piagetian constructivism but applied to interactional pattern. According to Raush, Barry, Hertel, and Swain (1974), this construct serves as a bridge between past and present, the intrapsychic and the interpersonal, communication theory and conflict theory. The schema not only organizes interaction, it also gives it meaning. Raush et al. show that there are schemas of reciprocity and schemas of escalation in couples. In the former, attempts are certainly made to coerce and attack the other, but the search for agreement and conciliation is also clearly present. "Harmonious" couples are those who, despite significantly differing points of view and often heated exchanges, send out a higher percentage of messages conveying the desire for reconciliation and consideration for the other's point of view. We could say that, when it occurs, interaction is a sense of "we-ness," the feeling of being part of a couple. By contrast, escalation manifests itself in attacks on the other's dignity and esteem, and in constant references to wrongs the accusing partner has suffered in a sometimes distant past. In these cases the action has no "turning-point" and the schema is impenetrable: "I" and "you" veer from attitude to another, allowing no sense of a "we-ness" to emerge and develop.

Of Rausch et al.'s (1974) two basic ways in which couples deal with conflict—avoidance and engagement—the latter is more germane to our purpose because it rests on the active, if usually unconscious, expectation that a mutual and constructive solution to problems will be found. Through engagement, partners fully express their feelings about an issue and pay more attention to their interaction and its real value, rather than content and outcome alone. However, the engagement is very different when the partners want to clarify their own points of view (self-interest) at all costs and resolve the conflict to their own advantage. And if the areas of conflict touch on delicate issues like sexual intimacy or relations with the family of origin, bitter battles are likely to break out that leave couples exhausted. In our opinion, this is clearly a perverse form of engagement that manifests itself in systematic attacks on the other and makes the partners seem uncannily like each other.

Epstein and Santa Barbara (1975) make a distinction between "dove couples" and "hawk couples." Interestingly, dove couples at first say that they want to exploit each other but quickly start using cooperative styles. They are able to express their differences, and even hostilities, but are also forgiving and supportive of each other. By contrast, hawk couples display a high degree of competitive reciprocity and mutual defection; the partners delude themselves into thinking that the other is giving in to their demands or needs and therefore go on taking advantage of them. We might say that the partners have the shared illusion that each is under the control of the other. Coercive tactics can take many forms (imposition, seduction, refusal), but they are all based on this illusion.

More recently, Markman, Renick, Floyd, Stanley, and Clements (1993) and Gottman (1994) produced a couple typology based on how couples manage conflict. They distinguish between couples that commit to cycles of listening and cooperation, and those that are stuck in a cycle of pursuit and withdrawal. For his part, Gottman distinguishes between couples that are able to validate themselves through cycles of listening and cooperation, and "volatile" couples who are unable to do this. The latter may in turn be divided into those that externalize their conflict and those that deal with it internally. The ones that externalize conflict involve their families of origin, their friends, and the groups they belong to, whereas those that internalize make the couple relationship itself the object of their destructive attacks. We might say that in the former case, the drama is enacted jointly and severally, whereas in the latter it is played out in solitude. In both cases, however, there is confusion, violence, and distress. These interaction styles are less noticeable in laboratory settings (which partners have more control over, and in which premonitory symptoms are present in any case) than in real-life situations, especially when the relationship is undergoing a serious crisis.

It should be stressed that the value of these studies is that they give priority to action. Obviously, partners have intentions and needs, but these are not seen as external to the interaction; on the contrary, they manifest themselves through the interaction itself.

As we have said, our approach is not cognitivist, whether of the constructivist or constructionist or interactionist variety, because it differs significantly from cognitivism in both its anthropological and philosophical assumptions and in its methodology. However, this does not mean that profitable exchange is not possible between relationalists and cognitive–interationists: all it takes is mutual respect and healthy curiosity.

For our part, our research into various types of couple relationships (Cigoli, 1997; Cigoli & Galimberti, 1983; Cigoli, Galimberti, & Mombelli, 1988; Scabini & Cigoli, 2000) has enabled us to identify the relationship's true task as that of making and renewing a pact. As can be seen, we accent the relationship itself, which is thereby accorded its own autonomous existence and features. We see the relationship as a third entity in addition to the two partners, in keeping with the trinitarian concept our approach is based on. The couple bond is not inalterable—it is constantly being renewed—and ethical/affective nourishment of the pact is the couple's permanent task during the various critical periods it goes through.

The pact should be seen as an organizer of relationships. As far back as the earliest Mediterranean and Central Asian civilizations, pacts have made it possible to heal social wounds, to mend divisions between peoples, clans, tribes, and individuals, and to plan ahead to a time when the rule of peace will be established. The couple bond is concerned with both these things: It can heal wounds, lessen pain, and make good the parenting deficiencies partners have experienced in their respective families of origin, while also rekindling trust and hope in the relationship with the other.

However, we are well aware that there are also "false" pacts and "evil" pacts. False pacts are made to deceive and abuse (a semblance of peace while preparing for war); evil pacts pervert the relationship in a variety of ways and are likely to be justified as concern for the other's well-being. Until quite recently, perversion of the pact was most often seen in relations between families or abuse inside the family (laws of inheritance; violence done to women). Today it is the cultural importance of the couple that makes it such a powerful magnet for sexual perversion, as well as for fully fledged mental and relational perversion (Hurni & Stoll, 1998; Racamier 1992).

Finally, a pact is different from a contract. A contract has legal status and is drawn up in accordance with the laws and cultural norms of its time. Its aim is to safeguard various types of economic and social interest. A pact has affective and ethical status and its aim is to lay the foundations on which the maintenance and development of the couple bond will depend. Its justice is not of the kind recognized by law; it derives instead from the promise that has been made, and relies on trust and hope in the relationship with the other and the commitment this generates. Pacts are strengthened when tests and problems are successfully overcome. These may include accepting one's own and the other's limitations, and being aware of the duality (ambiguity) of the couple bond, which is simultaneously permanent and precarious. Finally, there is acceptance of the fact that love can grow cold: there are times when the partners do not love each other, and times when they do not *want* to love each other.

Romano and Bouley (1988) describe the pact as the "bony tissue" the relationship needs if the partners are to understand each other's weaknesses and either deal sensitively with them or avoid dealing with them altogether. In other words, the pact creates an area of esteem and respect based on mutual sympathy and tolerance. As we have said, a minimum of trust is needed for this to work. The partners' weaknesses are the essential emotional and relational needs that neither can forgo. If these needs are attacked and violated, the ethical boundary between the partners begins to crumble.

Let us turn now to the ingredients of the pact, starting with the promise. Promising, like hoping, is predicated on an infinite future: The time will come when the partners assess whether the promise has been kept. But that is not the end of the story. They also move on to a new phase, as we see when we look at marital crisis and divorce. Arendt (1958) says that the desire to build a lasting world is a typically human trait, as is the ability to make promises and to forgive as a way of countering the unpredictability of action. A binding promise is one way of laying down "islands of security" for the future, without which even continuity would be unimaginable. In symbolic terms, maternal aspiration (continuity of hope, faith in the bond) and paternal aspiration (strength and constancy of commitment) become interconnected in this way.

One of the best known of the marriage vows is the promise to be faithful in joy and in sorrow, in sickness and in health, which is publicly witnessed in both

church and registry-office weddings. A promise made before witnesses is binding not only on the parties to it, but also in relation to the community. It goes
without saying that such a promise has a substantial ideal intent.

Unmarried couples avoid making this public statement of intent. In effect,
they are saying that their relationship is their own business and no one else's, so
the private promise they have made has to be looked for. It may, of course, be
out in the open for all to see, or, as we shall see, an integral part of the secret
agreement the couple has made. Whatever the situation, the couple bond
needs this promise if it is to stay alive; without a promise, it would be deprived
of the ethical matrix we have already referred to on a number of occasions.

The promise, then, may be regarded as a variable with several different
features: It can be formal, undertaken, or fragile. The variable is plotted as a
curve with formal and fragile at either end, and undertaken in the middle. We
consider these features separately.

A promise is formal when it is legally binding in its contractual terms. It may
be consciously drafted or else passively tailored to the conventional or fashionable contractual standards of the day. In other words, it is instrumental rather
than ethical in operation and intent. At the other end of the curve is the fragile
promise, whose ideal intent is of little real worth given that what the parties to
it value most is short-term emotion and experience in the here and now. As we
have said, it may be that the promise is feared, in which case the dissolution of
the bond is invariably seen as an instant remedy to an unacceptable situation.
Culturally speaking, the formal promise is a throwback to the past, whereas
the fragile promise belongs to the postmodern age where the emotional and
affective life of the individual is what matters most. In the middle of the
curve is the undertaken promise. Such a promise is taken seriously, in the
sense that the partners are committed to the bond and take concrete steps to
ensure that it functions properly. The promise's value lies in ethical factors like
commitment, support, forgiveness and reconciliation, which we have already
discussed.

However, a promise is not a hard-and-fast decision or choice. It should be
seen more dynamically, in the sense that the parties to it are, to an extent, unaware of its full significance and consequences, which tend to resurface during
periods of crisis.

The other variable—the secret agreement—is also plotted as a curve extending from impracticability to *rigidity*, with flexibility in the middle. We
prefer to say "secret agreement" rather than "collusion": We see agreement
as the basis of the couple and its destiny, and collusion as the mechanism that
generates pathological conditions. The "secret contract" has been a major
concern in psychoanalytic studies (Pincus & Dare, 1978). By means of this
contract, the partners meet and interlock through the projective–introjective
identification of their needs, desires, expectations and fears. The contents of
their inner worlds are transferred to the other, along with hopes and expecta-

tions—positive aspects of the self as well as unhealthy, negative ones. When we say that the other person is "my other half," we acknowledge that this mutual exchange of mental contents has taken place, and that the two halves form a "whole" that is the couple bond. This is further confirmation that the mind works through relationships, and that the couple bond—the third party to the contract—draws its substance from this fact. Norsa and Zavattini (1997) termed this third element "we-ness," a reality of a higher order than individual mental reality that draws identity and nourishment from intimacy with the other and mutual acknowledgement of difference.

In the literature, the secret agreement is often seen as a leftover from the past, an unconscious burden that weighs on the present and denies freedom of action. However, the new birth ushered in by the secret agreement is a genuinely new phase, not simply a repetition of past relationships, because it affords a certain margin of freedom, and therefore of risk. The secret agreement works rather like the camera obscura used by Vermeer and the other 17th-century painters to extend the possibilities of their art: It lays bare untapped potential and unexpected resources in people. Literature, like life, offers numerous examples of this. The secret agreement also has its own dynamic—it is forward-looking from the start, and this start is the plot's point of no return. There is no going back once the agreement has been made, even if the partners deploy imaginary "selves" and rhetorical "buts," and often refuse to accept that they can only go forward.

So the couple relationship may be defined as a new birth, a renascence of the bond (Cigoli, 2003a). As with any birth, a new couple relationship drinks from Lethe, the river of forgetting, before it emerges into the light. If origins are not forgotten, there can be no adventure, no moving forward, and therefore no true plot, although origins do still play a part in the new adventure, as we said in our discussion of bond antecedents. However, not all origins carry over into the couple agreement. The partners make a selection of the mental themes and relational problems that come together to characterize that particular couple bond *as* a couple bond. The main purpose of the clinical intervention model we have developed over time is to seek out the couple's specific secret agreement so as to avoid falling into the trap of using an abstract, general model of the generational unconscious.

The couple's secret agreement is an interlocking set of specific affective themes and problems, and it is also purposive—it does have aims, although they may be unconscious ones.

We are now in a position to define the features of the circumflex variable. The impracticability of the agreement is due to the fact that the partners are fighting hard to impose themselves on each other. Each wants his or her own needs to be satisfied. The result is a perverse circle of alternating domination and subjection, seduction and indifference. In this state of discord between the partners, the secret agreement can never become a reality because exchange itself is impossible. The existence and needs of the other are not acknowledged; what are noticed, if anything, are the other's defects, limitations, and shortcoming, which must be attacked and derided so that the other can be humiliated and enslaved. The other has to be possessed as such, and as a way of satisfying one's own needs, and all methods of achieving this—bribes, threats, deprivation of status, humiliation—are employed.

It is here that something unexpected occurs: Although there has been a starting point, the agreement is never actually made because this other force—discord—is what binds the partners together. Deep down, the couple's unity is based on a terrifying fear of the other, and anger at needing the other in order to satisfy one's needs. Instead of the charmed circle of love, there is a cursed circle of hate. There are various reasons for this, and they can easily be confused: Needing the other is unacceptable precisely because the need is so strong; the other is dangerous and a source of evil; the other must be controlled and possessed. As we shall see, not even divorce can dissolve this hard kernel of discord; on the contrary, it is more likely to make the fratricidal struggle eternal (Selvini Palazzoli, 1986).

Rigidity in the secret agreement is due to the fact that the partners are unable to renew and revitalize the agreement. Once made, the agreement is gradually eroded as needs and mutual expectations develop, and it eventually ceases functioning. It has made possible exchanges of needs and expectations, and the partners have protected each other from danger, but they are unable to espouse something outside themselves, not even the other as such.

Thus, the agreement becomes a dead weight, the bond no longer inspires hope and trust, even though the words actually used tend to be "I don't like him/her any more," "I'm not interested in him/her any more," "I don't love him/her any more," "We've got nothing more to say to each other," and so on. The alternative is for the couple to separate, but this is a difficult undertaking because, as we shall see, the interactive styles typical of impossible, impracticable agreements may suddenly kick in.

Impracticability and rigidity are very different things. In the latter, the agreement has had time and space to take hold and the partners have exchanged not only weaknesses and limitations, but also support and affection.

Finally, the secret agreement is flexible to the extent that the partners are able to satisfy well-defined mutual needs (thereby meeting the expectations of the other) and reformulate/revitalize the agreement itself. Flexibility is something that most people know and understand: Popular wisdom has always taught us that in life you go on marrying again and again, that is, the secret agreement adapts to changing affective and relational needs.

In our discussion of the factors that fuel the couple relationship, we have stressed the importance of communication, closeness (i.e., mutual openness) and idealization. Keeping ideal intent alive, and helping each other to cope with the obstacles that life places in our path, is one way of choosing the other in and

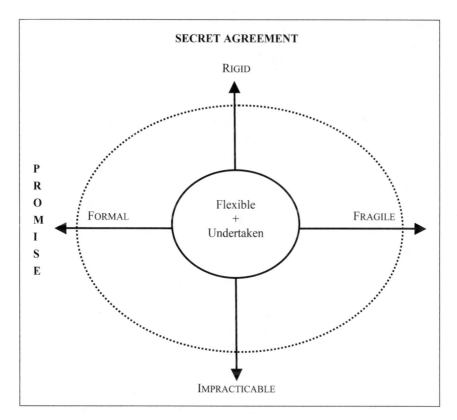

FIG. 5.1.   Types of couple pact.

for himself or herself, for better or for worse—the other is profoundly like me, and I appreciate and esteem the bond between us.

The couple's constant search for renewal may have a solid or fragile basis in reality, but the outcome is not predetermined; the search is an adventure. Moreover, temptation is always lying in wait. In the past, the temptation was to keep the couple under surveillance and straitjacket it in the constraints imposed by relationships with the families of origin; nowadays the temptation is to feed on emotion and keep commitment to the other at a safe distance.

We are now in a position to cross-correlate the promise and the secret agreement with their respective forms. The result (Fig. 5.1) is a circumflex model of the couple relationship based on two dimensions that reveals relational areas of particular interest. The central area affirms the existence of the pact and indicates that the couple bond is functioning creatively (Fig. 5.2). It includes responsible acceptance of commitment and the flexibility that enables the secret agreement to adapt to the partners' changing needs. It should be said here that the transition to the couple pact is neither quick nor straightforward; it is a series of problems that have to be coped with, some predictable others not. Obviously, the couple bond reflects the personalities of the two partners, but it also has a certain unpredictability because it taps into a specific period in the partners' lives and is shaped by how they met (by design, by chance, etc.).

In this sense, we believe that the couple bond is a new entity in its own right, with its own characteristics and aims. Its characteristics are the promise and the secret agreement; its aims are to draw up a pact and renew it as time goes on.

The pact is a joint agreement between equals. One crucial difference between the couple relationship and the relationship with the family of origin is that its guiding principle is reciprocity, not hierarchical dependence on the other. In fact, it is much more than a joint agreement; it involves interdependence, personal enhancement, mutually supportive strength and value. Wynne Lyman (1984) locates "mutuality" at the peak of the relationship's development. No pact can be made if the relationship's guiding principles are domination and dependence.

Many partners succeed in generating and nurturing the "shared entity" that is the couple bond. They do so by valuing and desiring the other, appreciating the support that she or he gives and accepting her or his limitations. The partners may decide in favor of the pact at various times in their lives: the other is trustworthy, it is nice to share meals, and so on, so in addition to personal sacrifice, she or he deserves the gift that expects no repayment.

Beavers (1985) defines emotional disturbance in interpersonal terms. The concepts he uses are in line with Fairbairn's (1952) key postulate that basic human motivation is directed toward achieving a satisfactory relationship with the other. Beavers (1985) says that the features of a "successful marriage" are responsibility, integrity, and respect. We would also add a sense of humor and willingness to learn from the past. All these things may seem idealistic and far removed from the endless problems of living together. If they do, what this really means is that problems, arguments, mutual incomprehension, and relational crises are being confused with ways of coping with them. Creative couples under strain may also, among other things, seek clinical advice, but a competent therapist will never fall into the trap of lumping dissimilar things together. There are couples with abundant resources and couples with limited or even nonexistent resources, so consultation is always tailored to the specific couple in question.

To summarize, the bond's value becomes evident when the risk involved in an encounter with the other is fully accepted. The relationship is worth the risk because it demonstrates that love is stronger than hate, that mutuality and closeness prevail over envy and fear.

The other areas of Fig. 5.1 chart the risks the pact runs, and its failure. The bottom areas are dominated by discord and deprivation of value. Let us start with discord. When the promise is basically a formal one—stereotyped and lacking any real life, as in cases where status and roles are rigidly assigned—its formality may combine with the impracticability of the secret agreement. The promise may even be experienced as a noose-around-one's-neck function, or an oppressive totalitarian system: The promise has been made, the couple have gotten married, and this gives each of them the right to do exactly as they please with the other, hence the use of such "diabolical" tools as manipulation, humiliation, and attacks directed at the other's weaknesses. A secret agreement—a ludic space for the mutual satisfaction of needs and expectations—is impossible in such circumstances. It is replaced by perverse, sadomasochistic interaction that also manifests itself in the couple's sexual relations. Such discord is, in effect, a form of relationship hatred. The partners seek their own survival at the expense of the other, and are absolute masters of the victim–persecutor logic predicated on total mistrust of the other (the converse of which is an overwhelming need for security), the belief that life is ruled by abuse and injustice, and the belief that a person's value is measured by his or her ability to dominate the other.

On the opposite lower side of the circumflex model, the fragility of the promise combines with the impracticability of the secret agreement. Here the promise is deprived of value, and even derided, because it is seen as an unacceptable constraint. The only things that count are emotions and feeling "happy," so the pact is too weak to cope effectively with disappointment and negative emotion and is always on the verge of collapse. Deprived of the solidity that comes of coping successfully with problems, and lacking any real substance, the pact wilts in the face of pain. The partners have very little faith in the bond and adopt the defensive strategy of negative investment in the relationship. Defense against pain inflicted by the other may be disguised as a search for the "right relationship" or drowned in a tide of promiscuity.

Whatever the case, the fragility of the promise carries over into the secret agreement with it, which becomes short-lived and unadventurous as a result. The impracticability of the secret agreement is also evident in short-lived marriages: the couple may have lived together for a long time, but as soon as the binding nature of the promise becomes real they start to separate, either to get divorced or to find another partner.

Unlike discord, deprivation of value results in no tragic struggle between persecutor and victim. The partners simply abandon the field and start looking for new adventures. Obviously, painful emotions are involved, but they have become consumer commodities—excitement and the happiness of the moment, neither more nor less—as chat shows and celebrity magazines make abundantly clear.

Discord and deprivation of value may thus be seen as two different forms of antipact (Fig. 5.2). Both attack the fundamental ingredients of the bond, which begins to unravel as a result, and in both cases anxiety is the dominant emotion because the partners derive no sense of security from the bond. In the case of

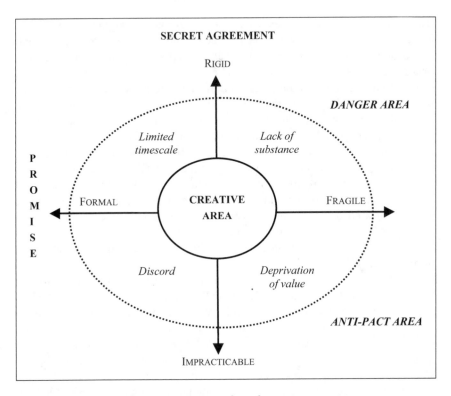

FIG. 5.2.   Types of pact functioning.

discord, they desperately try to impose it; in the case of deprivation of value, they prepare to get what they can out of the relationship because they have already prepared to abandon the field.

There are also cultural frames that can undermine the pact. Both the formality of the promise made in the name of social order and the power attributed to the families of origin, and the fragility and lack of substance of the pact made in the name of the individual's right to happiness, are ways in which the power of the antipact is brought to bear on the couple.

The situations linking the upper areas of the model are rather different. The first presents the problem of limited timescale that may result in the termination and collapse of the relationship. The couple has made its promise, which, although a formal one (i.e., ritualistic and stereotyped), gives the secret agreement time and space to develop in. There has also been an exchange of needs, especially protection from danger, but the couple is unable to get beyond this. Once these needs have been satisfied to a greater or lesser degree, the bond is emptied of meaning and no other reason can be found for espousing the other. The partners end up leading separate lives under the same roof (confirming the merely formal nature of the promise) or try to get out of the relationship in a variety of ways. It is usually one partner in particular who is aware of the gulf between them, the meaninglessness of the relationship, and the impossibility of going any further. This awareness may take the form of depression, or, more probably, a destructive attack on the other and assertion of the right to move on to new relationships.

The reasons that bring the relationship to an end are very similar to those that gave it life in the first place. It is as if the relationship comes full circle: What united the partners now comes under attack. Overdemanding needs and unrealistic expectations damage not only the individual's integrity but also the unity of the couple. The limited timescale is also evident in cases where mature and aging males embrace "antideath" relationship styles and start going out with much younger women. Today this is also true of upper class women. Obviously, it is the specifics of the encounter between the partners (i.e., their secret agreement) that should be considered. However, the real problem is that the partners have no way of restarting the relationship and taking responsibility for it. As we see when we look at "despairing" relationships, each partner always waits for the other to take responsibility for the situation: As the other is the repository of the guilt and suffering the couple has gone through, it is up to the other to put things right and inject new life into the relationship.

Finally, there is the pact's lack of substance resulting from the combination of a fragile promise and a rigid secret agreement. This can happen in couples who chose each other because they had both experienced suffering and/or serious emotional deprivation in their respective families of origin. Both partners are looking for mutual support, so the secret agreement is rigid. Often their feelings of impotence—Can the deprivations and shortcomings of previous relationships ever be made good?—carry over into the promise, which is fragile not because it is deprived of value and imposed on the partners, but because it lacks the foundation of devotion and trust the relationship calls for. The pact's lack of substance is also evident in cases where the expectation and birth of a child tests the couple relationship and then causes it to disintegrate. Males in particular fear that the equilibrium that makes them the center of attention will be upset, causing them "suddenly" to reveal previously unseen aspects of themselves.

To summarize, this model (Fig. 5.2) uses the variables of promise and secret agreement to define different kinds of pact. There are creative pacts, just as there are antipacts and pacts in danger of dissolution. An antipact is characterized by discord and deprivation of value. In the former, it is merely a tool to win the upper hand over the other: The other must be at my beck and call. In the latter, the pact is belittled and at the mercy of the individual's right to emotional satisfaction.

Pacts in danger of dissolution lack substance and have a limited timescale. In the former case, the relationship is largely a matter of commiserating with the other; in the latter, the pact is temporary, unsatisfactory, and may collapse when it has to cope with new relational needs.

Our model focuses on specific actions and motivations inherent in the couple relationship, namely making a promise and coming to a secret agreement. The aim of these actions is to make a pact, which may either succeed or fail. Thus, the model reveals not only the force lines—promise and secret agreement—but also the difficulty of transition, that is, making the pact. It may usefully be thought of as a sphere in which forces are at work that either attract the bond (the creative area of the promise and secret agreement) or repel and dissipate it (the antipact and danger areas).

Building and maintaining a couple relationship is a serious undertaking, and few couples make a success of it. Once the couple has freed itself of the constraints imposed by its families of origin, its extreme relational ideality and its extreme fragility come to the surface. Think, for example, of the problems the couple have to face. They include "leaving mom and dad" (i.e., managing the separation from families of origin); investing in the other as an erotic subject while simultaneously relating to him or her as father, mother, or sibling; wanting to have children, and bringing them up when they eventually arrive; and coping with illness, economic and work problems, the death of loved ones, and, in not a few cases, the death of the partner or spouse. This is why the couple relationship, for all the hatred it can inspire and all the pain it can cause, deserves to be approached with wonderment, compassion, and affection.

BEYOND THE BREAK-UP OF DIVORCE

We have seen that, as couples become increasingly self-centered and increasingly unsupported by family and social networks, the uncertainty and difficulty of the couple pact is making divorce an ever more frequent event. Faced with mounting disquiet over mushrooming divorce rates, especially in Western countries, researchers have reacted defensively to the distress of divorce by trying to "normalize" it as a predictable phase in the couple life cycle. Hence, also, the need to monitor it by identifying the phases partners must go through to restore balance to the situation (adaptation). Kaslow's studies (1980, 1987) of the stages of divorce are fundamental in this respect.

Divorce may also be thought of as one (though not the only) outcome of crisis in the marital pact, and as the outcome of not being able to make a pact in the first place. Because it is the break-up of a relationship, divorce is a traumatic event that manifests itself as cognitive–emotive confusion and a gradual spreading of pain, in the sense that the break-up involves many other relationships (with families of origin, with friends, with the people one mixes with in everyday life). Despite fashionable appeals for "good divorce" and "civilized" ways of managing it, divorce easily can degenerate into eternal discord.

In short, divorce is a painful experience: As well as giving people an opportunity to change (*kairos*), it exposes them to the risk of repeating certain types of relationship with the other. L'Abate (1997), for example, claims that most divorces are merely the latest expression of an increasing unwillingness to accept responsibility for relationships, and Lemaire (2002) uses the term *mild divorce* to describe the failure of many couples to arrive at any real cognitive and affective understanding of the seriousness of the decision they have made.

Another perspective draws attention to the resources of individuals and the strategies they use (in this case, their children) to cope successfully with traumatic situations in a given context. Here the operative concept is resilience. Psychosocial studies have shown that some 75% of adolescents and young adults with divorced parents suffer no serious mental problems, and that around 40% live in a state of mental well-being (Amato, 1999). However, a clinical study by Wallerstein and Lewis (1998) offers very different results: Years after their parents' divorce, all the young adults who took part in the study were suffering from a general malaise that could take a variety of forms.

Kelly and Emery (2003) recently conducted an in-depth review of studies over the past 30 years dealing with how well children adapt to their parents' divorce. In particular, they compared the risks children are exposed to with the protective factors operating in their favor. For our purposes, the most interesting aspects of this major study are the features of the couple relationship it describes. There can be no doubt that the most painful thing for children is never-ending conflict between their separated parents. This conflict was probably there well before the divorce, and divorce itself cannot and does not alter its nature. In our view, it is here that what we term the discord-based relationship manifests itself.

Recent studies of divorce do not blame persistant conflict merely on serious personality disorders in the partners. That would be a reductive approach that denies the real nature of the relationship. The partners may have perfectly acceptable interpersonal, social, and working relationships with others, and, when taken individually, reveal an impressive array of mental resources.

Psychosocial studies have clearly shown that a group can drastically limit as well as amplify an individual's resources, and the same is true of relationships between partners. Gottman (1994) in particular offers an illuminating account of the warning signs that divorce may be imminent. Complaint, criticism, denigration of the other, denial, and stonewalling (bloody-mindedness) form the ingredients of a reactive vicious circle based on attack (complaint, offense, contempt, criticize) and counterattack (calling foul, denial, obstructionism).

In other words, two interactive styles interlock, which cannot be attributed simply to the personalities of the partners. Gardner's studies (1989) of the parental alienation syndrome—the condition in which one or more children refuse to meet one of the parents (usually the father)—show that the syndrome can also be the outcome of a particular kind of couple bond. Denying the existence of the other, attributing all things evil to him or her, and claiming the right to ultimate power over the children (who will otherwise reject and desert the other partner), are all signs of discord motivated by despairing anger with the other and the inability to accept the end of the relationship and its implications. The divorced couple has to perform the difficult and delicate task of ensuring that their children have access to their origins (both parents, both families of origin). This is certainly not a matter of deciding which psychological parent (Solnit & Freud, 1973) should be placed totally in charge of the children's upbringing, but of cooperating to ensure that the children are not prevented from building a relationship with the custodial parent and his or her history, and that they are allowed access to both their families of origins if they so desire.

Studies have shown that, in addition to the 12% or so of couples caught up in serious, persistent conflict, a further 50% or so are engaged in "average conflict" (Booth & Amato, 2001). In our view, this means that a good many of the couple's problems are and will continue to remain unresolved for years to come, flowing onward in time like an underground river.

Let us now consider the results of research into protective factors from the relational point of view. Kelly and Emery (2003) identify these protective factors as a low level of conflict between partners, and joint custody of the children that is firm, competent, loving and supportive. Obviously, these ingredients are exactly the same as those needed to bring up children in intact families, confirming that divorce in no way alters or diminishes the parental tasks that have to be performed: There is no way out of generational ties and the responsibilities that go with them. We might hypothesize, therefore, that a low level of conflict shows that the partners have worked out a *modus vivendi* that enables them to feel they are still united as parents, despite the break-up of divorce.

Returning to the divorcing couple, Emery (1994) draws attention to the differing situations of the person who leaves and the person who has been left, and, most importantly, to the divorce grief cycle.[3] Love, anger, and sadness form a triangle in which, Emery says, the fate of the relationship is decided. Guiltiness and hopefulness are signs of love; anger and rage are signs of having been rejected and the refusal to accept it; and sadness is a sign of mourning for the failed relationship and the pain of finding oneself alone. Recurrent outbursts of anger are a sign that unresolved grief has been avoided, and has become, as the author puts it, a "toxic residue."

According to Emery (1994), being able to renegotiate boundaries depends on how all these complex emotions circulating within the relationship are

---

[3] "Emotional cycles" and "stages in the divorce" are not the same thing. The cycle involves the couple as such, whereas stages involve single individuals. Both need to be seen as part of a circular process of mutual influence. Whenever there are bonds, each with its own defining features, there are also people who occupy individual positions within those bonds.

managed. However, the partners are often exposed to the risk of being caught up in a power conflict, which is a visible manifestation of the difficulty, and even impossibility, of managing these emotions. The conflict (who has power, and over what) inevitably spreads to the "goods" caught up in it—the children and the couple's assets. Conflict conceals and represses the pain of no longer being close to the other. Divorce is the breaking of a tie, a loss of influence over the other, and therefore the removal of the other's presence from one's life. The standard solution offered by psychologists is to separate the couple's marital and parental roles, but this is a major undertaking that, unfortunately, has little to do with the relational aspects of the situation.

With the benefit of these studies, we can now move toward an understanding of divorce and its generational consequences, starting from the couple pact and its destiny. The theory of bonds rests on two major foundations: that bonds must be transferred if they are to survive, and that events are irreversible. The features of a bond (resources, limitations, failure) can be transferred generationally or interpersonally. An event breaks a relational continuum and opens the way to new kinds of relationship. For this to happen, however, a passage or transition is needed. In our view, divorce is as much a stressful situation that has to be coped with as it is a traumatic situation harboring a bond-related task. In other words, even when the partners have separated, there is still a family task to be performed: managing the end of the relationship in such a way that the something of it can be retained. This is certainly not a process of preservation, but a thoroughgoing mental review followed by reconstruction and restoration of the relationship with the other. Divorce sets the partners thinking about their generational history and the investment they have made in the relationship.

Let us now consider the end of the pact in the light of the different kinds of pact generated by the promise and the secret agreement we looked at earlier.

In the case of discord (a kind of antipact), the partners have been operating either on the same wavelength in their efforts to impose on the other the right to satisfy their needs, or have been trapped in the negative complementarity of an abuser-and-abused situation. However, the abused person allows him- or herself to be abused because the idea of ending the relationship—seen as a distressing, shameful, ruinous event—is simply unbearable. For both partners, ending the relationship is as unbearable as continuing to live together.

Thus, when divorce happens, it can only bear out what the relationship with the other has always been. It is one of the many ways of attacking the other's weaknesses in order to subdue and destroy him or her. Basically nothing changes; at most, the roles are reversed so that the victim becomes the persecutor.

Generational relationships (with families of origin and children) and social relationships (with courts, social services, psychologists, and friends) are caught up in the discord, and the result is utter desolation; the relational landscape looks like a bombed city or the aftermath of a terrorist attack.

In short, the failure of the pact also spells the impossibility of a constructive divorce, unless at least one of the partners conducts a searching reexamination of self and rediscovers the value of the relationship. This is where individual differences come into play.

As we have seen, the other kind of antipact involves depriving the relationship of value. Where does divorce figure in such relationship? We said earlier that, in such cases, the promise is deprived of value and makes for overinvestment in feelings and emotions. So attributing some defect to the other, or experiencing some kind of disappointment or disillusionment, or simply being bored with the relationship, can be enough to cause a split. It should also be remembered that depriving the promise of value is a way of warding off the pain inflicted by the relationship. On one hand, there is fear of imprisonment and subjection, on the other, dread of abandonment, so the partners separate to avoid being abandoned.

Although perhaps unconsciously, the couple attacks the continuity of the relationship and, with it, the shared memories that bind it together. Memory and hope carry too little weight; much more important are fear (of entombment, of abandonment) and assertion of the right to experience powerful emotion.

In such cases, divorce leads to something very specific, namely annulment. It is as if the relationship, which was never truly proclaimed by a promise, vanishes into thin air. Filial and social relationships are also part of this. People simply disappear and start a "new life."

However, there is another kind of annulment, directed at the other's very existence. We have already mentioned the well-known phenomenon of parental alienation, which first hinders access to the other parent and then makes him or her disappear altogether. And yet, the fact that this phenomenon has its own logic in the drama of married or cohabiting couples is little understood. As we see when we consider despairing relationships, this kind of annulment makes sense only to the extent that by annulling the other, I can also obliterate any responsibility for what has happened and thereby salvage my self and my value.

Here, too, divorce can give people the opportunity to take a long, hard look at themselves and their relationships with others. Relationships with children as "the other" may be the most effective in bringing about this searching review of self.

As we have argued, these two forms of antipact share a link. Because they both fall within the antipact (bond hatred) area in the model, there is no reason why desolation and annulment should not combine, although there is a difference between the two: with desolation, the other is needed if the eternal battle is to continue; with annulment, the other must either vanish or be made to vanish.

Let us now consider the danger area in the model. Through careful assessment of these situations, we have discovered not only that the various kinds of bond form a continuum, but also that there are crucial differences between them. Some end-of-pact coping styles may seem similar to those we examined earlier, but they are based on a couple pact that did at least offer the partners *something;* they were able to share and satisfy a certain number of each other's needs. Examples of this include wives who have helped their husbands in their careers, thereby realizing the dream of making their own fathers, while their husbands have either gone on being the apple of their mothers' eyes, as they were when they were children, or, if that was not the case, are now making good the deprivation thanks to the attentions of their wives (mothers). There are also those partners who give each other support because both have suffered in their respective families of origin. Others may at last have found in their partner's family the family of origin they never had, so that the other partner can never leave his or her own family. Although it is easy to see them negatively, secret agreements like these do have some value, and they do strengthen the pact.

Thus, whereas partners in antipacts have hated their relationship and deprived it of value for a variety of reasons, here the partners have been fully committed to it. In these cases, the problem is the end of the relationship and how to cope with it. Some pacts have run their course and cannot be restored and revitalized; others lack substance, so a new encounter with another partner could be a way of lending more substance to the relationship. Here the partners find themselves at a crossroads: Should they accept or refuse to accept that the relationship is at an end? It should be noted, incidentally, that an antipact does not allow for a crossroads, that is, an alternative and the possibility of choosing. The partners' shared perception of the pact's lack of substance, or the feeling that it has come to an end, helps them in making the move toward divorce. They can cope with Emery's (1994) cycle of emotions by drawing on their own resources or on the help of relatives, friends, groups they belong to, and experts. For example, family mediation may be effective in such cases.

The situation is rather different when the end of the pact is unbearable, and therefore unacceptable. Here, only one of the partners—the one who most feels the claims of the bond and the dread of ending it—needs to refuse. Using the construct of the "despairing bond," Cigoli (1997; Cigoli et al., 1988) has shown that the forms the refusal to end the bond can take depend either on being unable to stop hoping in the other, or on wanting to annul the bond so as to salvage the self from extinction. In the former case, the dependence that has always been a feature of the bond reveals itself to the full: It is the other who gives life, so it is up to the other to change. If one is the cause of the suffering, that one may also and always be the cause of the transformation. In the latter case, it is impossible to implicate oneself in what has happened to the bond. The partner must break free, in whatever way possible, from the person who has attacked the relationship and caused such disappointment. This is the only way of preserving the self as the source of the bond.

Two considerations need to be made here. The first is that we should avoid falling into the individualistic trap. It is no accident that dissolving the bond is a joint task. It took two to make the bond and it takes two to separate; the verb is plural. However, this does not alter the fact that different people cope with suffering in different ways.[4] The second is that separation confirms that the various types of bond form a continuum. Their refusal to dissolve the bond makes these couples similar to those who have made an antipact, including those extreme cases that end in suicide or murder. When psychic collapse precipitates somatic collapse, one of the partners may commit suicide either because he or she feels unworthy or because he or she wants to make the other partner—the persecutor—pay forever for what he or she has done. Similarly, one of the partners may kill the other in order to be free, at last and forever, of the persecutor. As can be seen, this "always and forever" hovers birdlike over the relationship because it truly is the soul of the relationship that can bring either life (promise) or death (deceit).

However, there is a crucial difference between the antipact and danger situations, and it can be used clinically to help couples to cope with the pain of ending their relationship. The partners have exchanged some good things, the relationship has borne some fruit, but this is difficult to see when you are blinded by pain. Can any of these fruit be recognized, acknowledged, and salvaged? A good way of moving beyond the pain is to leave the relationship with something that proclaims it had value: I did this for the other and the other did this for me; you did this for me and I did this for you. In a study of divorce, Bohannan (1973) speaks of the disenchantment that, it should be remembered, is typical of the tragic state of mind. A divorcing couple is often on the verge of tragedy, but it can also opt for comedy, that is, decide to revitalize the relationship, and this can happen vis-à-vis children (an external bond), new partners, or social activity.

In short, only some divorces have a negative effect on the couple bond, and most importantly, not all divorces produce the same effects. As we have said, some are not really divorces at all, however paradoxical that may seem. Many more show that partners are having problems getting beyond divorce, and their relationship is stagnating as a result. Still others are useful because they point to the family's aim in making the transition, namely, to preserve some aspects of the relationship with the other. In these cases, the relationship with the children is the litmus paper indicating how well the transition is going. The children's access to the other parent and his or her origins (family, culture, groups he or she belongs to) is a characteristic sign that this is happening, and making it happen is a joint task.

The new pact that may form during divorce is one in which the existence of the other as parent is acknowledged and legitimized. The bond cannot be

---

[4] Cigoli (2003b) has drawn up five "provocative" questions designed to reveal the relational resources of separating or divorced couples who come for consultation.

divided, but it can be transformed and its properties transferred from one place to another. In divorce, the couple pact becomes a parental pact. This is the only way in which the partners can be spouses no longer but parents forever.

RECONSTITUTED COUPLES: BOUNDARIES, HIERARCHIES, TRIANGULARITY

We can now turn our attention to a new event: the reconstitution of the couple and family. The tricky question of the boundaries that must be built, respected in the other, and imposed on the other, has been explored at length in the literature, where the clinical and psychosocial concepts of "flexibility" and "management" have been reutilized. However, a spatial metaphor is inadequate unless it is combined with a temporal one. As we have argued, the transfer of the bond (its vicissitudes, its qualities) to a new partner should be linked to the new event, which is the reconstitution of the couple bond. On one hand, there is the reconstitution event (two people meet) that gives rise to a new love affair; on the other, the transfer of the bond with the other and its features. It may be, then, that the reconstitution event is unable to change the abiding nature of the bond. If, for example, a partner's "relational territory" has been abandoned, or else invaded and attacked by hatred and desperation, generating a new kind of bond will be no easy undertaking.

Like divorce, the reconstitution event reveals the triangularity of the couple bond. In divorce, the collapse of triangularity (mother, father, children; wife, husband, pact) is to be seen in single parenthood. Graphic research tools can be used to show that the divorced parents, especially mothers, often place themselves at the center of family life and new relationships, while the other parent is left out. The Family Life Space makes this especially clear (Di Vita & Calderaro, 2001). The children, for their part, tend to adapt to the split environment and side with one or the other of the parents. The result is a single point of origin (which is also disconnected from the family matrices) and one or more dyads. Thus, the price that has to be paid to safeguard the parental self and awareness of one's own value is the exclusion (disownment, annulment) of the other. We have highlighted a gender problem here. Males are unable to match up their couple relationship and their relationship with their children, so that divorce and leaving the partner also entails leaving the children. This can happen slowly or suddenly. On the other hand, there are males who become *more* aware of their paternal responsibilities precisely because divorce is so traumatic.

As the divorce grinds on, a very different situation may arise in which the other parent is located within the family boundary, albeit on its edge. However, the other parent is mentally present in the family's living space, so triangularity is preserved and the children can access their paternal and maternal lineages.

In short, isolation and dyadic inwardness are signs that the divorce transition has run into serious problems, or has even failed completely. We might say that there has been a trauma of triangularity and that the partners' relational resources have been insufficient to withstand its impact.

Reconstituted or step couples help us to appreciate the crucial difference between a bond in crisis and a bond that has failed. Crisis leaves room to review and revitalize the relationship: It involves bewilderment, dismay, confusion, contradiction, and collapse, but keeps faith and hope in the relationship sufficiently strong. By contrast, in a failed bond it is repetition that wins the upper hand, that is, the painful separation from the other, the need to annul the other, and profound mistrust of the relationship are repeated. Reconstituting the couple is not enough to revitalize the relationship. It is no accident that the divorce rate is higher in second and third marriages.

In a seeming paradox, one sign of successful revitalization is the legitimation of the other parent and his or her lineage, even as the boundary of the new couple is being laid down and fortified. Research has shown that the parental relationship may be negatively influenced by one of the parent's transition to a new marriage (Cartwright & Seymur, 2002; Hetherington, 1999). Relations between parents and children are fraught with betrayal, disloyalty, and the pain of rejection. In particular, pressuring children to accept a new partner (one of the ways in which parents try to reassure themselves that they have made the right decision) is a source of confusion and leads to conflicts of loyalty.

So in any clinical encounter with stepcouples, it is of paramount importance to join them in their search for the origins of the generational grief and the resources available to the partners and their family/cultural context. These resources may be difficult to discern, but making the most of them can serve as a beacon of hope and a rock of trust during the perilous times ahead. The case studies that follow are intended to illustrate this point.

Children's Power as an Antihierarchical Symptom

"How do you picture your children in ten years' time? Can you make an Identi-kit so I can get some idea?" The family mediator thus provokes Daniele and Raffaella, who have reached an impasse in the mediation process.

After a long silence, the answer the mediator receives is evasive and embarrassed. The present, fraught with impotence and frustration, hinders and befuddles temporality, that is, the ability to draw strength from the past, look to the future, and get a perspective on things.

Daniele and Raffaella got married 15 years ago, had a son (now 11 years old) and a daughter (8 years old), and have now been separated for about 3 years. The end of the marriage bond is linked to the affective relationship Raffaella has established with Sergio, a family friend, in turn the father of two children. Raffaella claims that her husband's selfishness was responsible for the failure of their marriage because his only concern is for material things and he has completely ignored her affective needs. Raffaella's protest is "incestuous" (Racamier, 1992). The new affective relationship involves the closest family friend who is already a de facto family member.

Daniele, betrayed and humiliated, has destroyed the photos and anything else that might remind him of Raffaella. She claims he also threw her out of their home, whereas he insists that she deliberately left and abandoned him.

At the time, the judge ruled that the father should have custody of the children, and that the mother should have the right to see them. The trouble was that within a very short time, the children no longer wanted to see her. In addition, the children (also school friends and playmates) of the new couple formed by Raffaella and Sergio had done their utmost to oppose their parents' relationship.

Thus, the two new partners have "reconstituted" an emotionally valid couple (their evaluation of their relationship), which nevertheless risks collapse because of the isolation it finds itself in. Both of them have left their children to their former spouses, and Raffaella, in particular, is utterly dejected at the loss.

As to Daniele, he now has a new, young companion who entered his life as a home-help but in due time won his sincere affection. He feels that he is in a position to look after his children in every imaginable way, and that he cannot possibly force them to see their mother if they do not want to. After all, it was she who left them.

When they meet in a mediation setting, and after much effort, Daniele and Raffaella do manage to come to a constructive agreement, but when the children are told about it they reject it out of hand. They take exception to every single aspect concerning them and assert their desire (and right) to make their own decisions, thus confirming their rejection of their mother. Their father gives them the companionship and security they need, and that is all they want.

Faced with the children's rejection of their agreement, the parents fall silent. It is as if they are completely at the mercy of their children. The collapse of hierarchy (and the responsibility that goes with it) is represented here by generational reversal. Significantly, the parents are unable to look ahead and "picture" their children in the future.

The trauma of divorce has made the boundary rigid: There are those who have a right to live at home with the family, and those who are denied it. On one hand, there is a family reconstructed around the father, his new companion, and the children; on the other, a couple exiled from parenthood and living in a hell of isolation.

What resources can Daniele and Raffaella fall back on? On the fact that they have struck a deal that enables them to make a fresh start and set about reestablishing and revitalizing the "hierarchical principle." This will be no easy matter, to say the least. Now it is no longer just a matter of coming to an agreement,[5] but of sustaining it and legitimizing it through action.

Disruption or Crisis of Passage

Lella and Mario both come from previous marriages. Lella has three children: The elder son and daughter live with their father, the younger daughter with her. Mario has two children, who live with their mother but see him at weekends. They have been living together for about 8 years, but their relationship is now strained because of the behavior of Lella's daughter, the *piccolina* ("little one"), who is now 16 years old. She has no esteem whatever for her mother's companion, and her constant quarrels with her mother are turning uglier.

Lella's separation from her former husband, Giulio, was indeed traumatic, with never-ending arguments and confrontations that Lella says are the fault of "that filthy beast, your father." Mario's separation from his former wife, Giuliana, was "more consensual" according to Mario, who found in Lella a woman who was livelier and more devoted to him, partly because at home there was just her younger daughter to take care of. Before meeting Mario, Lella had had an affair with Luigi, whom her children had liked very much, but she had decided in favor of her present partner. To crown it all, the new couple, Lella and Mario, had lost a child in the early months of pregnancy.

As a result, the stepcouple is faced with two sets of problems: sorrow over the loss of an unborn child, which prevented them from having "a family of their own," and sorrow over their children's delegitimation of them as parents. Both the elder children took sides some time ago, and the younger daughter has now started attacking the couple violently. Lella loses her temper when they argue, and her language and behavior deteriorate.

Mario, in turn, is attacked by his former wife, who accuses him of not being up to the situation and of dragging her children into the drama. But he, too, feels powerless and fears the situation's "contagious antieducational effect" on his own children. Caught between the quarrelling mother and daughter, he senses danger but feels at a loss, although he knows he cannot just sit on the fence and either do nothing or flee from the situation.

In short, through her own children, Lella has unconsciously raised the problem of how to detach herself from her own parents. We could call this *reverse disengagement* insofar as she has opposed her children's wishes (their preference for the man they liked) in the name of her own right to choose as *she* wishes.

---

[5] In terms of bond theory, family mediation is a space where creative paradoxes are activated: The partners separate as spouses, but succeed in salvaging the parental self. All this comes about through negotiation over the custody of children (or rather, who will have custodianship of the parental bond) in which the bond's ability to withstand the trauma of divorce and avoid sinking into chaos and despair is put to the test.

On the other hand, in choosing Lella, Mario has reconstituted his need for a "vital bond" all for himself that is not undermined by the children, although he now senses the serious risk of his own generational nonexistence and of dragging his own children into it.

Where is the resource here? Perhaps in acknowledging with the couple that there is a crisis of passage involving several generations. On one hand, the 16-year-old daughter's "disengagement" reminds Lella of her own problems of separation and individuation; on the other, the *piccolina's* provocations are driving the father to reconsider himself as a person, irrespective of his role as just a companion. This could be a good time for a personal review of both the family history and the values that govern their behavior and give meaning to their lives.

We are now in a position to describe the tests that the reconstituted couple has to pass.[6] In our relational–symbolic perspective, the bond is reconstituted by passing two tests. The first relates to how the divorced partners left their home-bond. As we have said, it is important to preserve something of the relationship one has lived through.[7] If it has been demolished by hatred and contempt, the only thing to do is escape and find something totally new. Significantly, the partners of reconstituted couples indulge in the recurring fantasy of starting from scratch, doing it all again. This belief is a defense against the fear of failing anew, a fear that profoundly undermines the perception of one's own value. On the other hand, if something of the bond with the other can be carried over positively into the new bond, there is more likelihood of getting through the divorce and building life-enhancing relationships.

The second test relates to the partners' willingness or otherwise to reactivate generativity. Having a child is one example; another is reengaging with children from previous relationships. It is well known that a bond demands exclusivity. It can be perceived and experienced as a single, specific relationship with the other, or as the other's sole possession of and envious attack on oneself. For the former to happen, considerable and consistent mental effort is needed to see what is specifically one's own (*ipse*) and what belongs to both partners (*idem*). If the adults-parents have not been able to experience the bond as specific to themselves, it is most unlikely that their children will be able to do so. Fortunately, children can identify with people other than parents, but the fact remains that parents serve as the "prime model."

Reconstituted couples or stepfamilies seem more prone to sibling and peer envy between their children, who come from different couples. This is evident

---

[6] Studies have often pointed to the lack of fixed rules for stepfamilies and the uncertainty of their roles. Obviously, the comparison here is with families that have not gone through a divorce. In reality, as we see when we consider adoption, we need to discover the exact nature of the tests the family faces, in terms of family history and relational situation.

[7] In Ancient Rome the household gods (Lares et Penates) accompanied family members on dangerous journeys and when the household was reestablished in some other place.

either in permanent conflict between the children over who should have the exclusive right to attention from the adults, which has long replaced primogeniture as the first priority, or in the older children's envy of the younger ones, which takes the form of harassment, abuse, and groundless accusation.

The role of the "third parent"—the parent's new partner—is important here. In the literature the new partner is seen mainly as a parental / child-raising alternative or adjunct. This is due to the well-known and widespread fact that fathers tend to make themselves scarce or even disappear completely when divorce occurs. On the other hand, a father's erratic presence or total absence is likely to fuel the female-maternal fantasy of fatherless parenthood. Mothers' efforts to pressure their children into accepting the new partners may be seen as an extension of this fantasy. Here, it is the mother who "decides" who can be and act as the father. For our part, we see the presence of a "third parent" as a sign that the attempt to reconstitute the family has either succeeded or failed (Cigoli, 1998a, 2002). The basis for this belief is that, in relational terms, third parents can never legitimize themselves. No matter what they do, they always need the other to legitimize their actions and efforts. This could be the situation of a father with no fears over his paternity, or a mother with fears over her maternity, who are therefore able to make room for a third parent. This brings us to the further paradox that it is respect for the relational hierarchy that makes room for the third parent and his or her contribution to bringing up the children. But in situations where the fantasy of replacing one parent with another is at work, the generational consequences can be fatal. In terms of the damage that can be done, this fantasy is matched only by indifference to the fate of the other partner's children. In such cases, third parents, irrespective of whether they are men or women, count themselves out of the relationship because they see it as no concern of theirs.

In other words, a parent cannot be deprived of a generational role and banished from the generational stage. Even when guilty of serious shortcomings and prolonged absence, the parent is mentally present precisely because of these defects and the grief they cause. Children can work through their grief in peer groups, in bonds with other adults (relations, teachers), by seeking psychological help, or by confiding in a "third parent," provided that he or she can deal with the malice and rage brought on by the parents' shortcomings and absences. Once again, we see that legitimacy has to be conferred by the people involved in the relationship; it is far more than just a question of social norm.

Finally, it should be remembered that mothers and fathers differ in the way they bring up children. Mothers are more prone to dangerously intense emotional involvement because they are closer to the "root" of the bond. For example, mothers are as likely to be objects of jealous possessiveness as they are to be angrily rejected and even totally repudiated by their children. Similarly, a father's new companion may be bitterly hated and rejected, despite her unwavering kindness and helpfulness.

In other words, the triangularity of the relationship needs to be revitalized in some way for a couple and family to be successfully reconstituted. The legitimation of the other that was operative early on, in the divorce, as the parents' mutual legitimation in the eyes of their children, is operative here in the presence of a third parent. This is a new triangle and it has to be legitimized by the parental couple and the children themselves. Third parents in no way relieve their partners of the responsibilities and pleasures of parenthood; they are more likely to pose a new relational challenge because they stir up doubts, fears, and fantasies of being ousted from the relationship.

In this chapter we have looked at couple pacts, divorce, and stepcouples in an attempt to establish connections between them. They are very often kept separate in the literature, perhaps in the belief that this makes research easier. But what it really does is deprive research of content. We believe that a bond-based perspective, of which the relational–symbolic approach is a concrete example, can lead to greater understanding of separated couples and stepfamilies, and give them support in coping with the problems they face.

CHAPTER SIX

The Parental Bond: Transitions and Tasks

BECOMING PARENTS: THE GENERATIONAL SCENARIO

The birth of a child is the family's most significant critical event and gives rise to its key transition (McGoldrick et al., 1993). As we saw in chapter 1, the most salient feature of the event today is the unprecedented importance of the child itself, and its much-exalted power to confer on the couple the sense of stability that was once conferred, as both a gift and an obligation, by their generational mandate and inheritance. Of its very nature, the birth event establishes generational connectedness and is therefore a form of action, although this is rarely acknowledged. New roles and relationships magically appear: Spouses become parents, parents become grandparents, parents' brothers become uncles, other new babies become cousins, and so on.

The hub around which all this revolves is the parental couple, which acts as mediator between the generations involved: As Hill (1970) observed some time ago, it acts as a lineage bridge that gathers up the heritage of the previous generation and has the task of handing it down to the next. The parental couple negotiates the transition successfully when it is able to cope with the new tasks it faces on the triple front of marital, parental, and filial relationships. As well as someone's spouse, a young parent is someone else's child, and the experience of having generated another human being affects all these relationships. To this should be added the family's new relationship with the community the child will grow up in.

So let us examine the tasks that the transition to parenthood entails and their attendant relational shifts. In line with our model, we look at both the affective and the ethical spheres, and our conclusions are supported by the results of our own research over the years.

126

Tasks as Partners

The experience of becoming a parent brings about profound changes in the marital relationship, and the birth of the child presents the couple with a real challenge. The arrival of a child may activate personal and relational resources and consolidate the couple's identity, but it can also have the opposite effect of preventing the couple from growing, and even of causing its break-up. Many studies have analyzed the effect a child's birth has on the marital relationship. Most of them recognize that the transition to parenthood involves a period of crisis for the couple that may nonetheless be interpreted as a necessary evolutionary phase enabling both partners to find a new relational equilibrium. The extent to which the birth crisis diminishes marital satisfaction is still controversial. Some evidence supports the view that the birth event causes a decline in the quality of the marital relationship (Crohan, 1996; Kurdek, 1993), whereas other evidence points to the gratification and positive consequences the birth of a child has on the couple (MacDermid, Huston, & McHale, 1990).

Huston and Vangelisti (1995) conclude, Solomon-like, that the transition to parenthood may worsen some marital relationships, improve others, and have only a slight effect on still others because the overall impact of parenthood on a marriage depends on a multiplicity of factors. The one that most obviously affects marital satisfaction during the postnatal period is the couple's success in redefining roles when the child's arrival throws the existing set-up into turmoil. A sufficiently equitable distribution of the workload between husband and wife, or the husband at least helping out with child care, is regarded more favorably by new mothers. As we have shown, today's ethos of equality is one outcome of cultural shifts in the nature of "family-ness."

In reality, the main task the couple faces in achieving the transition is the difficult one of *integrating* the marital and parental dimensions of their relationship so as to generate a new relational identity for themselves. The marital bond acquires new values: companionship, as the term is normally understood, diminishes in importance while partnership—the feeling of being involved in a joint enterprise—becomes correspondingly more important (Belsky & Pensky, 1988). The longitudinal study carried out by Pape Cowan and Cowan (1992) describes in detail the changes in identity that the transition to parenthood brings to the couple. Adults say a lot about themselves through their parenting styles. The marital and parental systems are delicately balanced, especially in today's families where, as we have seen, demand for and expectation of intense emotional involvement with the partner are matched only by equally powerful emotional investment in children. It is hardly surprising, then, that partners may have difficulty in drawing boundaries between the marital and parental systems at a time when strong family cohesion is making it more difficult to draw interpersonal boundaries.

These problems are exacerbated by yet another factor. The idea that the couple relationship can and should be separate from the parental relationship is quite recent in cultural terms. In the past the couple's role was primarily a parental one; bringing up children took most of their lives because families were large and the average life was short. Now, a falling birth rate and increasing life expectancy are enabling couples to devote substantial amounts of time to themselves during clearly defined periods in their lives. This is a new challenge: As their children grow up, couples are increasingly expected to redefine their objectives and find ways of revitalizing their marital relationship.

Considering the tasks required of the couple from an ethical viewpoint, the first thing to stress is that each of the partners must be able to cope with the new responsibilities that come with being a parent. This personal task is made easier if each partner acknowledges the other's trustworthiness, thereby legitimizing each other's new functions and indicating their respect for how they are being performed. In today's world, legitimation of the parental role is weaker, and therefore more clearly takes the form of interpersonal acknowledgement. Only through mutual legitimation can a shared parenting style develop that it is always the outcome of dialogue and negotiation. Thus, the parents' ability to cooperate with each other is one of their relationship's crucial resources. The studies we have done, especially of family crisis and divorce, demonstrate the crucial importance of mutual acknowledgement and legitimation. We look at this more closely in the next chapter.

At this point, the integration of the parental and marital spheres in the couple relationship may be redefined as *caring for the other's difference*, rather than simply adapting to the other. Obviously, the difference that each partner has to acknowledge, respect, and legitimize in the other is only accentuated by the new role identities that turn this particular man and that woman into a father and a mother. The more support the partners give to each other, and the more they help each other to become good parents, the better they will cope with the affective and ethical complexities of the birth event by learning to live with the conscious or unconscious ambiguities it brings out in them. We believe this is the way for parents to identify constructively with their child and its needs.

Tasks as Parents

Let us now consider the tasks the couple faces as parents.

Objectively speaking, the transition to parenthood begins at the moment of conception and lasts the length of the interval between the announcement of pregnancy and the birth itself. As Ruble and Seidman (1996) clearly demonstrate, getting the transition under way is a slow and lengthy business in which parental motivation plays a key role in determining the success or otherwise of the real transition that culminates in the birth of the child. The transition is more likely to succeed with highly motivated parents who truly wanted their child because they will find it easier to construct an adequate mental space for the child and their experience of parenthood, and will cope more confidently and competently with the radical changes triggered by the birth (Michaels & Goldberg, 1988). Although preceded by a period of conscious expectancy, the birth itself is always a powerful bonding event that ratifies the parents' generational shift. Insofar as the birth turns two adults into caregivers responsible for another human being's life, it also modifies the partners' identities.

Many of the problems couples face in becoming parents (e.g., struggles over who should take responsibility; refusal or inability to behave like parents with their children) are caused by difficulty in moving up a generation, which involves much more than simply taking on a new role. It also entails the construction of a new, hierarchically superior relationship. As we have argued, responsible caregiving lies at the heart of good parenting, and is symbolized by the maternal affective function and paternal ethical function. But what does responsible caregiving mean in concrete terms? What should parents always assure their children of as a matter of priority? The first thing new parents do is establish an affective bond with their child, so as to give the new generation trust and space to breathe in. The parental bond is paradoxical because parents have simultaneously to bond with and detach themselves from their children. Even as they give care, they must acknowledge that their child is other than themselves. In other words, they have to make room for a third person who has the right to a place in the family and cannot simply be dismissed as a way of filling void and satisfying its parents' needs and desires. As Winnicott shows (1965), subjectivity is built on the amazing and surprising discovery that the child is other than oneself. In the postnatal period, parental care basically consists of protecting the child and, above all, assuring it of a secure base from which to make its psychological functions more appropriate to the context it finds itself in. Research over the last decade has stressed how important mother–child attachment styles are to a child's well-being (Gloger, Gabriele, & Huerkamp, 1998). In particular, it seems that a secure style, unlike resistant (or ambivalent), avoidant, and disorganized styles (Ainsworth, Blehar, Waters, & Wall, 1978; Cassidy & Shaver, 1999; Main, Kaplan, & Cassidy, 1985), is able to ensure this well-being and the child's ability to establish good relations with people in later life. A child with a secure attachment style can cope with detachment without breaking the emotional bond with its parents. Attachments studies have also shown that parental competence (especially the mother's) is rooted in the parents' personal family histories, and in the attachment styles and internal working models they have developed in their own lives and/or inherited from previous generations.

However, attachment theory and research is mainly based on a dyadic model, whereas the parent–child relationship is never separate from the child's relationship with the other parent, or even from the parents' relationships with their families of origin. Whichever way one looks at it, the job of being a parent is always at the apex of a whole set of intersecting triangles.

Turning now to maternal and parental roles, the expectation nowadays is that parental functions should not be split between mother and father but shared by both. Maternal and paternal functions are felt to be interchangeable and no longer the prerogative of one or the other of the parents. However, studies of today's "new nurturant fathers" (Shapiro, Diamond, & Greenberg, 1995)—those who are willing to devote time and effort to child care postnatally—show how problem-fraught this sharing process can be. As Parke (1995) has shown in intercultural surveys of this theme, this declared shift in male and female roles is more apparent than real. It is the mother who is responsible for "managerial" tasks like housework, child care, and organizing the family's free time. In other words, roles become more traditional when children are born (Carrà Mittini, 1999; MacDermid et al., 1990).

Other studies (Belsky & Rovine, 1990; Goldberg & Perry-Jenkins, 2004) have pointed to the fact that the experience of parenthood can be different from what the couple expects. Difficulty in sharing child care can also widen the gap between parents. When mothers find that their share of the workload is greater than expected, they start complaining and rate their marital relationship more negatively than woman whose experiences match their expectations. It is important to emphasize here that it is not so much the workload that constitutes the problem as violated *expectation*. In this sense, traditional couples seem to have an advantage because their expectations of what the postnatal workload will be are not violated.

From our viewpoint, the couple's efforts to share things should be seen as a mental (ethical–affective) response to the need for a parental pact. As we have shown, the real problem is not the equal apportioning of workloads championed by advocates of equal parental rights and duties, but knowing how to react and cope when expectations are violated. This happens not only when the other does not meet one's expectations, but also, and most importantly, when there is no way of jointly renegotiating those expectations. Thus, sharing turns out to be not so much an equal apportioning of functions and tasks, as a pooling of the commitment that sustains the parental pact.

The transition to parenthood is repeated with each child that is born; even in large families, a birth is always a unique event. From the parents' point of view, however, the birth of their first child is special: The significance and surprise it engenders make it a wholly unique experience. People become mothers and fathers when their first children are born, meaning that first-time parents make a greater mental investment in the event. First children will also be correspondingly more aware of the mandate they received from their parents' families of origin.

Let us now consider the ethical aspects of the parental relationship. Parents have the task of ratifying their child's family membership by giving him or her a first name and surname that allow access to their families of origin in later years. This constitutes caring custody of the heritages handed down by their respective lineages. Transmitting family membership and allowing access to family origins certainly means legitimizing newborn babies as the children of these particular parents, but it also means making them feel part of a history going back generations by giving them access to their maternal and paternal lineages. In this respect, the family's sense of continuity and stability is guaranteed when the new parents perform, and therefore appropriate, some of the rituals handed down by their own families. These rituals may be linked to celebrations like Christmas, Easter, and baptism, or to family-specific traditions like birthdays, anniversaries, visiting relatives, and going on vacation. As Bossard and Boll (1956) pointed out, rituals are often an effective way of organizing family life because of the symbolic and affective significance they carry (Fiese & Kline, 1992; Wolin & Bennett, 1984).

For a young family, rituals are an element of stability they can hang on to and acknowledge in the period of maximum postnatal instability. A ritual stabilizes the family on two different timescales. In the here and now, it provides the support that helps the family nucleus to find a balance between familiar and new, unplanned and planned, and in the family's longer temporal perspective it has the power to link past and future, ensuring continuity and enabling individual members to realize they belong to a particular family, not just any family.

A recent study of couples with children aged 6–18 months carried out at our Research Centre (Guglielmetti & Greco, 2003) has shown that the young family's ability to identify their respective family rituals and use them to create rituals of their own without diminishing the original ritual's importance in any way, is a major protective factor in the transition to parenthood. On the other hand, failure to recognize what those rituals are, or having no rituals of their own, or adhering to the letter rather than the spirit of a ritual, may be taken as a sign that the couple-to-family transition is proving difficult.

So making the parental pact does not begin and end in parent–child interchange. A child is both an expression of its parents' history as a couple, and part of the larger family history, not just a source of the couple's joint and personal fulfilment. To the couple's relatives, the new child represents the new generation and a link with previous ones, even though they may no longer be alive. The new child *is* the larger family's future. We might say that the child's awareness of its own identity depends on being able to access and draw nourishment from its maternal and paternal lineages and the key values they have handed down. In Western culture, the ability to keep channels open with both families without annulling or compromising the child's dual membership of two families largely depends on the women, who actively organize parental and social relationships. In this respect, the relationship between mothers- and daughters-in-law is crucial to forging real contact between maternal and paternal lineages.

Finally, it should be remembered that a new child, although obviously the outcome of a couple relationship and a ratification of its unity, is also and inescapably *someone else*. The couple's ups and downs and the directions it decides to grow in will be a sometimes powerful influence on relations with the child, but the child can in no way be reduced to a mere product of the couple; a child transcends the couple that generated it, and is important in and of itself. That the child is of, and yet somehow greater than, the couple is a paradox that may have creative or fatal consequences for the couple. Children are generated, but they can also generate. In other words, they too are responsible for generativity.

Tasks as Children

A new generation's arrival on the family scene affects the entire "family body" and sets new tasks for both the new parents and the previous generation. Not-so-young parents become grandparents and go through a new transition. Thus, the transition to parenthood is associated with the transition to grandparenthood.

At the intergenerational level, the child/grandchild's arrival marks a key stage in the family relationship and enables the two generations (the child's parents and grandparents) to acknowledge each other's value through their common status as parents. Williamson (1991) points out that the experience of having children allows the grandparents and their grown-up children to explore new aspects of their relationship. For new parents particularly, experiencing parenthood brings them closer to their own parents, enabling them to see the man and woman behind the father and mother and appreciate the inner meaning of their experience as human beings rather than just as parents. Experiencing such closeness at the generational level may enhance the relationship and lead to greater mutual understanding, lending new depth and meaning to parent–children relationships.

However, the new parents' task is far more than this: They are also expected to carry the family history forward in some new way, meaning that the couple needs to see itself as connected to yet separate from its families of origin. Ethically speaking, this means that the earlier and later generations legitimize each other. The family of origin acknowledges that the new parents have prime responsibility for bringing up their child, while the new parents are expected to legitimize their own parents as grandparents and the grandchild's role as both a continuer of and a leading actor in their family history. The risks inherent in this task form a shifting continuum between the negative poles of intergenerational breakdown and mechanical, unquestioning repetition of intergenerational mandates, with positive value continuity in the middle. Couples who can count on a good relationship with their families of origin, while also maintaining an appropriate distance from them, also cope better with the challenges of parenthood.

Studies we carried out to ascertain the quality of marital and intergenerational relationships in a large sample of young parent couples and their parents

(Carrà Mittini, 1999; Scabini & Regalia, 1999) have yielded interesting results. A significant correlation between marital and parental relationships was found. In particular, high levels of marital satisfaction are associated with high levels of parent–child reciprocal support, whereas low levels of marital satisfaction are associated with low levels of parent–child reciprocal support. Moreover, high levels of marital satisfaction are associated with good continuity in the values parents receive from their parents' generation and intend to hand down to future ones, whereas low ones are associated with evident breakdown in intergenerational value transmission.

However, it was analysis by gender and generation that yielded the most interesting results. We found clear gender differences in the relationships with families of origin, with strong intergenerational solidarity in females rather than males. Women can rely on significantly greater support from their family, and from their mothers especially, than husbands can. On the whole, husbands had a less positive perception of their relationships with their parents, and with their fathers especially, and seemed to have difficulty in appropriating the resources of their families of origin.

This casts new light on the much-reported fact that fathers are becoming increasingly irrelevant in bringing up children. This problem goes back a long way and is linked to increasingly less reliable value transmission through the male line as family name and heritage, once clearly linked to the male-paternal line, become less important. Men's difficulties in appropriating their family's resources ultimately derive from this. At the opposite end of the scale, the current dominance of mothers in family relationships, based on affects and their social value, is being strengthened still further by the intergenerational sources young women can draw on.

However, the picture changes when we look at relations between the family and society, especially in terms of work. Analyzing a large sample of young husbands and wives (Margola & Molgora, 2002; Margola & Rosnati, 2003), we found that husbands invested more in their jobs than women did, and derived more satisfaction from their work. Moreover, wives appeared more affected by the influence of their family life on their jobs, especially when there were children. More specifically, women's perceptions of serious family–work conflict had a negative effect on their personal well-being and marital satisfaction.

So the woman's relational advantage vis-à-vis her family of origin could be seen as a way of "compensating" for gender imbalance in society. In Italy, and Southern Europe in general, women are certainly worse off than their husbands in terms of professional fulfilment and are more conscious of the need to reconcile working outside the home with proper child care, but are better off in terms of the intergenerational resources provided by their extended families. In particular, they receive much support from their mothers in performing their dual role when welfare support is poor or even nonexistent.

And yet, the importance to a woman of her relationship with her parents can also have a negative side. It should not be forgotten that women suffer more than men when relationships with parents cool, and this may even affect the marriage itself. This appears to confirm that women experience family relationships in terms of "relational coherence" (Sroufe & Fleeson, 1988), whereas men are able to keep their marital and intergenerational relationships at least partly isolated.

Moreover, frequent "forced dependence" on families of origin for child-care support may encourage inertia, so that the new couple runs the risk of remaining tied to its parents. In such cases, the transition to parenthood may be weak because the relationship shift any transition entails is either avoided or played down.

In Southern Europe there is the widespread phenomenon of "ongoing extended families" in which new families are very close to their families of origin, live near at least one of them, and have many contacts and exchanges. In clinical interventions, this means avoiding uncritical use of the "enmeshment" construct and taking full account of cultural differences. For example, Anglo-Saxon culture, unlike Latin culture, attaches great importance in the development of intergenerational relationships to physical distance seen as a sign of psychological separation (Vignoles, Regalia, Manzi, Golledge, & Scabini, in press).

Whatever the situation, when intergenerational transmission takes place along the female axis alone, the couple's successful transition to parenthood is threatened, placing a further obstacle in the way of the couple's joint performance of parenting tasks, which was the whole aim of the transition in the first place.

To summarize, awareness of the tasks facing both new parents and the preceding generation enables us to identify the following indicators of a successful transition to parenthood: (a) perceived sharing of parenting; (b) the ability of parents and their grown-up children to acknowledge and integrate the similarities and differences between the new family and its families of origin; and (c) enrolling newborn children in the family lineages.

Tasks as Members of a Social Community

The birth transition also faces parents with new social tasks, as well as those specific to the family itself.

There can be no doubt that the birth of a child is necessarily followed by a period of severely reduced social contact with friends and acquaintances. Running the family takes up much of the couple's time, and it is difficult to reconcile family time and work time, especially for mothers. The result can often be an abrupt break of contact between the family, its informal network of friends, and the outside world. As the children grow, however, social contact becomes an ever more powerful force in the family's life: The children start going to school, and develop their own networks of friends and acquaintances when they reach adolescence. This is another reason why parental couples have to perform social tasks.

As the children grow older, managing the interface between family space and social space (e.g., work time) becomes a key task. Many studies have explored the work and family interface in dual-career and, more generally, dual-income families (Allen, Herst, Brack, & Sutton, 2000). However, few have consistently used dyads (wife–husband) as the unit of analysis and data analysis techniques related to this unit of analysis (Mauno & Kinnunen, 1999; Windle & Dumenci, 1997).

Yet again, researchers have had difficulty in conceiving of the family as a unit, albeit a multifaceted one, and the difficulty only increases when the family is studied in relation to the social community and can no longer be regarded as a purely private phenomenon. Similarly, social responses to family–work relationships reflect the difficulty of seeing individuals as family members, and the family as a social subject with its own features.

Social policy trends in Europe are instructive here. The Scandinavian countries (Denmark, Norway, Sweden, Finland) are moving toward a welfare model based on providing assistance for individuals rather than families. Family relationships are seen as a private matter, and the individual's independence needs to be safeguarded if they are to be managed properly. Welfare agencies intervene in family affairs only to ensure that gender equality and children's rights are safeguarded. This is also the situation in continental Europe (France, Benelux, Germany, Austria), although more account is taken of the individual's family situation. For example, fiscal policies are tailored to the size of the family that has to be supported. Southern European countries like Italy and Spain already have rights reconciliation policies in place, if only in embryonic form for the moment.

In our view, however, current political and social attitudes still prevent the unique features of families from being taken properly into account. For this to happen, it is essential that people start thinking again in terms of generations, not individuals. Families themselves do typically think in this longer term way, but so should the communities they live in. A family is a result of intergenerational exchange, and its continuing vitality depends on whether those changes are generative or antigenerative. However, society itself is also a result of intergenerational exchange, and suffers accordingly if the exchanges are mistrustful rather than trustful, or based on inequality rather than equality.

In short, the intergenerational perspective is rarely if ever applied in the social sciences. The conditions of women, children, the elderly, and the poor are analyzed, certainly, but the people themselves are treated as demographics cohorts, or gender and status groups, not as individuals whose identities are expressions of generative relationships developing in and through time. Losing this sense of generation following generation, and reducing everything to the here and now, causes family and social relationships to implode. The dizzying onslaught of postmodernity has eroded society's longer temporal perspective, so that families and communities have lost their sense of generational rhythms. Concern for well-being is directed exclusively at the present moment, albeit an extended one.

However, there are some signs that the generation chain written into our DNA, and the cultural/symbolic nurturing we receive, may be making a comeback. For example, such topics as intergenerational fairness (Williamson, Kingson, & Watts-Roy, 1999) and children's rights (including those of unborn children) are now being discussed. In some European countries, ways and means are being debated of bringing the family into politics, perhaps by weighting the votes of couples with children so that children are indirectly given a say in policymaking. Similarly, some Far Eastern countries thinking of planning introduce People's Tribunes for future generations in order to move politics toward a more responsible form of democracy that takes future generations into account, rather than merely responding to the concerted demands of today's social actors (Takeshi, 2003). As a result, families will be accorded full citizenship for the first time.

At the community level, these developments are encouraging families to take an increasingly active and confident view of their social responsibilities. However, they can act effectively only if they turn their backs on isolation, start trusting in the other, and generate associative forms that can promote family and social well-being by encouraging solidarity at all levels. It is through concerted "caring" that family associations can successfully play an active role in the community by responding to emerging as well as traditional family needs. "Traditional" needs might be those of a particular family struggling to cope with a child's sickness or disability; responding to "emerging" needs might mean an association's advocacy of family concerns based on actively defending the rights of families as social subjects. Decisions about the raising and education of children, and family health and quality of life, may be among these concerns (Rossi, 2003).

THE ADOPTIVE BOND: A RADICAL KIND OF PARENTHOOD

We see adoption as a radical and extremely important form of parenting because it highlights the themes that underlie parenthood. For this reason, we devote an entire section to this subject. As a community response to the problem of sterility, adoption is among the oldest forms of human generativity. The first historical references to it are in the Code of Hammurabi (Mesopotamia, 18th century BC). In ancient Egypt, Greece, and Imperial Rome, adoption was widely practiced and had the mainly patrimonial function of guaranteeing the inheritance rights of children born out of wedlock, and sorting out problems of succession in families with no heirs. The aim was to keep the specter of posthumous oblivion at bay while also dispelling the anxiety of knowing that one might die without provision for inheritance. In ancient Rome, adoption involved a ceremony called *emancipatio*, a fictitious "act of sale" that formally terminated the power of the original paterfamilias over the adopted child and ratified his or her new bond with the adoptive father, whose official child he or she now became.

It was in the Hellenic Age that private forms of adoption began to emerge, as middle and lower class couples increasingly adopted exposed children,[1] often to replace their own children who had died. Justinian Law (6th century AD) brought about a major cultural shift when imported Greek and Oriental laws were combined with the precepts of rapidly spreading Christianity, which regarded adoption as a form of *charis* toward one's neighbor and saw adoptive status as somehow part of the human condition itself (Had not St. Paul said that Christ's coming had made all men God's adopted children, who would share God's inheritance with Christ Himself?).

Thus, adoption, or *affiliato* as it was often called, was increasingly likened to biological parenthood. In time, the idea that adoption was a form of affective "repair" or "reparation" for children who had been abandoned, maltreated, or had lost their parents, emerged alongside its existing patrimonial and legitimizing functions. In today's society, this is the most visible aspect of adoption. Its peculiarity lies in the fact that it establishes a parental relationship where there are no ties of kinship, so that the biological level is absorbed into the cultural–symbolic level.

The family relationship revolves around human beings' primitive mental categorization of reality into "mine" and "other-than-mine." As psychosocial studies of ingroup and outgroup perceptions have shown, "mine" is associated with closeness and similarity, "other-than-mine" with distance and difference. In this perspective, adoption reveals the true nature of challenge inherent in the family relationship: how to hold "mine" and "other-than-mine" together by turning something that is different into something that is literally familiar, a part of the family.

In adoption, this difference is one of lineage and origin, and is often associated with ethnic difference (traditions, values, social class, religion, and race). In biological families, lineage difference is inherent in the couple itself, which unites two lineages whose histories and traditions were separate until the couple formed; in adoptive families, lineage difference is also built into parent–children relationships.

As we have seen, in order to turn an outsider into an insider, a stranger into a member of the family, adoption has to operate at both the patrimonial level by

---

[1] The abandoned child was adopted by publicly witnessed decree in the city-state's main square.

ensuring survival of family name and continuity of lineage, and at the affective level by offering warmth and affection. The former, a typically paternal gift, dispels anxiety that personal identity and value may be lost, whereas the latter, a typically maternal gift, dispels the pain of having been abandoned. However, this does not alter the fact that adoption has often been a form of exploitation and abuse. It is significant that the plots of so many fairy stories, fables, and novels center on the exploitation of children as free labor, and repeatedly depict their social and psychological humiliation and exposure to various kinds of abuse.

As we saw in chapter 1, the *matris-munus* has become more important than the *patris-munus* over the centuries, and a similar shift has also taken place in adoption. The decision to adopt is seen as a response to abandonment, and adoptive parents see their task as giving the abandoned child the warmth and affection it needs. However, the reality is more complex than this. It should not be forgotten that, in most cases, adoption is a response to a dual lack: the couple's lack of maternal/paternal fulfillment (caused by infertility), and the child's lack of a family.

So the aim of the peculiar transition we call adoption is to construct an adoptive pact to which both parents and children, and the ethical–patrimonial as well as affective spheres, are parties.

Up to now we have used the term *pact* to mean the basis of the marital and parental bond, but we believe that, in the case of adoption, it can usefully be extended to include the bond between adoptive parents and children because it highlights their shared commitment to constructing a viable family relationship. The adoptive pact is a curious and unique amalgam of needs, expectations, and the personal histories of all those who enter into the contract—the child, the couple, and the parents' own families of origin. The pact's outcome is not simply the reciprocal satisfaction of need: It involves more than merely subtracting deficiencies from and adding resources to the family equation. To be constructive, a pact has to assimilate these reciprocal deficiencies and transform them into a generative project/commitment of which both parents and children are part.

The etymology of "adopt" underlines this dimension of choice (in Latin *optare* means to choose, reinforced by the prefix *ad*). The couple may perceive choice as an element that characterizes only the initial phase of the adoption process. But faced with the real child, always different from the one they longed for and imagined, the adoptive couple must again choose to be father and mother of *this particular* child (or these particular children) and must go on making that decision in future years.

The child is also called on, over time and above all during adolescence,[2] to make a choice and decide to be the son or daughter of *these particular* parents.

[2] The advisability of allowing or denying adopted children access to their families of origin when they come of age, and its psychological consequences for the child's social adaptation and the adoptive parents themselves, is the subject of heated international debate. In some U.S. states

However, the reciprocity of the choice must not obscure the asymmetry of the responsibility that always flows from the first generation toward successive generations.

The key factor in the transition to adoptive parenthood is the difference between fecundity and generativity. The aim/task is to achieve generativity in the absence of fecundity, while also maintaining a "symbolic balance" between the affective and ethical levels in the relationship. The parents' task is to ensure that both the affective and the ethical are present, even in a culture like today's that prioritizes affective rather than ethical aspects, and all this has to be done without losing sight of the fact that the adoption pact is specific and exclusive: An adoptive family can never be the same as a biological family (Cigoli, 2001).

The couple's ability to come to terms with infertility and to reconcile parents' and children's similarities and differences are the main protective factors highlighted in the literature. Coming to terms with infertility is a joint task, irrespective of which partner is its "cause." The psychoanalytical literature has made much of this theme of grief: Learning to deal mentally with the deficiency or lack that infertility represents is conceptualized as an elaboration of grief. Our view is that this process is more than a one-off mental operation that can be kept separate from the decision to adopt once it has been completed. As a life-altering decision, adoption is a way of coming to terms with grief over infertility by investing trust and hope in one's ability to be generative.

On the other hand, reconciliation of similarities and differences is a task not only for the marital couple, but also for the children and the families of origin. We examine each of them in turn.

The Parents' Tasks

According to Brodzinsky and Schechter (1990), the coping strategies adoptive families employ form a continuum between the two extremes of rejection of difference and insistence on it. At one extreme, differences are banished by the family and are strenuously denied; at the other, families tend to blame the child's adoptive origin for all the difficulties and problems that sooner or later arise in the parent–child relationship, with peers, or at school. In the middle of the continuum, there is a functional area where differences are acknowledged. This strategy is founded on the acceptance of differences that are acknowledged and then incorporated into the family history.

In other words, it is all a matter of establishing a dynamic balance between two equally risky scenarios. At one extreme, the risk is that cognitive and

---

it is already legal in order that adopted children may know who their biological parents are when they come of age. Such "open adoption" is also legal in Italy for Italian adopted children, although severe restrictions apply. The possibility of knowing who their biological parents are, and even contacting them, should not detract from the task facing all adopted children, whatever their situation: the realization that the decision to belong to their adoptive family is theirs, and theirs alone.

affective acceptance of the adopted child as the equivalent of a biological child is achieved by denying that the situation is in any way unusual: Similarities are stressed, differences are played down. At the other extreme, the risk is that similarities are played down and differences accentuated in order to stress the child's adoptive origin. If difference is experienced as the child's *being an outsider*, the result may be that the child is not acknowledged as a son or daughter and may even sometimes be expelled from the family.

To make adoptive parenthood work, the parents also have to legitimize each other. The title of parent is conferred in a legal sense by the courts, but there is also an inner process for the assumption and legitimization of the parental role, namely *entitlement* (Cohen, Coyne, & Duvall, 1996), the term indicating that one has the moral and affective right to exercise the role of parent. The construction of adoptive parenthood implies, therefore, the legitimation of oneself as the parent of that particular child with full acknowledgement of his or her own history and different origins.

Such a process of inner legitimation is also required in the case of biological parenthood, but in adoption it can be undermined by the absence of a shared genetic history, or by the fact of not having experienced pregnancy and the first moments of the child's life. When these "first moments" run to years, as is often the case, it becomes even more difficult to construct the pact.

This means that adoptive families have greater need of legitimation than biological ones, and in this respect the father has a special role to play in relation to both his wife (the mother of the adoptive child) and the child itself. Because there is no biological matrix, the mother's warmth and affection are especially important and need to be encouraged. A mother's presence and importance can never be merely self-referential; these qualities are attributed to her, and acknowledged and affirmed by significant others. So the father's task is also to support and legitimize the mother's function as generative rooting that transcends biological origin and the couple's sterility.

The father's relationship with the children is also very important. Rosnati and Marta (1997), collecting data from large samples of (mostly non-Italian) adopted children, have shown that adopted adolescents communicate more easily and more freely with their adoptive fathers and regard them as more supportive than their peers' biological fathers. Sobol, Delaney, and Earn (1994) have also shown that adopted young adults think their fathers are emotionally closer and more supportive that those of their nonadopted peers. For their part, Levy-Shiff, Zoran, and Shulman (1997) found that when the adopted children are foreign, fathers are more involved in bringing them up than when they are of the same nationality, so much so that researchers now speak of adoptive enhanced fatherhood as a feature of interracial adoptive families in particular. So here, too, the father plays a crucial role in legitimizing the child.

The unusual nature of the adoption event also has an effect on the couple relationship. Couples function in significantly different ways depending on whether their children are biological or adopted. In a longitudinal study comparing a group of couples before and after adoption with a similar group of couples before and after the birth of their first child, Levy-Shiff, Goldsmith, and Har-Even (1991) found that adoptive parents cope better with the physical and emotional stress of looking after a small child and are more satisfied with themselves as parents than are biological parents. However, as the authors themselves warn, this may reflect the long period of deprivation they have had to spend coming to terms with infertility and then waiting for the adoption to come through. Once it has, there follows a kind of "honeymoon" period in which the couple tends to minimize the problems it is having, in order to reassure itself and others that adoptive parents are no different from biological ones. In minimizing its problems, the couple may even go so far as to deny any involvement in parental responsibility.

Adoptive parents are less likely than biological ones to associate symptomatic behavior in their children with dysfunction in the family or couple itself. They are more likely to attribute their child's problems to biological/hereditary factors and the child's earlier experience, thereby exempting themselves from the need to think seriously about the role parental or marital dysfunction may have played in the origin of the problems. Significantly, adoptive parents of symptomatic children may see getting rid of the child as a way of solving the problem, whereas biological parents would see their own separation as a possible solution in extremis (Cohen et al., 1996).

So it would seem that adoptive couples are reluctant to blame themselves when problems arise, preferring to shift blame on to the adoption itself and the child's early negative experience. It seems likely that their long wait to have a child, and the sheer effort and difficulty of bringing the project to its longed-for conclusion, tend to strengthen the couple bond, which to them seems somehow exempt from parenting problems and totally (therefore pathologically) separate from their relationship with the child.

The Children's Tasks

The children's affective and cognitive behavior also has an effect on the reconciliation/appropriation of similarity and difference. Although generational responsibility is clearly hierarchical—earlier generations look after later ones—adopted children gradually come to realize that they too have responsibilities. It is mainly during adolescence, a good time for personal rebirth, that they find themselves in a position to decide whether they want to be the children of those particular parents, and members of and heirs to the history of that particular family.

Our research shows that adolescent adopted children tend to value their relationship with their parents more highly than do biological children of similar age (Lanz, Iafrate, Rosnati, & Scabini, 1999). This could be interpreted as an effort on the part of adopted adolescents to be "more like" their parents. Distressed by not knowing who their parents are, or by having been abandoned, or by the deaths of the parents and relatives they knew, it is as if they need to be reassured of their identity. However, the risk in overidentification is that the process of individuation, an integral part of being an adolescent, is hindered.

We believe that another crucial event in helping adopted children to feel they have at last been truly adopted, and are now members of their own family, is having children of their own, because generational continuity finally becomes a reality to them. Very few studies have addressed this topic, however. Later on we look at a case study that centers on the achievement of this continuity.

The Family of Origin's Tasks

The parents' ability to reconcile similarity and difference and incorporate it in the family is certainly influenced by their relationships with their families of origin and their memories of childhood. This has been practically ignored by the literature. In some of our studies, we inserted "relationship with family of origin" as one of the variables affecting the construction and effectiveness of the adoptive pact (Greco, Ranieri, & Rosnati, 2003; Greco & Rosnati, 1998). We summarize here the results of the qualitative assessment carried out in the first of these studies.

In addition to a semistructured interview, adolescent adopted children (from different ethnic groups) and their adoptive parents were given the Family Life Space (FLS) test. The verbal and graphic material they produced enabled us to generate the following "pact typologies" in which, apart from the last two types, which clearly point to relational pathology, the pact can also be seen as a relational style that may change in time.

The *pact of acknowledgement and appreciation of differences* was found in families where adoption had not only been integrated into the family history, but had also brought with it a richness enjoyed by all. They believed they had had an experience that had given "something more" to all involved, compared with other families. This pact is based on shared and often painful awareness of the realities of adoption. The drawings made reference to the story of the adoption and the context the child lived in before being adopted, and the affective aspect of family relationships clearly emerges from the verbalizations accompanying the drawings.

In these families, one sensed a certain freedom not only in the retelling of the adoption story, but also in expressing both positive and negative emotions connected to it. The children, by now adolescents and supported by their parents, had succeeded in assembling the disparate parts of their life stories and in giving them meaning as they undertook the difficult mental task of reappropriating their own origins and accepting the abandonment that had scarred their personal histories.

On the whole, the parents seemed grateful to their families of origin for what they had received from them, while also acknowledging any deprivations or shortcomings there may have been, and adoption was seen as a way of handing on what had come to them from previous generations. In the drawings, members of the families of origin were placed near the family nucleus, surrounding and almost embracing it as they "chorally" welcomed the new arrival. The family of origin's total approval of the decision to adopt was made evident.

In such cases, we could say that the "adoptive graft" has taken and that the things that had previously been lacking (maternal and paternal fulfillment for the parents, a family for the child) have been turned into a generative project.

In the *mutual assimilation pact,* the adoption event and the child's obscure origins were kept in mind but for the most part neutralized The event's peculiarity was acknowledged, but immediately "bracketed" in an effort, on the part of the parents, to resemble a biological family as much as possible. Significantly, adoption was seen as a "physiological fact" and equated to birth. The drawings referred to the adoption as an event, but any reference to the period prior to adoption was left out, and the adoption's emotional impact was never verbalized. The effect was to turn the adopted child into a biological child by trying to hush up anything that might point to the child's different origins. The difference of origin, although not denied, was juxtaposed with the family's history and only superficially integrated into it. The extended family usually gave the adopted child a warm welcome, but the adoptive parents did not manage to personally assimilate the heritage passed down to them by previous generations because emotionally they were still too close to their families of origin. Quite often members of the families of origin came first in the sequence or were placed very near compared to the spouse and children.

The adopted children adhere to the pact by trying in turn to hush up any reference to their different origins and representing themselves as their families' children in every sense.

An *imperfect pact* is a touch-and-go pact in which there is no reciprocity. For example, the parents may offer the child an assimilation pact ("Make yourself part of the family") but the child, especially if adolescent, is still too busy setting his own history in order and connecting up disparate parts of self and self-history, and cannot accept the pact. In short, adoptive parenthood is actively proposed, but adoptive childhood is still being constructed or has run into problems. In the drawings, the children often either failed to indicate relations with their adoptive parents, or indicated that they were definitely conflictual and positioned themselves at some distance from and "out of alignment" with the family. Interaction styles with previous generations were positive on the whole, and the adopted child had been well received by the extended family.

In the *denial of difference pact,* both the parents and the child refused to engage with the adoption story, which had been an exceedingly painful experience for all concerned. For the child, coming to terms with abandonment seemed as impossible as coming to terms with sterility/infertility was for the parents. That the adoption story was mutually repressed by parents and children was evident from the FLS, in which neither the child nor the parents made any reference to the adoption.

In such situations, the parental couple seems overwhelmed by the pain of their wounds and the grudge they bear their families of origin. In many instances, adoption was a move to underline even more clearly their separation from previous generations. Because adoption is a generational act, the parents were able to make their own parents the gift of continuity as well as using the adoption to assert their "freedom" and total separation from them. They were the new start and therefore had nothing to do with previous generations! The parents' difficulty in acknowledging and accepting the child's obscure origins was clearly paralleled by their difficulty in setting about separating themselves from their own family (their own origin).

In the *impossible pact,* the parents and children were so psychically distant from each other that it impossible even to make a pact. The discrepancy between expectations and reality was great in both cases. In the drawings, they omitted to indicate the relationships between them, so that the parents and children seemed suspended in a void and so distant from each other that no shared relationship style could be agreed on. The children were mostly seen as outsiders and the negative aspects of their behavior were blamed on their origin. For their part, the children confirmed their outsider status by leaving links between members out of the drawing.

As in the previous pact, the marital couple had difficulty in differentiating themselves from their families of origin, whether by breaking away or, the exact opposite, moving in so close that they could no longer be distinguished from them. This confirms the chaotic nature of pathological relationships, which may reveal themselves in alternating phases of enmeshment/confusion and distancing/indifference that these families unfortunately seem prepared to undergo.

It seems clear from this brief discussion that families of origin also play a fundamental role in determining the nature of the adoptive pact. Some couples see adoption as a way of passing on to the next generation the abundance of gifts received from both their families of origin. In other families, however, the couple's relationships with one or both families of origin are unresolved—there is still unfinished business to be done—so adoption is seen by the couple as a way of distancing itself from the families and making the break from their parents.

We could say that, in these cases of unresolved relational difficulties between the generations, there is an associated difficulty in establishing satisfactory relationships between parents and adopted child on one hand, and grandparents and adopted grandchild on the other. Indeed, difficulty in adequately addressing the issue of difference is often connected to difficulties experienced by the parents distinguishing/differentiating themselves from their respective families of origin, whether through excessive closeness or, at the other extreme, a severance of ties.

Grandparents have an important role to play in supporting and maintaining their children's commitment to such a difficult and risky undertaking as adopting a child. Moreover, the support that grandparents give to the adoptive parents, whether emotional, affective, organizational, or material, is an irreplaceable resource. They must also welcome the adopted child as one who will carry on the family's history, and must accept that the family legacy, including the material inheritance, be entrusted to a genetically foreign individual. The bond that is established between grandparents and adopted grandchild is critical to the process of his or her integration into the family unit. It is evident, therefore, that the construction of the adoptive bond does not depend exclusively on the relational network within the nuclear family, but on the larger context of the extended family as well.

One final consideration regarding methodology: It should be emphasized that very few of the studies published in Italy and other countries are truly family-oriented and reconstruct the family's unitas multiplex starting with parents, children, and families of origin. It should also be noted that there now exists a stereotype of the adopted children's well-being. For decades, researchers have seen adoption in pathogenic terms, drawing attention to the drawbacks and risks associated with it. A substantial number of studies have compared adopted children (sometimes from nonclinical samples) with those brought up by their biological parents, reporting more behavioral problems (especially in externalization), poorer school performance, and lower social competence in the adopted children (Brand & Brinich, 1999; Brodzinsky, Smith, & Brodzinsky, 1998; Miller, Fan, Christen, Grotevant, & van Dulmen, 2000; Priel, Melamed-Hass, Besser, & Kantor, 2000). Studies of this sort have certainly supplied a lot of useful information, but they refuse to recognize the special nature of the challenge and all the many obstacles that families have to face and overcome.

The result is uncritical acceptance of research data on adopted children's problems, so that problems experienced by just a small number of cases are wrongly attributed to adopted children as a whole. Although confirming that adopted children have more behavioral problems and are more likely to be referred to mental health centers, Brand and Brinich (1999) have also shown that differences between adopted and biological children do tend to disappear when the small group of subjects with extreme scores is "temporarily excluded" from data analysis. This suggests that most adopted children have the same problems as biological ones, and that the differences between them may be attributed to a small number of subjects with serious psychological adjustment problems.

Palacios and Sanchez-Sandoval (in press) also emphasize that, compared with biological children, adopted children invariably seem more at risk than their peers because the background variables are so different. Genetic factors, variables relating to the child's biological parents, traumas they have suffered, and the quality of the care they received when infants, inevitably mean that adopted children are more disadvantaged than others. On the other hand, these disadvantages disappear when adopted children are compared with children of similar backgrounds who for a variety of reasons have remained in institutions or orphan communities.

Few studies have dealt with this because sampling is so difficult. One notable exception is the study we cited in the previous paragraph, which shows that children who have remained in institutions or communities display more behavioral problems and much lower self-esteem than children placed in adoptive families, and that if there are differences between adopted and biological children, they are relatively slight and confined to just a few specific areas. In the light of these results, adoption seems a valid way of giving deprived children the affection and stability they need. For our part, we would like to stress that in family research, one has to know how to recognize the differences between families. As we have said, adoptive families are faced with the double challenge: for the parents, coping with infertility or, in some cases, the loss of an expected child; and for the children, coping with the abandonment they have suffered.

This certainly does not indicate any desire to overlook the risks inherent in the adoptive transition, whose difficulty should not be underestimated. On the contrary, our claim is that the decision to adopt, when adequately supported and properly prepared for, may be a viable option for children and their families. In this respect, it is essential to stress that the community must assume some responsibility for preparing and supporting families that have embarked on adoption, for example by developing enrichment and enhancing programs to help strengthen and enhance the adoptive bond in its various stages.

To conclude, we could say that in order to bring several lineages and families together under one roof—which is what happens with an adoption—parents and children must be willing to face their respective problems of infertility and lack of a family so as to get beyond them and make the shift from negativity to generativity. The following variables seem important in making this happen (Cigoli, 1998b, 2001):

1. The adoptive couple's image of the *family lineage:* traditions and values worth renewing versus debilitating injustice and violence that the couple wants to be free of;

2. The couple's present relationship with its *families of origin:* a relationship based on presence and support that may also include criticism versus a relationship based on absence and mere formality or rejection;

3. The *adopted child's image:* positive attribution to the child, resources to be discovered and nurtured, despite the pain this may cause versus negative

attribution to the child, total absence of resources, which remain entirely in the hands of the parents;

4. Emotional willingness to deal with *basic deficiencies* (infertility, genetic angst) versus denial of basic deficiencies;

5. *Paternal legitimation* (support of the adoptive project, concrete commitment in childrearing) versus paternal irrelevance (no support, father's disengagement, mother's distancing of father).

When the adopted children reach adolescence, another two variables become crucial:

6. The child's affective and cognitive attitude toward the adoptive family: attribution of value, identification with family versus rumination over abandonment or, its opposite, excessive identification with the family and almost total support for it;

7. The advisability of asking about origins: the child can express feelings, plan action and journey back to his/her origins versus suppression of questions and refusal to address the issue on the part of both parents and children.

Although risky for the reasons outlined, adoption pacts are successful in most cases. Becoming an adoptive family and making an adoption pact is definitely worth the effort it takes, although this does not mean that the risks should be either played down or overlooked.

THE ADOPTIVE PACT AND CLINICAL INTERVENTION

The reciprocal process of choosing and deciding that the families of origin, parents, and children who are parties to the pact they are bound up in, can also be seen in clinical intervention. It is worth pointing out that, etymologically speaking, *decide* means "cutting something away" and thus considering and accepting the limitation that the removal of possibility (deciding) entails. For the parental couple, the limitation is the one imposed by infertility, the impossibility of generating something new, or the lack of a male or female child in the family. For adopted children, it is having to acknowledge the reality of a past in which they were abandoned for various reasons (poverty, death, parental fecklessness, or violence) and then putting it behind them and learning once again to value and believe in the bond that has been forged. As we know, this process is far from straightforward and sometimes even impracticable.

The reciprocal nature of the decision to adopt becomes evident enough during the long period of the child's adolescence and early adulthood, and is equally plain to see when adopted children have children themselves. So when we talk about "tasks" that have to be performed, we mean not so much duties and mere moral principles, as the tests and challenges the family members have to face, which are much more important. It is important to acknowledge their existence and give them a name so that everyone knows what is going on, but what the family members do to each other is even more important.

Obviously, the challenge can be avoided and even denied or perverted. In such cases, it is the task of clinical intervention to help family members (including the families of origin) to acknowledge the challenge and find the resources to deal with it.

One of the guiding principles of clinical intervention is to do "just enough" to bring family resources into action. This is not the kind of quantitative principle that translates into, for example, a fixed number of meetings with family members; it is an ethical–affective principle that leads us back to the symbolic level that underlies and directs the things family members do. With adoption, "doing just enough" means helping parents and children with their process of reciprocal legitimation. As we have seen, this is a radical process in the sense that it is the root and sap of the family relationship.

Is It Possible to Relive One's Own Birth?

This is the dream: "It's Sunday afternoon. I'm at home with my mother and Ale, my baby boy, and we are getting ready to go to Mass. As soon as I'm in church, I realize I haven't brought the baby's pacifier with me and I decide to leave. At the door I meet my uncle, a priest, who asks me why I'm leaving, and I explain why.

"I'm back home again with my mother. I realize that outside, in the oratory, there are people who would like to see me. Since there are so many of them, I decide to save time by flying there. I notice three colored kids. I don't know them, but they keep on staring at me so I decide to go down to check them out. We talk for a while and then go back to the church where I find Marisa and Fabio (a young couple she knows) who have been waiting for me to see an eclipse.

"It starts to get dark and we go into the garden with our cameras. I try to take a photo of the eclipse while it's over the bell-tower and I see there's a shooting star too, but my camera doesn't work so I grab Fabio's and fly upwards to get a better shot from higher up, but there are trees and I can't manage it."

Anna is a mixed-blood young mother. She was adopted in South America through some missionary priests the family knew. Her adoptive family already had two boys, but they also wanted a girl to keep the mother company (the father, a very busy politician, was often away) and help her run the house, and also to take care of the uncle, a priest, who would have no one to look after him when he grew old.

The account the parents gave her of her origins was that she was brought to the mission by her mother, who ran off immediately, leaving her near the entrance. The mother was probably in grave danger because she may have been a guerrilla or revolutionary. At any rate, she was in no position to look after her baby. At the mission, Anna was cared for by a young woman she still vaguely remembers. There was said to be an old photo somewhere showing them together.

She married one of the brothers' friends who often came to visit. By doing so, Anna had tried to deal with, at a stroke, her own social isolation ("I never talked to anyone . . . I kept myself to myself, and so did other people . . . even when I was at high school no one ever came to see me . . . it was like being surrounded by scorched earth"), and the suffocating relationship with the mother, whom she felt totally dominated by.

The marriage had been possible because Mauro was already "one of the family" and the priest uncle (whom she would eventually have to care for) had approved and supported it. Her marriage to Mauro had produced Alessandro (Ale), her son.

During family consultation, which the priest uncle had also taken part in, what emerged was the mother's fear of isolation.[3] In her philosophy, males were destined to lead their own lives, so once a woman finished looking after her men, her life became a void. Her relationship with her husband sustained and confirmed her philosophy, given his numerous political and cultural commitments.

Thus, the uncle's fear of a lonely old age and Anna's social isolation seemed a way of giving the family's problem a name, and a way of dealing with it through a third party so as to keep it at a suitable distance from the mother. The aim in shifting all her distress onto Anna was a contradictory one: Deal with the problem, drive away the problem.

The Anna–mother relationship could be seen in turn as an antidote to the fear of isolation, and its cloying nature as a way of keeping family time at a standstill. Finally, the male group (father and sons) was able to turn the unalterable mother–daughter bond to its advantage as a way of dealing with their guilt feelings over leaving their mother-home. Now there would always be someone there to fill the void.

When faced with a family problem (trauma), one must always take the available resources fully into account. In this particular case, the trauma was the prospect of isolation, that is, the mother's feelings of emptiness and insignificance. It is by no means always true that the person concerned acknowledges the trauma as his or her own (it's a *family* problem, after all) or that this person wants to deal with it or would benefit from doing so. In the case in question, the family's resources[4] were revealed to be the priest uncle who had supported his

---

[3] Consultation is always concerned with a number of different triangles, in this particular case the one formed by mother–uncle–Anna, mother–father–Anna, and parents–brothers–Anna.

[4] We define "family resources" later in this chapter.

nephew's marriage, and Anna herself, who had openly said that she wanted to "be clear about herself to herself." Anna was supported in her "selfish move" by both the uncle and father, and the mother aloofly declared she had no objection to it. So there was room for an individual clinical encounter within the context of a family mandate, in the sense that the existence of the trauma-pain affecting the entire family had been acknowledged.

The dream quoted earlier came toward the end of an encounter with Anna a year before. It was a genuine gift she had given to herself, the therapist, and (why not?) those involved in the generative adventure of adoption.

As we said, Anna had not been a mother for long, and motherhood was leading her back to her origins. In her dream she was in her mother's house, in the Mother Church, and went into and out of her mother's house and Mother Church. This entering and leaving was controlled and authorized by both the uncle and the mother. Anna, for her part, wanted to see things from above and thereby possess them at a glance.[5] When she does so, she focuses on color difference, reinforced by the fact that there are three colored people. In fact, it is difficult to see her as colored because her skin color is only slightly darker and looks typically Mediterranean. The issue here is difference of origins, as Anna realizes full well in her associations.

As for the birth, it assumes the nature of an extraordinary, miraculous event, as the arrival of each person in the world should be. This explains the eclipse and the comet-like shooting star. Also, it was a couple, not just a single individual, who took part in the event: It was forming a couple and getting married that brought the question of her origins back to the surface.

The dreamer's attempts to see and get a fix on her origins are unsuccessful because a number of obstacles present themselves. In their conversation, Anna and the therapist explore this idea of wanting yet being unable to see. Her concern for her origins as an abandoned child is an obsession that adopted people frequently have to cope with, and having a child of one's own is a golden opportunity to connect the mysterious and traumatic event of being abandoned and the need for the miraculous event of birth. Anna has no one to tell her the story of her miraculous birth, but she can see her miraculous origin with her mother's eyes and those of her baby boy, which seek her out and hold her gaze.

The Deadly Secret

"Never, but never, will my daughter know she was adopted," hissed her father. "I'll take the secret to my grave . . . no one will ever convince me it would be

---

[5] In the Gupta culture of India, the "genie of the air" is a bearer of wisdom. He is depicted with one leg under his body and the other slung out behind to suggest the idea of flight. In Christian culture, too, the winged cohorts of angels are bearers of knowledge and the power to overcome Evil.

right and proper to tell my daughter she isn't my daughter—*we* brought her up, she's *ours*." The mother said nothing, but her silence was so absolute that the therapist's hope that she might see matters differently from her husband was denied.

The couple had come to the consultation on the advice of a psychiatrist colleague who had met their daughter, Luisa, an 18-year-old girl of extremely fragile identity, haunted by fears of all kinds and with little sense of personal boundary and "skin." Talking to the parents eventually brought the secret out into the open: Luisa had been adopted when only a few days old, but knew nothing of the event, which was why the parents had been advised to find someone to help them.

The therapist's first task was to understand what had happened and what kind of life the family was leading. The drama, as it emerged from clinical dialogue, was as follows. Luisa had been adopted after Caterina, the mother, had twice given birth to a stillborn child, or as she put it, a child that "died as soon as it was born." Petrified by the idea of giving birth to death rather than life, the couple was even more united in its rejection of the event. Some years later, they applied to adopt a child, went through the usual procedure, and, with the fatal collusion of social workers, were assigned a little girl just a few days old who had been premature and underweight and was speedily abandoned by her birth mother. It could not be ruled out that the birth mother had actually been urged to do this.

The parents, who had prepared for the adoption well in advance, had kept Luisa's origin a secret by saying that Caterina, having problems bringing her "pregnancy" to term, had gone to a specialist pregnancy clinic a long way from home and had stayed there until the child was born. The incredible thing was that the couple did not live in a world apart. There were numerous relatives who knew all about the adoption, but the prospect of bringing more suffering to the couple who had already suffered so much filled them with dread. In short, there had been and still was almost total assent to the couple's wishes and to its attempt to solve the adoption issue through denial.

"Everyone knows she's our daughter," said Ernesto, the father. "A couple of years ago she came home saying she'd heard she wasn't our daughter, but I had no trouble persuading her that my wife and I were right. I said there were people who had lost touch with us around the time of her birth and were now inventing these fantasies about it." Attributing what is yours to others brings the deadly process of denial full circle!

However, the meeting with the therapist enabled the parents to acknowledge their problems and fears. It was learned that the mother, a competent teacher, had taken early retirement to devote herself to helping Luisa, but had been humbled to discover how little she could do to improve her daughter's learning abilities. Luisa's premature birth had probably affected her mental development, but this was something else no one was prepared to talk about.

Luisa's premature birth was too close to Caterina's "original sin" of having given birth to dead children.

Ernesto, the father, realized that his daughter had no mental space of her own, was too easily influenced by others, and was even incapable of managing small sums of money, despite her age. So he agreed to her receiving psychological help, but on condition that her adoption would never be mentioned and everyone would pretend things were normal. The adoption issue was unimportant anyway, he said. This was a malign pact that the therapist was unfortunately unable to abide by. What was offered instead was time and space for the husband and wife to work through their distress and, in particular, their need to feel they were generative parents and their desire to be acknowledged as such. They were asked if anyone else could be brought along who might be able to help them, in addition to the therapist.

It should be borne in mind that when adoption is intolerable to the parents[6]—the case we examined here is an extreme one—it attacks the identity awareness of children predestined to live a borderline existence. This was Luisa's psychic situation. As can be seen, *denial,* which is an attack on reality, and *scission,* which attacks the bond, are fundamental pathological ingredients. However, we also have to take account of denial situations brought on by adopted children. The affects of this denial explode in adolescence and early adulthood, when the generational shift occurs, and often take the form of antisocial behavior (thieving, gang membership, attacks on the family's validity and heritage) and challenging the family's "good name" (poor performance at school, inability to hold down a job). Obviously, the ability of the family (i.e., the parents and their families of origin) to rise to the challenge counts for a lot, but the internal strength of the adopted adolescent's internal, undeclared bond should not be underestimated. We might say that they give either *mimetic* or *deep assent* to family models. The mimetic sort reveals itself in assenting to the logic of consumer society and theatrical declarations of good intentions, or through first acknowledging the family's values and then regularly ignoring them. By contrast, deep assent is rooted in the child's ties with his or her biological parents, a kind of imprinted love of people attendant on his or her origins. Thus, a son might continue stealing to please his mother or imitate his father's blackmailing violence.

In short, it is not only ruminating on the pain of abandonment that blocks the adoption process, but also this incredible loyalty to origins, irrespective of how wretched and unsuitable they may seem from the outside. Nor is making the child consciously aware of this loyalty sufficient to break the bond. Equating "discovering" with "changing" is a form of magical thinking. The reality is that discovering something—drawing attention to a crucial aspect of the

---

[6] Of the two cases presented here, the first is an example of an *imperfect pact,* the second of a *denial of difference pact.*

generational issue—only leads to dramatic relational conflict whose outcome cannot be known in advance.

It is the generational shift that presents adopted children with the crucial choice of who to be loyal to, which family to belong to, whose child to be. For natural children, the generational obstacle is knowing how to reconstruct and accept one's origins, their dramas and their resources, and then to move on, whereas for adopted children it is knowing how to choose sides, knowing which relationship to value and nurture.

One of the tasks of clinical intervention is to restore awareness of these obstacles in family members (parents and children) and decide with them where the resources to overcome them are to be found.[7]

By "family resources," we mean willingness to care about the relationship with the other. In the relational–symbolic approach, "happiness" lies in valuing the relationship with the other and living it to the fullest, and, as we have stressed, the "other" is our destiny. This also means being aware of danger (perversion of the relationship is always lying in wait) and acknowledging one's own and other people's limits and shortcomings, rather than expecting to refashion the other in our image, as we would like him or her to be. It also means being ready to help the other, and being willing to be helped in return.

In this sense, family consultation is a fundamental way of dealing with generational problems. By widely adopting the systemic approach, one of the mistakes family therapists have made is their failure to take full account of differences between individuals, and to realize that these are the stuff relationships are made of. The consequence of this has been a visible decline in family therapy and an upsurge in so-called individual systemic therapy. Family consultation, which lasts as long as it has to, has the dual aim of involving a set of people in a problem instead of blaming it on someone (therapists are all too prone to siding with the "poor children" and blaming the problem on their parents), and deciding which family members are best able to shoulder responsibility for it. Some may be more willing to do so than others; some may be less suitable. In the first of our case studies (Anna), there was a double resource; in the second, none at all, or at least not in the current situation. People have to be asked who they think might be able to help them deal with the family's problem. It could be a relative or, just as easily, a friend or some religious or moral authority figure. On the doors of some medieval French and Spanish churches, there is the wonderful image of a man carrying another man on his shoulders. Another common image is the Atlas figure carrying the weight of the church on his back. This is very much what we mean by "family resource": acknowledging there is a load that needs carrying, and doing something to support the family tree by giving it direction and vitality.

---

[7] Clinical intervention is certainly not the only form of relationship support. Some family members (especially women) are already attuned to relationships and their cause. There are also religious and voluntary groups, as well as various kinds of self-help.

ASSISTED PROCREATION: A NEW FORM OF PARENTHOOD

Now we come to a totally new family scenario. One of contemporary culture's stranger transitions to parenthood is its ever more frequent recourse to assisted procreation, in which the critical transition is increasingly seen not as a matter of *having* children, as of *how* to have them.

Unlike time-honored adoption, choosing assisted procreation is a new solution to the old sterility problem. And yet, although it may relieve the couple's distress by offering the prospect of generativity, assisted procreation is not without its risks. In particular, the predominantly medical nature of its procedures precludes discussion of the pain of sterility. As we have seen, sterility inflicts a deep narcissistic wound that also boosts faith in the magical power of medicine to satisfy the longing for a child, once the couple has opted for this kind of treatment. In reality, however, a certain proportion of successes (estimated at around 25%) is offset by a significant percentage of failures, even after repeated attempts. This is extremely distressing for the woman concerned, and therefore for the couple, too.

The psychological cost of such failure has barely been investigated. Those few studies that have addressed the issue show that couples find themselves at a cross-roads: The challenge the partners share either weakens them as a couple or brings them closer. In some situations, repeated attempts at assisted procreation contribute to the couple's break-up, whereas in others the couple stands fast and tends to use the marital relationship as a refuge from pain and distress. Failure can easily be blamed on external factors, especially lack of adequate support from medical staff (Weaver, Clifford, Hay, & Robinson, 1997).

When the treatment is a success, however, it becomes very important to distinguish between couples who have used homologous fertilization (usually IVF) and those who have used heterologous fertilization (usually donor insemination). In the former case, the effort spent analyzing the couple's functioning leads to an improvement in the relationship as soon as the child is born. This is understandable when one realizes that the couple has achieved its goal of having a child, albeit by "unnatural" means. Such positive effects can also be observed in other procedures like adoption, where the couple's massive investment in the event, and achieving the goal of having a child to call their own, binds the partners together and strengthens their union. Couples who have been successful with assisted procreation may even be happier with their marriages than those who have had an "unassisted" child (Levy-Shiff et al., 1991). As with adoption, this may be because the birth event was preceded by a long period of deprivation. There may also have been a long honeymoon period in which future problems were underestimated, or an attempt was made to deny the partners' differences by reassuring each other of their adequacy as parents (entitlement to parenthood).

It should also be said that assisted procreation studies are difficult to interpret because the couples were in a sense selected before success was achieved. As with adoption, it seems likely that only strong cohesive or denial-prone couples have the will to see such a difficult procedure through to the end, and we know little about those that drop by the wayside. Studies of parental relationships in couples who used homologous fertilization agree that these parents, especially the mothers, are more emotionally involved with their children (Hahn, 2001) and are also better parents.

As in many studies of adoption, this can be explained by the parents' massive investment of time and effort in the generative project. Their eagerness to become mothers and fathers makes them highly motivated in their efforts to give the child an upbringing commensurate with the investment they have made.

What we still cannot say with any certainty is what the generational effects of the child's "artificial" origin (usually shrouded in secrecy) are likely to be. Moreover, present studies are based on samples of children aged 4 to 5 years, and there can be no significant differences between naturally and artificially conceived children of this age (Golombok et al., 1996; Golombok & MacCallum, 2003). However, longer term negative consequences have been reported. At school age, artificially conceived children (especially boys with older-than-average parents) seem more vulnerable than others in terms of social and emotional adaptation (Levy-Shiff et al., 1998). At any rate, it seems clear that longer term (i.e., generational) studies need to be done.

This brings us to heterologous fertilization, which has a good many psychological consequences for couple who opt for it (Chatel, 1993). For women, the most common is disappointment with the partner, who seems discredited by the donor's greater potency, and the unconscious feeling of betraying the partner while simultaneously feeling aggressive and guilty toward him. The man's situation is no easier because accepting heterologous insemination means accepting his own sterility once and for all. Here the commonest risk is that a sort of insuperable rivalry develops toward the anonymous donor, whose potency and fertility induce feelings of inferiority, jealousy, and even persecution fantasies in the sterile man.

The effects of donor insemination on children are also insufficiently known because the relevant studies are still too short-term to provide any convincing answers. At any rate, the crucial point is the secrecy of the child's origin (Bonnie, 2002; Golombok & MacCallum, 2003) which, as we already know, is a key consideration in the decision to adopt and makes revelation (both inside and outside the family) of the method of conception a major issue. Other studies have emphasized that revelation is a ticking bomb waiting to go off when children start wondering who their "real" fathers are (Blum, 1996; Klock & Maier, 1991; McWhinnie, 1996; Rangell & Hrushovski, 1996). The situation will certainly be no better if the question is never asked owing to suppression and denial. Clinical experience tells us that the question will necessarily circulate within the family under some other guise before resurfacing in symptomatic form.

Moreover, a number of distinctions need to be made regarding the type of donation. With sperm donation, both the donor's identity and the father's sterility are secret. It should be remembered here that men often identify impotence with sterility, so the secrecy about it serves not so much to protect the child as to protect the father against doubts about his virility and preserve his faith in generational continuity.

Egg donation is quite another matter. Here secrecy is less important because by carrying the child, the women puts part of herself into the procreative process and therefore feels that the child is her own. However, there are obvious psychological risks in nonanonymous donation, such as from a sister or a friend. Although the donor's intention is to help the sterile woman become a mother (Bydlowsky, 1994), the ambiguous presence of the dual female figure does remain a problem.

In our view, one of the key considerations is that assisted procreation seems yet another incarnation of the fantasy of self-generation always present in families, a new form of the myth of autogenesis. Separating conception from sexual union pushes the couple into the background so far as being a biological and affective vehicle of generativity is concerned. Moreover, the couple loses definition and eventually disappears from view when heterologous fertilization is chosen. One of the partners suddenly becomes inscrutable and noticeably "absent." Usually it is the father, who in Western culture acts as the symbolic bridge with lineage and, as psychoanalysts have repeatedly stressed, opens up the mother–child relationship to a third person and the world. The old saying *mater certa pater incertus* (mother certain father uncertain) reappears in a new guise, and by choice, not as a result of uncontrolled procreation. The perception is that the child has been generated by the mother and is being drawn into the black hole of the self-generation fantasy. As we have shown, this fantasy is a postmodern form of the mythical-religious theme of the Great Mother. One example is Shakti, the Indian female deity who originates the world. Another is the Mater Matuta of Mediterranean culture, whose many breasts allow her to suckle an infinite number of children. Finally, the early Middle Ages (4th to 5th century) saw the cult of the church as the Great Mother.

Associated with these myths, there is another, present in the Bible, of being able to conceive in old age, thereby challenging the laws of nature and causing wonderment. It should be said, however, that the individuality myth in today's fantasy of self-generation has subsumed the collective religious bonding of the Great Mother myth's earlier manifestations.

Whether based on undervaluation of lineage (the family stories behind the couple who generate the child) or, much more dramatically, on the (biological–symbolic) absence of the other parent (especially the father), the fantasy of self-generation brings generation and reproduction so perilously close as to make them virtually indistinguishable. The prospect of human cloning, which would be *literally* reproductive, suggests a new and disturbing form of "reproduction."

Irrespective of the important differences in the situations we have examined, assisted procreation does invite reflection on how the meaning of "transition to parenthood" has altered in step with the disturbing shift from natural to artificial conception. Because it bypasses the procreative act, this new kind of parenthood makes symbolic mediation difficult. Assisted reproduction encourages a split between sexuality and procreativity, biological parenthood and the meaning of having children, whose general effect is to fragment the transition to parenthood and undermine the relational and symbolic meanings that represent the species-specific aspects of human generativity.

This tends to strengthen the postmodern couple's self-centeredness, its belief in its own self-generation and correspondingly poor appreciation of the fact that it was generated, and its imprisonment in a perpetual present in which relational history and process of gift and obligation linking it to previous generations, are only dimly perceived. Significantly, recent studies (Golombok & MacCallum, 2003) have noted that most couples prefer not to tell either their children or parents that they have used assisted procreation.[8]

Parenthood through assisted procreation poses dramatic questions for parents. Therefore, these couples should be helped to nurture the symbolic aspects of fatherhood, motherhood, and having children, so as to compensate for possible imbalance in the couple, especially when heterologous fertilization was chosen and only one of the parents—usually the mother, who has gone through pregnancy—feels like a biological parent in every respect.

---

[8] "Generate," "procreate," and "reproduce" are all ways of saying "give birth," but the first two are used of human beings, while the third generally applies to animals or is used in scientific discourse ("human reproduction"). Significantly, the terms *assisted procreation* and *assisted reproduction* are both in common use today.

CHAPTER SEVEN

Becoming an Adult:
A Generational Impasse?

In postmodern society, the transition to adulthood is an extended period covering around 20 years of an individual's life. Adolescence is increasingly starting earlier (at around 11 or 12 years of age) and lasting longer (until the age of 19 or 20), and we are witnessing a new phase termed *postadolescence* or, more properly, young adulthood, which may last until the age of 30. It is in this last phase that the true passage to adulthood takes place.

The transition to adulthood is thus a double transition: from adolescence to young adulthood, and from there to full adulthood. The former is, therefore, a preparatory phase for the true transition that the young person will accomplish in the following phase. This process is a gradual one in which the young person moves from the totally marginalized social status typical of adolescence to the partially marginalized status of young adulthood, and then to the fully acknowledged social status of adulthood.

The transition to adulthood has thus assumed new features, even compared with the recent past. Until a few decades ago, it coincided with the brief "launching children" phase in family life (McGoldrick & Carter, 1982), characterized by a rapid generational shift, precise "passage markers" occurring in a precise sequence—end of schooling, finding a relatively stable job, marriage—and the impossibility of a "return" to the preceding state. Today the transition to adulthood has become a long moratorium phase: The timescale is much extended, the importance and symbolic meaning of traditional rites of passage have diminished or even disappeared, the temporal sequencing of the rites has been lost, and the cultural paradigm of experimentation and reversibility of choice is becoming increasingly widespread. The result is that the transition to adulthood is now a shifting sequence of numerous microtransitions (Breunlin, 1988). Rather than the transition itself, it is the transitory aspect of the event that dominates. Arnett (2000) has called the period sandwiched between adolescence and adulthood "emerging adulthood," and has shown that this new life-cycle phase occurs only in cultures that allow young people to live a long period of relative independence from social roles and prescriptive expectations.

The prolongation of the transition to adult status has been noted in recent years by many researchers belonging to different schools of thought, demonstrating that this is a very widespread phenomenon in Western societies.

Iacovou and Berthoud (2001), in an analysis of data gathered by the European Community Household Panel, identify two behavioral models in young adults. In the first, the Mediterranean Model of the Southern European nations (Italy, Spain, Portugal, Greece) and to some extent Austria and Ireland, individuals leave the parental home either when they marry or when they become parents; in the second, the North European Model (Germany, Denmark, Scandinavia, the Netherlands, the United Kingdom, France, Belgium, Luxembourg), individuals leave the parental home much earlier and pass through several intermediate stages, such as living alone, living with a partner, or a long period of childless marriage.

Significant differences between these two transition styles begin to appear around the age of 20 and lessen again around the age of 30. Up to 18 years of age, the vast majority of young people in Europe and the United States live in their families of origin, and are single and childless. Five years later, however, at the age of 23, 72% of Northern European women have left their family of origin as opposed to 27% from the south of Europe, and 47% of Northern European men leave home at that age as opposed to 15% of their peers in Southern Europe. This trend increases proportionally until the age of 30. In other words, between the ages of 20 and 30, young Europeans differ very noticeably in their relationships with their families of origin. However, there are no significant differences between young Europeans in the phases before and after this period. Things are different in the United States, where most young adults leave home by age 18 or 19. One third of emerging adulthood go off to college after high school and spend the next several years in some combination of independent living. Here too, however, there is evidence that the age at which young people are still living at home is steadily rising, although to a lesser extent than in Europe (Goldscheider, 1997). Furthermore, as a result of the steep rise in divorce rates, one often sees a return to the family of origin after the failure of a marriage, the so-called "refilled nest."

In this context of extended young adulthood and postponement of binding personal and working decisions, the family of origin acquires greater prominence. This is especially typical of the Mediterranean Model that has produced the so-called "ongoing family," in which two adult generations live together. The family of origin's enhanced value is evident from the importance young people attach to it, and by the influence it has on their lives. More than in the past, today's families play a central role in children's lives because children remain in their families longer and because significant adult figures outside the family, once a constant presence in adolescents' lives, are practically nonexistent today (Lanz, Rosnati, Iafrate, & Marta, 1999).

Thus, the transition to adulthood is increasingly a "joint developmental enterprise" of parents and children (Sroufe, 1991; Youniss & Smollar, 1985). In this type of family, young adults enjoy considerable freedom and leeway in negotiation and, unlike some decades ago, live in a supportive, conflict-free family climate. This is partly due to the fact that parents and children know they will have to spend a long time together before the younger generation's transition to adulthood comes about. A key element for both generations is the presence or absence of a clear goal to be achieved, and a positive meaning attached to it. The transition is successful if the family perceives itself as being on the move, in "transit," and does not lose its sense of striving toward a goal during the slow process of transition. Examples of loss of purpose include young people who, while dependent on their families, achieve their professional goals but indefinitely postpone their affective choices and family responsibilities, and young people who believe that they must walk the path of personal growth in extreme solitude, and can achieve the transition only by severing all ties with their families of origin. They may leave the parental home but still have accounts to settle with their families of origin (Furlong & Cartmel, 1997), so the separation does not entail personally working through one's family history. On the other hand, as we see shortly, parents may also obstruct their children's emancipation and may implement strategies to "detain" their children for as long as possible in the family. Thus, the theme of separation is prominent in this transformation.

To varying extents, every transition is marked by two major affective themes: the grief over losing what has to be left behind, and hope/trust in what will be acquired and achieved by doing so. In this transition, grieving over loss is dominant because, as we have seen, what is acquired through the transition—the child's new adult identity and the establishment of a new family—seems "remote" and uncertain. Thus, the pain of separation is felt not only by the child (who leaves the security of childhood–adolescence for an ambiguous, uncertain future), but also by the parents, who will have proof only in the long term that their child has achieved true adulthood by deciding to start a family and carry generational history forward.

On the other hand, there is also a close connection between family and community during this phase. Children are "handed over" to the community as fully fledged, responsible members of society. The community, for its part, is expected to make room for them in a variety of ways. In Europe, for example, where social leadership is gerontocratic, the relationship between the generations is biased in favor of adults and the elderly. The different generations in the family and community are, therefore, expected to undergo a generative transformation. This transformation affects a variety of relationships and gives rise to specific tasks whose outcomes may affect each other.

TASKS AS PARTNERS AND CHILDREN

The partners' most important task in this phase is reinvestment in their relationship as a couple, that is, as a marital couple and not just a parental couple, with an eye to the fact that the child will eventually leave the parental home. Freed from the burden of everyday child care, the couple has more space and time for itself *as* a couple: The partners can communicate more and move toward a new, more supportive marital relationship.

It also becomes important for the couple to strengthen or initiate relationships with the community, reactivating or reinforcing their relations with friends and society. In short, given today's extended life expectancy and better health, reinvesting in the couple relationship is one of the tasks of our age. If it is neglected, the couple may find itself in crisis; it is no accident that divorces of couples with late adolescent and young adult children are on the increase.

In this phase, women find themselves in a particularly critical situation in that, having often sacrificed their careers in order to raise their children, and having invested a great deal of energy in their upbringing, they find themselves more prone than their husbands to experiencing an identity crisis when the process of the child's separation begins. Her husband's support is, therefore, a crucial factor for a woman during this difficult separation.

New family and work responsibilities contribute to the couple's redefinition of its aims. Once again, women are at the center of these changes. In some cases, they may return to the careers they abandoned in order to raise children, and they are more often involved in caring for the older generation.

During this time of life, middle-aged partners must face, as children themselves, the ordeal of their own parents' illness or death. This highlights the fact that the family life cycle cannot be described in terms of the individual life cycles. In reality, family bonds are simultaneously tested by a whole series of crucial events. The middle generation's task as children is to accept their parents' aging, take care of them if they are ill, and receive from them their legacy. The woman's greater involvement in all this challenges the couple's equilibrium, which needs to be restructured if an overall breakdown of the family system is to be avoided.

TASKS AS PARENTS

Let us now turn to parent–child relations in this new context of decelerated transition. The task of parents of young adults is to support their children and guide them toward the assumption of adult responsibility, which includes a commitment in the field of study and work as well as in the affective sphere, with all its generative consequences. As we have argued, in the current cultural context this is rendered difficult by the increasing emotional closeness between the generations that tends to weaken the challenge represented by the transition and the generational leap.

Let us now look more analytically at the features of intergenerational relationships during this transition. Responsible care giving, the symbolic core of the parent–child relationship, turns into a "flexibly protective" attitude and a capacity for personalized guidance when the children reach adolescence (Scabini, 1995). Protection and support become flexible by taking into account the gradually increasing independence that characterizes the long period of adolescence and young adulthood. Today such direction and guidance in making choices needs to be "tailored" to the specific situation of each individual. We could say that we are now more aware of personal differences than of the gender differences that until recently largely dictated both the timing of marriage and choice of partner, and still do in some non-Western cultures.

The acquisition of adult identity is encouraged whenever adolescents know they can count on a family environment that provides support as well as direction and guidance for growth. All the numerous studies of parenting styles reiterate that an authoritative style best fosters growth, unlike laissez-faire (no rules) or authoritarian (no warmth and support) styles (Steinberg, 2001).

In the ongoing family, the gradual process of acquiring independence may weaken if parents and children use the process to satisfy the same needs in each other, producing a dangerous stability that prevents differentiation and the achievement of full adult identity. We call this phenomenon *reciprocal relational advantage*. The relationship between generations always presents a certain ambivalence: Previous generations often fear but also care for those that follow. In the past, this fear was expressed by subjugating the younger generations, denying their demands for differentiation, and underestimating the value of personal growth. Today we are in an opposite situation: The younger generation is guaranteed ample space for personal development and differentiation, but a new and devious kind of ambivalence has appeared, in the form of ambiguous intergenerational stability.

The following brief description of reciprocal relational advantage is based on the results of in-depth interviews we conducted on samples of young adults and their parents (Scabini & Cigoli, 1997). On one hand, young adults stake out for themselves a completely autonomous and private "free zone" inside the family home. They can thus enjoy the support and resources of the family of origin without any particular constraints. Faced with an uncertain future, their families of origin represent their one fundamental certainty. From this supportive context, young people can venture forth a few steps at time into the community and gain "controlled" experience of work, which is what they are most worried about. At the same time, they venture into affective experience while constantly postponing the decision to start a family. In this way, they have a long moratorium in which to test their affective and working capabilities without having to shoulder the burden of the ties and responsibilities their choices would necessitate.

Our studies show that young adults especially perceive the advantages of prolonged cohabitation with parents in terms of emotional security, while also sensing its potential risks. The interviews show very clearly that, paradoxically, young people would like their parents to be less tolerant because this would free them from a task many of them are aware of, that of "weaning" their parents, coping with their "empty nest" fears, and helping them to move on.

For their part, parents appreciate the relational truce that characterizes this phase, and indirectly enjoy its effects, deluding themselves in turn that they will be parents forever. When they say, "It's right for children to leave home," they are playing a typecast role that masks the fear of solitude they truly feel. Our interviews with parents revealed that this condition is reinforced by strong identification with their children, in that the latter enjoy a life that is free and rich in possibilities, a life their parents have not been able to have, even though they wished for it. Moreover, by being sympathetic to their children's needs, parents achieve an ideal parent–child relationship that was denied them during their own youth. A double identification thus binds parents to their children: They are the young adult children their parents would have liked to be (desire) and, at the same time, they are the parents they wish they had had but did not (need).

Furthermore, parents and children have shared representations about their future. They are drawn together by a negative representation of adult life characterized by uncertainty and precariousness, whether on the social level — the difficulty of achieving one's working aspirations — or the family level — the difficulty of finding a trustworthy partner.

The world of work is the principal focus of young people's personal investment, the assumption being that it will meet their expectations of it. Parents and children thus share an idea of self-fulfillment based on emotional self-centeredness severed from generativity and its concomitant responsibilities toward a future family. Work and emotional life are seen as areas for self-expression and much less as areas in which one accepts commitments and acknowledges bonds. Once again, affective aspects are dominant while ethical ones remain latent. Thus, the value of family genealogy becomes latent, although the child is significant as an expression of its parents' self-fulfillment, motivated in turn by their self-centered fulfillment needs.

The long transition to adulthood within the family of origin is, therefore, the outcome of the combined movements of parents and offspring: Both gain a psychic and relational advantage from the process. This "solution," which prolongs the transition, may be a functional answer to a host of social problems, and thus a resource. However, it may pose a threat to the children's successful separation from their parents if it becomes a form of intergenerational impasse. So, the principal task of parents and, more in general, of the adult generations is to oppose this generational impasse, encouraging and legitimizing their children's ability to demonstrate new social and familial generativity.

However, this generative transformation is again relational because it personally affects parents, who are themselves expected to make a crucial transition. When a child moves into adulthood, parents too must undergo a radical change that takes the form of a changed generative perspective, that is, parents are expected to invest more heavily in the social community the generativity they once exercised in their family.

What do parents do with the generative verve that has accumulated over many years of nurturing and rearing children? Is it enough to be supportive of their children at a distance and to busy themselves with what few grandchildren will be born?

Until several decades ago, short life expectancy, large families and correspondingly longer periods of child care, and a constant succession of generations (when the youngest child left home, the others already had children of their own) made this question less urgent. For women especially, it meant moving from one form of caregiving (their own children) to another (their grandchildren). But today's middle-aged parents, who can hope to live for many decades to come, cannot fail to ask this question, at least implicitly. Examples of the problem include the increasing frequency of adult identity crises and midlife divorce, and ever more widespread forms of depression.

But the passage from parental generativity to social generativity is as decisive today as it is crucial, given the cultural individualism that permeates both the parent–child relationship and the relationship between adult and young generations in the community. On one hand, children tend to be a form of adult self-fulfillment—parents mirror themselves in their children and support them in their need for self-fulfillment—so that parental generativity is crippled by overprotectiveness and failure to encourage children's independence. On the other hand, adult society—particularly in Europe—is definitely biased against the young generations, a condition that has been justly labelled *generational disequity*.[1]

This is true of Southern European countries like Spain (Cordon, 1997) and Italy (Donati, 1991),[2] where in past decades the welfare state greatly favored the active population, which is now adult or elderly, but is unable to do the same for present younger generations on the verge of adulthood who are faced with the

---

[1] We follow Donati (1991) in attributing three meanings to the concept of generational equity: (a) equity as the just distribution of material and nonmaterial resources between the generations in a given historical period; (b) equity in the relationship between present and future, that is, how much one generation leaves to the next, how much one generation consumes or saves or creates for the next generation; and (c) equity within a generation in relation to the family burden of whoever shoulders responsibility for reproduction.

[2] In a macrosystemic perspective, the discussion could be extended to the relationship between the rich North (composed mostly of adult/elderly populations) and the poor South (composed mostly of young people and children).

difficult and laborious task of integrating themselves into an environment that is both competitive and greedy in its allocation of resources tightly controlled by the adult and elderly.

We might say that, in the social context, adults have acted and continue to act as if they have forgotten their identity as parents. They have lost their capacity for generative investment in future generations and have functioned corporatively in order to safeguard themselves at the expense of young people. We are faced here with the evident paradox that the generations seem to be strongly united in the family yet strongly opposed and competitive in society.

Systemic exchange between family and society is, therefore, based on schism and compensation rather than cooperation. By prolonging the family's protectiveness, parents compensate for the social injustices they help to produce, albeit unconsciously. In this way, parental generativity only marks time and does not transform itself into social generativity.

PARENTS AND CHILDREN COMPARED

The relational entwinement that emerges from our the interviews is borne out by our numerous questionnaire-based studies. In line with the methodological observations described in chapter 4, we have always used several family members as informants in these studies, so as to articulate similarities and differences between children's and parents' points of view (Scabini, Marta, & Lanz, in press). We employed such variables of overall perception of family functioning as cohesion, family satisfaction, family collective efficacy, and other variables aimed at detecting the quality of the relationship between dyads (mothers–fathers, sons–daughters, fathers–sons/daughters, mothers–sons/daughters) such as filial and parental efficacy, communication, and support (Caprara, Pastorelli, Regalia, Scabini, & Bandura, 2004; Caprara, Regalia, Scabini, Barbaranelli, & Bandura, 2004; Scabini & Galimberti, 1995; Scabini, Lanz, & Marta, 1999; Scabini & Marta, 1996). As regards support, in our most recent studies we used a relational version more in keeping with our theoretical perspective, aimed at probing the relationship between received and given support (Branje, van Aken, & van Lieshout, 2002). Moreover, the comparison between received and given support provides important information about the intensity and equity of exchange, which is just as important (especially between two generations of adults or near-adults) as the quality of communication (an affective variable). Given the centrality of gender and generational difference, the following interpretation of our findings is based on this perspective.

Family relations were generally perceived as positive. In effect, the family is a place that the vast majority of young people feel they can count on, whereas for parents it is a focus of positive investment: Communication levels are medium-high between family members, and levels of cohesion, satisfaction, and support are good (Scabini, 2000a). However, this positive perception shows significant differences when analyzed by gender and generation.

Let us first look at generation difference. In all our data sets, and in line with the literature (Noller & Callan, 1991), parents show a positive bias in almost all the variables. We might say that parents overestimate the family's "efficacy" and the quality of their relations with their children, whereas children seem more critical. More specifically, we think it is important to consider differences in the variables relating not only to the closeness and trustworthiness of the bond, but also to its autonomy.

In a study comparing generations of parents and children in a time frame extending from late adolescence to young adulthood (17–25), we obtained two interesting results. The first is that, whereas parents report very high long-term given-and-received support and perceive a fairly low level of independent decision making in their children, the children's perceptions of these same aspects are "inverted." We might say that parents know that closeness is important and voice the need for connection, whereas children see their own emancipation as important and voice the need for autonomy (Scabini, 2000b).

This discrepancy tends to lessen over the years, however: At the end of the transition, the two generations are much closer. Young adult children's acknowledgement of reciprocal support is pretty much like their parents', while parents acknowledge a degree of autonomy very close to that reported by their children. The two generations are also more similar in terms of discrepancy indices and communication problems, especially in father–son dyads.

It should also be said that, in general, change in the parents–children relationship is reported more often by children than parents. Children report different levels of communication and support in age ranges from early adolescence to young adulthood, with a negative spike around 16 to 17 years, whereas there are no significant differences between the parents of adolescents or young adults. In short, the transition and its attendant changes are experienced and perceived more acutely by children than by parents. This is further confirmation of what we noticed in the in-depth interviews, the fact that parents play a not insignificant role in delaying their children's emancipation and generational shifts (Lanz, 1998; Lanz & Rosnati, 1995; Scabini, 2001).

The results we obtained from our studies of future orientation are in line with our preceding observations. Jointly faced with a larger number of positive elements (hopes) than negative ones (fears), the two generations differ in the timing of their achievement of positive objectives, and in the real likelihood of achieving them. It should be said that parents are more optimistic about their children's abilities and their likelihood of achieving their goals, but postpone the moment of actual achievement well into the future where work is concerned. On the other hand, the children—in particular, the girls—locate the achievement of goals closer in time, although they are less certain that they really can be achieved (Lanz, Rosnati, Marta, & Scabini, 2001).

However, the most interesting ideas emerge when gender and generation differences are connected. Most importantly, we find once again that parents and children differ in their attitudes. Unlike children, who report differences in the quality of the relationship (measured in terms of communication and support) according to the parent's gender, parents in many cases do not appear to perceive significant differences related to their children's gender (Scabini, 2000b). This tells us that, for parents, the child's status *as a child* overshadows any gender-related considerations, and this at a time in their children's lives when gender plays a decisive role in shaping identity.

More specifically, we can use our data set to describe the relational scenario of Italian families. The mother is the dominant figure and is at the center of the relational network; the children indicate her as their principal reference point for communication and their most supportive parent. The father seems a less influential background figure. Children turn to their mothers not only for personal advice, as was to be expected, but also for academic and career guidance, where she clearly exerts an influence on both sons and daughters. We believe, therefore, that the Italian family carries to extremes the matrifocality reported in studies of Western families with adolescents, especially in Southern European countries.

However, if we compare the data for each parent with each child, so as not to lose sight of specific relational bonding in each family, the picture changes. Mothers' perceptions of their children appear significantly less accurate than fathers'. A study comparing communication and support with level of psychosocial risk for the adolescent clearly showed that mothers failed to identify their child's level of psychosocial risk, especially if it was intermediate, whereas fathers were accurate predictors of it (Marta, 1997; Scabini & Marta, 1996). It seems likely that the mother, overinvolved in family relations and overburdened with tasks, loses the objectivity that the father has precisely because he is more distant. So we might say that the mother is partially blind to negative elements in the relationship with her child, and has difficulty in perceiving and accepting the changes involved in the transition. Mothers do not seem to grasp that the level of family cohesion has to change, and that family boundaries need to be more flexible to accommodate children's growth, whereas fathers, in agreement with the children, do seem to grasp this. Moreover, mothers want more family cohesion, making them a centripetal force in the family (Scabini & Galimberti, 1995).

The exercise of paternal function is certainly less visible than in the past, and methodologically more sophisticated research designs are needed to reveal it. An effective paternal presence certainly makes the difference in some significant moments in the transition to adulthood, as shown by our study of young people at the end of high school faced with the problem of choosing whether to continue their education or find a job. We analyzed the data by constructing family typologies based on level of family functioning, and found that the father's effectiveness in helping adolescents reach a final decision was typical of high-functioning families with high levels of satisfaction. When the father performs his paternal function at certain critical moments, especially as a mediator with the social world, he redresses the bias in favor of the mother, to the advantage of the family's overall functioning (Scabini, Lanz, & Marta, 1999). We could say, then, that the exercise of the maternal and paternal functions produces a variety of relational configurations based on their effect on the overall level of family well-being in both normal and at-risk families.

As far as children's gender differences are concerned, the most interesting finding comes from comparing correspondences between self-perception and how one is perceived by others. Daughters are better than sons at discriminating between relationships. Whereas the sons' communication indices for both fathers and mothers correspond, daughters' perceptions of communication with a parent correspond more closely to the communication perceived by the parent than to the daughter's perceptions of the other parent. This shows that daughters regard reciprocity in relationships as more important and are able to discern it, whereas sons are guided more by the principle of relational coherence (Sroufe & Fleeson, 1988), which tends to iron out gender differences in maternal and paternal roles. This discriminative ability, which is undoubtedly a resource, may also be a potential cause of family problems and a source of dissatisfaction.

Another interesting point emerges when intergenerational relations are analyzed by gender. There are clear similarities between mothers and daughters on one hand, and fathers and sons on the other, especially with respect to ease of communication and support. However, the female line is the stronger of the two, with higher indices of agreement and goal sharing. The goals may also be quite ambitious where future work is concerned, confirming the marked tendency (already noted in the in-depth interviews) for parents to mirror themselves in their children, which to us seems to derive mostly from the mother. Rapidly changing female roles see mothers and daughters united by an identity transformation that mainly affects daughters but indirectly affects mothers as well, thereby fulfilling their ideal selves. Although this overview may seem wildly optimistic, it does point to signs that the difficulty of the game at stake has been perceived. The female dyad is significantly less satisfied than the male one, in contrast to the findings of American studies (Graber & Brooks-Gunn, 1999). Both mothers and daughters have lower family satisfaction indices than fathers and sons. The mother's position at the center of family relations evidently carries with it a price to pay and is even perceived as a burden. Moreover, expectations play a far from secondary role because, as we have seen with cohesion, they are so high that the gap between the real and the ideal inevitably leads to some disappointment. In addition, fathers also have significantly higher scores than mothers in terms collective family efficacy (Caprara et al., 2004).

But if this is the relational picture of the so-called normal family, what are the variations within specific family typologies? The literature mostly compares "normal" and clinical families. With regard to adoptive and divorcing families, we have already noted the limitations of comparisons aimed at detecting discrepancies between supposedly "normal" families and all other families, which are deemed "failures" by the same criterion that makes the others "normal." We are not interested in these comparisons, nor do we wish to deny the difficulties that specific typologies present, but we do think that comparison is very useful in helping us to understand how families can be described, whether in more common situations or more specific (although not necessarily problematic) situations, and where their risks and resources are to be found.

Let us look more closely at some crucial points for analysis by gender and generation, drawn from two opposing situations: the separated family with young adult children (we have done many studies of them over the years, especially clinical ones focusing mostly on the young people); and the family with young adult children involved in voluntary social work. The former is characterized by relational deficit, the latter by a surplus of relationality. The remarks that follow summarize our observations of the family relationships of young adult children living in divorced families.

An examination of relational intertwinement during this phase of the family life cycle is particularly important because it allows us to highlight the long-term effects of the parents' divorce on their children (feelings of danger in close relationships) that were never voiced in previous years (Wallerstein & Lewis, 1998). Over time, there has been a decisive, and we think very interesting, change of direction in research. From a perspective exclusively centered on adjustment–maladjustment following divorce, and its immediate effects in the short term (the period of time immediately after the family break-up), attention has shifted to what happens during young adulthood and the ethical as well as cognitive/affective coping styles of subjects involved in the divorce situation. Thus, some studies have taken into consideration the feeling of injustice that pervades family relations following the break-up of divorce (Jurkovic, Thirkield, & Morrell, 2001), whereas others have considered whether and how adult children and parents have sought confrontation and reciprocal clarification over the years (Arditti & Prouty, 1999).

Placing our findings along two axes—the risk–resource relationship, and gender and generation difference—produces a more or less predictable picture in line with the international literature. The children of divorced families have more fearful and uncertain perceptions of the future, especially with respect to marriage (Giuliani, Iafrate, & Rosnati, 1998). Moreover, they evaluate the quality of family relations less positively than intact families. More specifically, whereas communication levels with mothers are positive (even if lower than those in intact families), the relationship between children and noncustodial fathers is more problematic (in the vast majority of cases, the father is the noncustodial parent.) Here the resources would seem to be located on the maternal axis and risks on the paternal axis (Lanz, Iafrate, et al., 1999).

However, it was the qualitative data (interviews and Double Moon graphic–symbolic drawing) that supplied the information that helped us to reconstruct the families' relational interplay in greater detail (Cigoli, Giuliani, & Iafrate 2002; Scabini & Cigoli, 2004). While openly declaring the difficulties of their current situation, young people do acknowledge that they have received something good from their families. The most common scenario sees the mother occupying center stage for both males and females: She is identified as the source of well-being because she is supportive and caring even at the cost of personal sacrifice, and she transmits ethical and spiritual values. The father is seen as distant or totally disengaged and is often omitted from the drawing. The mother is a resource in the sense that she behaves as a single parent, that is, she combines the maternal and paternal functions, while the father fades into the background.

In a few cases, however, the parental couple is perceived as the source of well-being (the children speak about "my parents") and as able, despite the marital break-up, to provide care and transmit values, although here, too, there is evidence that the parental couple is not seen as a stable reference point. At any rate, in both situations the children see the difference between their family's past and their own future as their parents' fault, and in relation to their own desire for freedom.

How do children position themselves in relation to paternal and maternal figures? Sons and daughters have different attitudes to paternal "absence" and maternal "excessive presence." Sons notice the absence and seeming irrelevance of a father who sets rules and gives direction, and they create an emotional distance between themselves and their mothers. Daughters, on the other hand, especially miss the presence of a partner at their mother's side to protect them from her excessive intrusiveness, which they perceive as dangerous, and from a mixture of feelings related to identifying with their mother's suffering. Thus, sons lack awareness of their obligations to their mothers, whereas daughters are highly sensitive in this respect.

In young adulthood, therefore, divorce foregrounds identity as a process of identification with whoever is similar to us (comparison within the male and female lines), and relationships with the opposite sex, which are certainly more keenly perceived by daughters, who, as is well known, are particularly sensitive to relationships. When imagining their future family life, sons identify critically with their father and therefore fear that they will repeat his mistake, whereas daughters, who are decidedly more oriented toward starting their own families, are afraid they will not find a trustworthy partner, or will be unable to bind him to them. Thus, it is through what is absent and irrelevant—the father—that young adult sons and daughters reveal their specific problems.

Now we come to a situation of affluence rather than deprivation: the family with young volunteer social workers. Our specific interest in this topic is the transition to adulthood which, as we have seen, is marked by shared, family-specific representations of mistrust of, and danger in, the social community that makes the family-to-social shift difficult. We wondered, therefore, how relational interplay unfolds in families whose young adults have achieved the transition to adulthood unaided and of their own volition. What are the benefits, and what, if any, are the possible risks in these situations? Our studies of this are quite recent and some are still in progress. We created cross-sectional and longitudinal designs supplemented by questionnaire interviews, diaries, and graphic–symbolic production (FLS).

Our findings may be summarized as follows. The young volunteer social workers and their families showed a marked typological spread, but we can definitely say that the most widespread and positive family typology includes young people whose highly prosocial behavior is fuelled by both self- and other-oriented motivation. Other-oriented motivation—the most prevalent kind—is an indicator that they will see their social commitment through to the end (Pozzi, 2003). These young adults come from intact families and have parents who, for the most part, are themselves involved in volunteer social work or are active in their neighborhoods. Less positively, there is a second family typology with a problematic relational situation attributable to the paternal figure and predominantly self-oriented motivation in the children. And there are clear weaknesses in a third, numerically minor, typology of problematic families with fathers who are completely marginalized. In this case, it seems justifiable to conclude that the commitment to volunteer social work, which is fragile, discontinuous, and promoted by reference figures outside the family, fulfills a need for belonging that has not been satisfied elsewhere.

We might say, then, that there is a link between capacity for social commitment and the quality of family relations, especially when they are sustained by parents' actual involvement in the community (Marta & Pozzi, in press). It is the twin presence of active involvement in the community on the part of family members, and their ability to offer mutual support within the family, that creates the ideal context for the transition to adulthood. In particular, analysis of our findings makes clear that, unless supported by good family relations, parents' involvement in the community is insufficient in itself to promote prosocial behavior in young people, which is the classic antecedent to volunteer social work (Guglielmetti & Marta, 2003).

Now let us consider gender difference, which is especially visible in parents. What are the roles of fathers and mothers? With high levels of prosocial behavior, and higher self-transcendent scores in volunteers' mothers than in control-group mothers, plus lower self-enhancement scores in volunteers' fathers, we find once again that it is the father who plays the crucial role in the sample of families with volunteer social workers. The antecedents to the young volunteers' prosocial behavior include the father's prosocial behavior and the support he provides. We can say, then, that if the mother plays an important role in her children's becoming socially involved, her role is made effective when accompanied by a paternal generative function (Dollahite et al., 1998). In such prosocial families, social involvement is not an escape from difficult close relationships, but an extension of the generativity experienced in the family. These families are a crucial resource in opposing the intergenerational impasse or dangerous, false intergenerational stability that in the long run may compromise young people's acquisition of a true adult identity that makes them responsible for their actions and sensitive to the destinies of others.

To conclude, it is clear from the overall picture that emerges from our studies that the critical element in the transition to adulthood is not so much the prolonged cohabitation of parents and young adult children, as it is the relational imbalance within the family and the behavioral split in adult generations who overprotect young people in the family and but exclude them in society.

We know that parents hold primary responsibility for their children's growth, even when they have come of age. Parents are expected to support their children and direct them toward new goals outside the family. The current relational bias toward the mother, which expands her sphere of influence well beyond its limits, is not helpful in addressing this task. In the postmodern West, the centrality of the maternal figure extends beyond the phase of child-rearing into adolescence, as many American studies have also found, and carries over into young adulthood, especially in some Southern European countries.

The mother's centrality is also amplified by the spread of divorce. As in the vast majority of cases the mother is granted custody of the children, she is a stable, enduring element by comparison with a plurality of paternal figures. In our view, this centrality should be seen as pertaining not just to the mother, but rather to the symbolic aspects of maternal function. The maternal aspect and its intrinsic affective and protective elements is so dominant partly because it originates in a specific tendency in Western culture, as we noted in our introductory remarks. In other words, the imbalance in favor of the maternal relationship and the feminine line indicates an imbalance of affective over ethical elements. Whereas in divorced families we tend to see "single parents," in intact families we see "undifferentiated parents" with predominantly maternal functions, and both of these figures are a constant feature of the long transition to adulthood. In this situation, it is difficult to detect the paternal function, which is very much a latent one: When it does emerge and researchers are able to see it, it does truly make the difference in a symbolic, rather qualitative sense because it enables the ethical–affective components of family structure to be rearranged, and generativity to be produced as a result.

In effect, it is the weakening of the symbolic–generative core at the family and community levels that makes the transition to adulthood problematic. At the family level, it limits young people to the status of sons or daughters, and makes parents' mirroring themselves in their children (a sort reverse identification) more important than the search for generational renewal. At the social level, it tends toward disproportionate reinforcement of closure and generational self-referentiality. The modern autopoietic family, limited by its illusion of self-referential communication, seems to encounter structural problems when it is called on to convert its human capital into social capital.

From this point of view, the prosocial family, which combines responsible commitment to the other (even when the other is not a family member) with trusting openness, appears to have an advantage when negotiating the transition to adulthood because it shows through its actions that it has already laid claim to a portion of the social sphere, the one toward which it has directed its care. Despite occasional ambivalence, such families concretely and symbolically represent a positive way of shifting relationship-caring from the family to the community.

CHAPTER EIGHT

Beyond Family Boundaries:
Illness and Migration

CHANGING SCENARIOS

The fact that several generations—sometimes up to four—coexist within a family, which we then call the *multigenerational family,* and the fact that changing migratory routes have reversed the situation in many countries including Italy, constitute far-reaching changes within the family and the social scenario.

Let us consider the first point. Here, a number of factors have reversed the generational balance. The first is a gradual lengthening of the lifespan thanks to medical breakthroughs and improved living conditions in general, together with a decline in the birth rate. As stated in the first chapter, this is particularly true for Italy. Population aging, however, is a European phenomenon applicable to the "old continent." Now immigration is changing the demographic situation, bringing it closer to equilibrium. This means that a small number of children are surrounded by a large number of adults and elderly of different ages.

Moreover, families are experiencing the new phenomenon of aging together. Family members of 60 years and over live together with and care for other family members who are in their 80s and over. They may have adult children who live with them, or who are married and may have one or two children, who nevertheless refer back to their family of origin for any number of reasons. So, the middle generation, which in the past corresponded to 35 years of age as the Italian poet Dante Alighieri (1307/2000) said ("Midway this way of life we're bound on"), now comprises people in their 50s and 60s, and it is this generation that mostly bears the family burden. In brief, the coexistence of several generations causes a shift in the family balance and dynamics.

Shanas (1984) has spoken of a "silent demographic revolution" and introduced the distinction between elderly and overelderly (over 75 five years of age). The silent aspect of the revolution has significant social implications. These include difficulties in distributing resources within the community (with

174

the latest generations clearly penalized with respect to previous ones) and the difficulties of the chronic and disabling diseases that are often associated with aging and involve heavy family burdens (with a smaller number of children able to support these burdens).

It should be noted that the typically Western concept of the person as a separate individual has led to the acquisition and extension of individual rights, but it has also led to the denigration of all forms of personal limitations and dependence on others. In many cultures, an elderly person is venerated as a "sage," but not in the West. Indeed, he or she is the individual who *must* live life to the full and *must not* be in need. In this respect, the cognitive approach in clinical psychology aims to provide individuals with all the strategies necessary for being fully oneself and for having all situations under control. So the risk that spreads throughout social relationships is the following: Elderly people, rather than feeling themselves part of a story that contains the succession of generations, believe they are at the center of the story, and the limitations set by disease are at times an intolerable affliction.

The danger has been perceived, however, and it is no accident that psychology has been increasingly concerned with generativity. Erikson (1982) paved the way for this concept, and worthy researchers and clinicians such as de St. Aubin, McAdams, and Dollahite have followed in his footsteps and opened up new horizons.

We are taking the same path, employing the psychosocial and clinical approach described in this book. In dealing with family generativity, we opted to focus our attention on serious diseases that affect the elderly. What happens to a family when one of its elderly members becomes seriously ill, or the specter of death hovers over the relationship? How do family members cope with the situation and how do they manage, if they do manage, to get "beyond death"? The answers that the families give help us to distinguish between family generativity and degenerativity.

Before presenting the findings of our study, we need to take a look at another kind of change: the change in the migratory route. Europe, in particular, in the encounter with the other culture, finds itself having to come to terms with its colonial past as well as with its position as a migratory starting point. Throughout history, Europe has both exported its culture worldwide and at the same time forced its inhabitants to seek new lands. It has, therefore, expanded in the tentacular fashion peculiar to "dominion," but has also expelled the roots of its identity, whether for economic or religious reasons, or for reasons of customs and language.

The United States, on the other hand, has been free of "dominion" in its identity roots, and prides itself as the New World and a new land. In light of the Founding Fathers' beliefs, and in the name of those civil rights deemed natural and consequently universal, anyone wanting to settle in a new community is welcomed to the new land.

As we have shown, the relationship with the other culture (ethnic group, religion, traditions, and customs) is affected by differences between identity roots, but it remains a challenge and an adventure characterized by repeated violence and setbacks. It lies at the very heart of mankind, in both the constructive and the tragic sense.

We have attempted to deal with the problem from the point of view of the family rather than that of the individual and of ethnic grouping. We asked the following questions: How do the families that migrate keep their ties with their origins? What is their attitude toward, and how do they cope with, encounter with a different culture? Finally, what kind of reception do they get?

Because migration is seen as a family enterprise, we examined the exchange between generations by focusing on the migrant parental couple. We know that the effects of an encounter between cultures should always be considered over long periods of time, that is, over two or three generations. However, there are indicators that can show if the way to encounter is open, if there are glimmers of hope in the difficulties that the family encounters, or whether the road is a dead end right from the start.

In brief, changes in social scenarios suggest new challenges for family ties. Besides, these challenges cannot but exist within a matrix that, as we have tried to show, deals with the issues of differences (of gender, generation, lineage), of meaning and basic values (the ethical–emotional triangle represented by trust, hope, and justice), and the incessant movement between giving, receiving, and reciprocating. So, changes come up against what is permanent: Renewal and repetition constitute the two sides of the same coin.

CLINICAL INVESTIGATIONS IN FACT AND FICTION

Wisdom is pungent and salty. Without salt there is no flavor, and salt also preserves from decay. But wisdom must be pursued; it is not clear-cut like knowledge, nor does it accumulate like research. Now, psychosocial and clinical investigation of the family is aimed not only at identifying the difficulties the family may encounter, and its different forms of relational pathology, but also at discovering its resources and its wisdom — the flavor of its ties and the methods used to preserve them from decay. Illness and death are critical events and transitions crucial to the acquisition of "family wisdom."

It is worth noting that psychosocial research investigates family relationships through constructs, dimensions, and categories by collecting data from large samples. Clinical research's task is to focus on the specificity and peculiarity of each case. As in the previous chapters, the consequent advantages of comparing the two types of research outcomes will be highlighted.

Because we see culture as a major force in shaping the meaning of life, we start with a brief historical–cultural digression on the theme of death.

According to Vovelle (1983), in the Middle Ages the elderly died surrounded by members of their family and various members of the neighborhood. These could include comembers of guilds (guilds had knots and ties as symbols) as well as members of other families. The dying person was expected to give a final message, and also an example of how to face the final and most important journey.

However, actual manuals on the *ars moriendi* were circulating throughout Europe between the 15th and 17th centuries. The dying person turned his face to the wall, so turning his back on life and urging everyone to keep his memory alive. Those present recalled the qualities of the dying person and commended his soul to God. If he belonged to the political or religious elite, he would be guaranteed a monument among the living. This could take the form of a sepulchral monument or a painting depicting the funeral and the dignitaries of the period. One splendid example can be found in St. Mark's Church in Florence. Almost all the congregation at the funeral of the bishop-saint have their heads turned toward the observer so as to meet his eyes, day after day, year after year, century after century. As can be seen, immortality was pursued on Earth even before Heaven, and by an act of recognition that took place through the meeting of the eyes, even though the dust of ages settles on the fabric, slowly wiping away all memory. The funeral was a solemn event in the theatre of life and was juxtaposed with a convivial moment. Refreshments and hospitality were given to those who came from far and near to prove that, in life, bonds of family and friendship prevail over the grieving of death.

In big cities especially, where everything moves incessantly and time is always short, the dramatic aspects of dying have been superseded by obscure death. Obscure death is secret and fast, and declared after the event, as if nothing had happened, and is accompanied by cemeterial devotion, that is, dialogue with a person who no longer exists but lives on through us. Ariès (1960/1962) wrote that society has expelled death, except for the death of statesmen. Recently, however, a Neapolitan group introduced the first virtual cemetery on the Internet, which has the added advantage of resistance to wear and tear in time. Everyone, therefore, can have a funeral according to his rank. Furthermore, collective devoutness is rare; what counts is private sorrow, with its myths, inner sorrow, and noncommunicability.

But we must beware of commonplace descriptions. The large metropolitan cities are not representative of the entire world, and the lives of families in large cities do not correspond to the historical–sociological analyses that focus on individual and collective behaviors. So, there could always be a *Spoon River* round the corner, a place where every grave tells a story just waiting to be told.

Let us now look at the psychological family research. In line with our objective, we leave the research dealing with aging and the differences in coping with aging in the background, together with the research dealing with the "satisfaction" of elderly couples and the interactions and exchanges between parents and children. We focus instead on the "generational perspective" in an attempt to connect the present of family relationships tried by illness with their past.

In this respect, marital and intergenerational bonds have crucial roles to play. Kramer (1993; Kramer & Lambert, 1999), for example, highlights how the negative effects incurred by the wife caring for an elderly husband, and vice versa—physical, emotional, financial, and interpersonal costs experienced by wife caring for older husband, as well as the negative outcomes among husband caregivers—should not be attributed solely to caregiver strain but also to the quality of the marital relationship. The more critical the relationship, the greater the effect on the care tasks. In a couple who have a sound, consolidated relationship, on the other hand, caregiver strain is seen in terms of "sharing" (Spitze & Ward, 2000). In our view, this is a sign of the fulfillment of the marriage vows to live together for better or for worse, in sickness and in health.

Whitbeck, Hoyt, and Huck (1994) and Zarit and Eggebeen (2002) report that the history of a parents–children relationship has long-term consequences and a significant influence on the relationship between elderly parents and adult children. It is not the frequency of the exchanges between them that sets the quality of the bond; it may, in fact, be influenced by a sense of obligation deprived of all sense of reciprocity, and therefore a sign of unresolved issues between the parties. Parents may be convinced that their children have an everlasting debt toward them, and so are unable to nurture the reciprocity inherent in exchange. It is mothers especially who have the greatest expectations of help from their adult children. The extent of these expectations is inversely proportional to the parents' subjective well-being. The greater the expectation, the greater the disappointment (Lee, Netzer, & Coward, 1995). Here again, we should see this in terms of the history of the relationship. The expectation may include feelings of guilt and defense tactics such as denial, together with a feeling of exclusive possession of the children, which, as we know, hinders generational transmission.

Blieszner and Hamon (1992) and Hamon and Blieszner (1990) carried out studies on filial responsibility to parents and found a significant convergence of opinion between both parents and adult offspring. This included the feeling of closeness, emotional and tangible support in certain situations, and the willingness to deal openly with issues as they arose. Thus, there is intergenerational agreement when it comes to fundamental values.

Lee, Netzer, and Coward (1994) identified a positive correlation between help given and help received in intergenerational exchange between parents and children. However, there is a hierarchy in the relationship that must be respected. The help given by children is the result of an exchange that happens over the course of time. Furthermore, a mere listing of the giving and the taking should not be made: The preceding generation may offer much more support than it receives and not have particularly high expectations (Zarit & Eggebeen, 2002). It is in time of difficulty, and need of the other, that the parents–children relationship shows itself as it really is. Illness should be considered an epiphany of the relationship and, at the same time, a possible renascence of the bond.

As we have said, psychosocial and clinical studies have their distinctive features. Clinical studies in particular encounter as many cases that confirm what is expected on the basis of previous findings, as those that do not. Consequently, not only do they take into account psychosocial research findings, but are also to consider books and films that deal with the same subject—life.

Dermer and Hutchings (2000) consider cinema as one of the mediators of popular culture, or rather, of the "collective mind." We, too, can use the cinema to compare couples and families with different types of problems. Sequences with specific affective and ethical content are shown to the family members. As example, here are two cases taken from the cinema.

> • Iris Murdoch, the novelist and philosopher considered the most brilliant woman in England, dies of Alzheimer's in 1999. Her last, successful book came out just 3 years before. John Bayley, a respected literary critic, has been her partner for 40 years. While Iris is slowly wasting away, John remains unconditionally devoted. Although he has difficulty in looking after himself, given his age and limits, he does everything he can to help Iris. But what resources does he turn to? It is the memory of the past and their younger days together that serves as a rock against the disease that has made his loved one unrecognizable. (Eyre, 2001)

> • Remy, a highly cultured professor who has led a life devoted to pleasure (sexual, cultural, culinary) is affected by a devastating tumor. Within a short period of time, he finds himself alone, abandoned by his friends and his women. But there is Louise, his ex-wife. Although he cheated on her many times, she has never forgotten her bond with him. She persuades their son Sebastien, who lives far away and is a "new barbarian" (according to Remy, all business and financial people who dedicate their lives to wealth and technology are barbarians), to look after his father.

> But why should he? Why should he devote care to a selfish man who hardly cared for his son and spent his entire life cultivating his own interests? The fact is that Sebastien does so in many ways, including bribing people to stay by his father so that he does not feel alone.

> What is the resource in this situation? The fact is that the son is willing to risk a new bond with his father, despite the disappointments of the past. The father–son bond is regenerated: Their foreheads touch, followed by a hug and simple words of love, and both father and son experience a renewal of the bond (Arcand, 2003). Being aware of one's mistakes, like Remy, and being in the right for having been abandoned, like Sebastien, are no longer important. What is important is the possibility of being able to renew, reweave, and regenerate the bond. And so, even the most painful moments can be "good moments."

In short, psychosocial studies of family relationships attempt to identify the crucial variables that enable us to highlight how relationships work, and the probability that they will work as predicted. Clinical research does not deny the crucial variables, but uses them to examine the unpredictability of living. So, in light of the story of their bond, we expect devotion and care from Iris and John and we are moved. From Sebastien, on the other hand, we expect a denial of the father who abandoned him, but instead father and son weave a bond just when the father is close to death.

But can we exclude sibling relationships from family relationships? There are many studies that show how siblings' affection and closeness are highly significant in old age. It is as if they give each other support and make their lives less lonely. Again, illness plays a crucial role and furthers the relationship. Here is an example from the world of cinema:

• Old Alvin has decided. He will go to visit his brother whom he has not seen for many years. There has been resentment and misunderstanding between the two. He has heard that Lyle, his brother, has suffered a heart attack. Alvin does not drive, and so he decides to use a lawnmower and a trailer. Before arriving at his destination, after a journey full of colorful encounters such as the girl who ran away from home (see chapter 1), he stops at the cemetery. There he meets a minister who knows Lyle, and Alvin tells him he wants to be reconciled with his brother.

When the two brothers finally meet, they just look at each other. There is no need for words, there is only a need for joint action. The brothers sit out on the porch together, looking up at the star-studded sky, just as they did when they were young. It is this shared experience that enables them to acknowledge and resuscitate their bond. (Lynch, 1999)

Cicirelli (1995) notes that siblings are not at the top of the hierarchy in family help. First comes the spouse, and then the adult children. Support between siblings seems to be more important in the case of unmarried family members, widows and widowers, and when there are no offspring or the children live very far away. Wegner and Jerrome (1999) examined the "confident relationship" in the elderly in an important longitudinal study. The elderly depend above all on the spouse; in the absence of a spouse, they prefer the relationship with their daughters, and in the absence of daughters, the relationship with their sisters.

For both males and females, the feeling of having a close bond with a sister is linked to feelings of well-being in the elderly and a decrease in depression. On the other hand, reciprocal conflict or indifference between brothers and sisters increases the risk of depression.

Gold (1989; Gold et al., 1990) uses quality interviews to highlight how hostile and indifferent relationships among siblings have common roots in intergenerational relationships characterized by unfair favoritism, excessive preferences, and serious lack of attention and care on the part of the preceding generations. Such generational exchanges can result in resentment and envy, as well as reciprocal emotional detachment and indifference within the sibling relationship.

Research has outlined the crucial variables, which are grouped into dimensions and are useful in understanding how families deal with serious illness of an elderly member. Recent studies by Li and Seltzer (2003) and Lieberman and Fisher (1999) have clearly shown how quality in the relationship between generations and the ability to manage conflict (present and preexisting) are crucial factors in the management of a chronically difficult situation, such as illness in the elderly. Above all, the past relationship clearly plays a significant role. It influences exchange in the present in the sense that old grievances are reawakened and resources originating from ties come into play. Family members can brood over these sorrows, suppress thoughts and feelings so as not to suffer again, forcefully foster a happy memory of the past, and not revisit the hazardous ground of relationship. In such cases, the illness and loss of a family member will most probably be incorporated into the past relationship, but this is not the case if the family members have access to a whole range of feelings and memories, share rituals, and have managed to draw trust and hope from the relationship with the other person.

Trust and hope, therefore, amalgamate with justice, that is, with all the just and fair things that the family relationship has to give family members. Illness and the foreboding of death are still painful and sorrowful, but the bond is renewed. Silverstone and Hyman (1982) maintain that illness in an elderly family member could be positive for the other members when it reinforces preexisting bonds and develops new ones. To examine this subject more closely, we must assess the meaning of illness and the consequences it has for family members.

How do families see illness? For some, illness means "bad" or "evil"; the word "ill" comes from old Norse *illr,* meaning "bad." At the root of the word, therefore, we have the idea of evil performed by the very fact of being human, as in the Judaic–Christian tradition. For others, illness is connected with higher forces (divine or fate) that hate human beings and strike them down unjustly, or to a higher force that is gloomily awaited. For others yet, illness is a test of the bond—a trial to test whether they are able to bear the burden (Cigoli, 1992).

However, the representation of illness (the world of ideas and feelings it arouses) is not sundered by family members' experiences of bonds. This involves a specific dimension in the family relationship—*time management*—expressed in such variables as the quality of historical family bonds, the expression of ideas and feelings about illness, and the acknowledgement of resources and their use or nonuse. Furthermore, illness "forces" family members into movement. Faced with illness, the family member may be numb with astonishment and anguish, and if this persists, it highlights the impossibility of movement. This may be termed family member *space management,* expressed in variables such as the ability or inability to identify the issues to be dealt with, the relationship between the family members (roles, leadership, task assignments), and the relationship with the outside world (neighborhood, relatives, and, above all, the social and health services). An important study conducted by Davies, Reimer, and Martens (1994) identified the following variables in family function: integration with the past, feelings management, problem solving, use of resources, consideration for other members, family coping styles, assumption of roles, and toleration of difference. We have focused on the two dimensions of time management and space management, and there is a third, latent dimension that involves family values. Family values are, however, included in our consideration of the other two dimensions.

CASE STUDIES BY FAMILY

As we said in the chapter on methodology, it is important to "think in terms of family," meaning that the family must be observed directly and considered as a unit of analysis. Different research methods may be used, but the family must always be considered as a single unit. In particular, the serious illness of an elderly person is considered an event that throws light on the quality of the family relationships and shows how the family group as a whole deals with this difficult transition, that is, how to "climb the steep slope" of a family member's illness and/or death. When we consider the individual differences of the members faced with illness, we should also bear in mind the fact that the family is a living and operating whole, a "body" with its own peculiar interweaving of relationships. By interweaving, we mean that which unconsciously binds family members together and constitutes a specific organization of meaning within the generational fabric.

In the following two cases, the findings of the Family Interview (Cigoli, 1992) are presented with the findings of the Family Life Space (Gozzoli & Tamanza, 1998).[1] The families were interviewed in their homes, and all the members—spouses, children, grandchildren—were invited to participate. Each family is a "world" unto itself, but we are able to identify the typical recurrent forms (a kind of typology) through which families deal with the critical event of a family member's serious illness. This is especially important if we want to offer support to the families. The serious illness in question is Alzheimer's Disease, which may be considered a *disease of recognition* (Tamanza, 1998). The more the sick person fails to recognize his family, the greater difficulty the family has in recognizing the person (mother or father) who brought them into the world.

Each to His Own Way

Giacomo, a 66-year-old former builder, lives with his 64-year-old wife Claudia, a housewife, and their three sons. The eldest, Luigi, aged 30, is a free-lance engineer. The second, Gregorio, aged 26, works in sales. The youngest, Ferdinando,

---

[1] These have been reproduced on the computer for easy comprehension.

aged 24, is in his final year of engineering at university. Claudia's 92-year-old mother lived with them until she died 2 years before after a long period of illness during which the daughter cared for her.

After an initial underestimation of the symptoms and visits to various specialists, Alzheimer's disease was hypothesized for Giacomo, and 2 years later the diagnosis was confirmed.

Giacomo has been going to a specialized day center for 3 years. At present, personal autonomy and cognitive abilities are seriously impaired. He is hyperactive and tends to wander about without destination or purpose. All members of the family are present at the meeting, including Giacomo.

The Interview. The meeting with the family takes place in an atmosphere of apparent tension, and this causes the family members to outwardly display their emotions. The mother tearfully expresses the pain she is living through and the sons vent their hostility, especially toward their mother.

The mother paints a picture of a depressing family situation characterized by two aspects: on one hand, isolation and solitude vis-à-vis the disease and distance between the various components of the family itself; on the other, the chaos and confusion of everyday life. She says she cannot confide in or depend on anyone (*"I can't depend on any of my children . . . and everything is emptiness, emptiness and no one . . ."*). The sons say they are busy with their work. They spend all day out of the house and claim they have no time or opportunity to get together. The father, who is present, is completely omitted from the family description. The second son abruptly says: *"There's only the four of us!"* and the mother adds: *"Their father no longer exists for them."* We can see a generational rupture: The mother has almost exclusively taken on the caring task (*"I don't do anything, I'm here with him and that's all"*). Her world has been turned upside down by her husband's illness and she feels at the mercy of daily events. And then there are the children, only marginally involved in the caring and for whom *"life continues as normal,"* making evident their denial of the effects the disease is having on the family relationship.

The social and health services were only involved at the beginning of the illness, but the family says it cannot rely on them because Alzheimer's is an incurable disease for which there are no drugs, and against which *"nothing can be done."* The Day Care Center, which Giacomo has been regularly attending for almost 2 years, has no real professional standing. It is used only because it removes the father from the family, albeit for a brief period of time, and gives the mother a break, which is indispensable to her in recovering the energy she needs to survive (*"So I too can have a moment of respite"*).

The researcher's request that the family members try to imagine what the family will be like in the future causes much tension. They consider it a nonsensical question. Everyone is obviously aware of the pathological course of the disease, and their refusal to express expectations for the future is also evident. The mother stresses that the situation does not allow for projects, but forces them to live day by day. The eldest son's curt suggestion that a full-time nurse should look after his father in the future, or that his father should be put in a home, leads to serious conflict between siblings and mother. In aggressive and accusing tones, the sons for the first time berate their mother for all the inconveniences and difficulties they had to bear during their totally disabled grandmother's prolonged stay with the family. In brief, the sons are punishing their mother for her lack of care toward them, due to the fact that she chose to care for her mother (and now her husband). This goes beyond the issue of illness–death in the elderly, but none of it is voiced.

Family Life Space. The symbolic diagram clearly shows the breach between the family members and the deficiency of their relationships (Fig. 8.1). The family life space is clearly separate between the mother and the three sons. Moreover, there is no sharing between the presences drawn, and no bond can be seen between them. None of the family members place the father within the

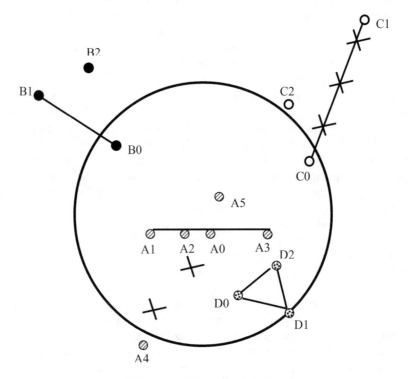

FIG. 8.1.   FLS: Giacomo's family.

life space, and the only reference to a serious illness event is the presence of an operator from the day care center (A5), placed in the center of the family life space by the mother. The mother places the three sons horizontally to herself within the life space, gathering them into a single segment. The mother then places a friend in the lower part of the diagram, just beyond the border, a friend *"who offers her help, but she too has her own problems."*

The sons' drawings are even more limited. Luigi, the eldest, limits his ties between himself and his fiancée (B0 and B1), overlapping the boundaries of family life. The youngest son, Ferdinando (D0), depicts himself and an uncle on the border. The third son shows the same uncle together with the aunt, the mother's sister, in a similar position but outside the circle, far from the family and marked by a conflicting relationship.

Overall, the diagram is characterized by a centrifugal movement that develops along four lines of escape, one for each family member. In particular, all the sons flee from the "care center," which is left in hands of outsiders (the Day Care person) and place themselves on the other side of the boundary.

Family Interweaving.   It seems that the family is breaking up when confronted with the devastating blow of illness. What we have now is a group of people with no stable reference point. There is no shared solid foundation, and what emerges is a drifting motion of separate lives and different perspectives. In such a situation, it is difficult to acknowledge the illness and provide care: People do not always seem to find sufficient resources, either within themselves or outside the family. It is as if death has been anticipated, and only flight and breaking off the relationship can provide protection from pain and sorrow. The mother's statement, *"This isn't living, we are at the mercy of what is to come,"* well defines the condition of the family bond, which is drifting as aimlessly as the father himself.

In short, the illness reveals what has happened to the family bond, which is haunted by an unsolved question: Who deserves to receive care? The mother devoted her care to her own mother and then to her husband, and the children therefore were bitter and resentful. The children now ignore the mother; similarly, the mother ignores them and does not take responsibility for the generational difference. This is a problem that the family members risk passing on from generation to generation.

Claiming the right to receive care, and resentment over what could have been, may leave children-siblings, although adult, in constant need of receiving, and so in serious difficulty when they have to exercise generational care themselves. What the clinical researcher can do after listening to the family is point out the serious risk the next generation is exposed to. Is there anything that might oppose it? Other bonds, for example, or a review of the history of family bonds (mother/daughter) could lead to understanding and forgiveness.

Who Inherits?

Vittorio, 81 years of age, has lived with his 87-year-old wife, Beatrice, for over 50 years. They have two daughters, Elvira and Maria Rosa, both married with children. The former lives in the same house as the elderly parents. Nine years ago, Vittorio started showing the first signs of mental impairment and a general degeneration of his psychophysical functions. Alzheimer's Disease was diagnosed almost immediately, and the course of the illness was very slow and gradual. At the present time, Vittorio suffers from severe cognitive impairment and total loss of personal autonomy. Behavioral problems, on the other hand, are not significant.

The wife, the two daughters, the two sons-in-law, Elvira's two children (Nicoletta, 22, and Davide, 12) and Maria Rosa's son (Sandro, 26) were present at the meeting.

The Interview. The researcher's request that they define their positions within the family causes animated discussion on the meaning of family. The family members adopt two different positions. Some perceive it as limited to their own restricted nucleus, whereas others perceive themselves as part of a single large family that includes the elderly parents. In the end, the concept of wider family prevails, especially thanks to the eldest grandchild, Sandro, who assumes a specific role within the family and is acknowledged. He is the firstborn of the latest generation, has a privileged affective relationship with his grandparents, and has continued in the traditional family business (restoration and trading of antique furniture).

In describing their role within the family, the daughters tend to underline the commitment given to helping the parents and the consequent hard work required, especially in terms of emotional involvement and supervising the course of the illness. The elderly mother is still able to perform the necessary caring, although she does need to have someone on call in case of need.

Unfortunately, the family members were already familiar with the disease and its effects because it had struck a member of one of the son-in-law's family several years before. The daughters stated that they were expecting something similar given the advanced ages of the parents. In this sense, the disease does not assume specific traits, nor does it cause any upheaval in the family order. It is associated with the inevitable deterioration that accompanies aging. In the eyes of the family members, the father is not "the patient" but is remembered as he was when he still had all his faculties.

Contact with the social and health services is seen with disparagement. The services are necessary for the assessment of the disease and for welfare contributions; otherwise they are useless. They do not have any therapeutic or diagnostic abilities (*"They didn't tell us anything we didn't know"*) and they are too different and too remote from the actual family needs.

The family members believe that the father's progressive deterioration may require increased assistance in the near future. Soon the mother will no longer be able to perform the caring she has given until now, and she too will require aid and assistance. Faced with this prospect, the conflict resurfaces and two different positions are established. The eldest daughter maintains that it is the family who should care for the elderly parents because admission to a home for the elderly would mean falling short of one's filial duty and, most importantly, the father has always dreaded the prospect. The youngest daughter, on the other hand, stresses the impracticability of their coping with such a heavy, all-embracing burden. It could lead to a neglect of their own families, which would be an even greater injustice.

The suggestion put forward by the eldest daughter, and seconded by her husband, is that she will care for the parents alone, taking them into her own home if necessary (they live in the same house as the elderly couple). This arouses resentment in the younger sister, who sharply comments: *"He's not just your father and you can't decide by yourself!"* The elderly wife says it is highly probable that she will spend her last days in a home; she is not only resigned to the fact, but also favorably disposed toward the prospect because she believes it is right to *"get out and leave the daughters free to live their lives."*

Family Life Space.   The impression given by the diagram (Fig. 8.2) is one of confusion and disorder. The internal space that confines the family environment

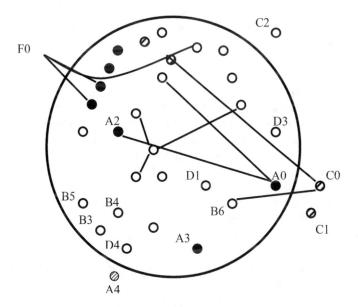

FIG. 8.2.   FLS: Vittorio's family.

appears completely full, but there is no well-defined form. However, more careful examination reveals a number of significant graphical elements. The bottom half of the circle shows a series of disconnected presences, while in the top half there is a series of identifiable relationships. These were drawn by the the younger daughter's husband and the grandchildren, and contain no other elements.

Let us now take a look at the individual family members. The second daughter (C0) places herself outside the family life space and links to her children (C3) and her sister (B0). The eldest daughter and her husband have filled the family life space with numerous presences, but they are for the large part disconnected. The elderly mother (A0) places herself at the edge of the family life space and links herself only to her husband (A1). The eldest grandchild (F0) places himself above and beyond the family boundary, opposite the aunt, and from there controls a whole series of ties.

It should be noted that the daughters do not draw either the father or the mother, though these are marked by the sons-in-law and two of the grandchildren at the center of the family life space (D5). Nonfamily presences indicate the personal interests of the family member, whereas there is no mention of the social and health services.

Family Interweaving.   Alzheimer's disease assumes specific patterns and features when it breaks into family life. Because of the long, gradual course of the illness, the advanced age of the victim, and the "familiarity" that the persons involved have with this disease, in a way it is both expected and anticipated. The illness is, therefore, recognized and accepted not so much for its distinctive pathological features as for its association with inevitable aging. What emotionally affects family members, therefore, is not the disease in itself, but the prospect of an imminent family reorganization due to the deficiency of the elderly generation.

The resulting movement is twofold: the upward one (upper part of the FLS) represents the attempt to control the situation, whereas the downward one (lower part of the FLS) represents the risk of disorganization that the family will face from now on. But what does this imply? It shows the breach between the sisters and their respective families. One lives close to the elderly couple and has a son who is the family heir. The other daughter lives further away, has two younger children, and claims possession (*"He's not just your father"*) as well as acknowledgement of the current family's value in relation to the original one. And so we have one family that places itself in the hereditary line, and one that risks exclusion. This is clearly represented by the counterpositioning of C0 (the younger daughter) and F0 (the son of the elder daughter). Both are outside the family boundaries, but C0 connects to her children (C3) from below and to the elder sister (B0) who is inside the family boundary, while F0 seems to be in a position of control. A series of ties flow forth from F0's position, as if he is able control family events from above. The elderly mother places herself within the life space boundaries and keeps a distance from her daughters' conflict.

The family breach, which this time is between persons of the same generation, is just around the corner. To counteract it, the researcher-clinician must be able to take the place of the elderly, sick father and, on his behalf, state his desire that both the daughters and their families should consider themselves family heirs, albeit in different ways. Furthermore, it should not be forgotten that the younger sister still seeks contact and/or a tie with her elder sister (C0 against B0). As Goldbeter-Merinfeld says (1997, 1998), taking the place of the absent third party helps the family members to review their relationships.

TAKING THE TOPMOST TWIG OF THE CEDAR[2]

Many prominent researchers and clinicians have studied the death issue and its impact on family relationships (Bowen, 1976, 1978; Byng Hall, 1995; Cicirelli, 2002; Kubler Ross, 1969; Walsh & McGoldrick, 1991). They all use different theoretical paradigms and research tools, but all have underlined both the importance of antecedents—that is, the quality of the relationships—and the effects that traumatic losses have on generational exchanges. Traumatic losses include violent deaths, suicides, the untimely death of children and adolescents, sudden deaths, and deaths following long illnesses.

We have focused our attention on serious illnesses of the elderly, applying the concepts we have presented in this book, which involve relational principles and relationship cores and settings. We have also highlighted the importance of focusing on specific events (as is the case with serious illness) because they challenge the relationship by revealing its characteristics and qualities and encouraging its renewal. In the case of illness in an elderly person, intergenerational exchange may be defined as "caring about acknowledgement," in the sense of knowing anew and showing gratitude.

But how is "caring about acknowledgement" displayed in the case of Alzheimer's Disease? And what can obstruct it? To answer these questions, we have used two dimensions: time management and space management. Time should be considered "the great sculptor" of family ties because it connects the present with the disease with the family's past and its future, whereas space should be considered "the realm of portrayal" because it reveals the links between closeness, distance, and even absence of family ties. Taken together, time and space are the means and tools that allow us to "take the topmost twig of the cedar."

The cases under study enable us to say that, although family members may or may not share certain features of the illness, it is the impact of the illness that

---

[2] Ezekiel, 17: 4, "The Holy Bible," Revised Standard Version, 1952.

tells us the truth about the generational tie, that is, its sorrows and its resources. Listening to "family wisdom," we can only acknowledge that the test of illness and the anticipation of death constitute a very difficult obstacle to overcome. To anticipate death is to admit (as did Adam and Eve) that we are naked and consequently frail and limited. Findings show that the family suffers hard, painful breaches: Family members flee from relationships, they are tormented by doubts, and old wounds are opened up.

There is no family history that has not been touched by misunderstandings, wrongs, and failings. However, some families have been hit particularly hard by problems arising from intergenerational exchange. In these cases, recognition, including gratitude to the previous generations, collides with ill-feeling and hatred, and runs aground in the wasteland of violence and wrongs suffered in the past. Illness in the elderly causes old wounds to open up. Their effect is intergenerational because the pain and sorrow suffered in the past are handed on, together with the feeling of being unable to cope with them. It is not the pain itself that causes the problem, but the feeling of helplessness.

On the other hand, other family histories leave space for the renewal of the intergenerational tie. One way is through continuity; the intergenerational tie is solid and capable of coping with the evil–illness by mobilizing its inherent care resources. The second way is through discontinuity; despite attacks on the family tie, the wrongs and the pain, there is one family member who is capable of forgiveness and reconciliation and of rekindling trust and hope in that tie. The shift in the intergenerational relationship also occurs through renewal of the bond between two family members. If we look carefully, however, we can see that there is always a third party who has facilitated the renewal of the family tie with his or her inspiration, encouragement, and support. That is, when the family dynamics that work around giving, receiving, and reciprocating have reached a dead end, there must be a "triangle" to release them. In psychosocial research into family relationships, we need to compare the information obtained from quantitative and qualitative data, thus assuming a "third-party position" (see chapter 4), and this is equally true of clinical interventions. Some triangles may already be present and active in the intergenerational exchange and so promote "caring about acknowledgement," whereas others have to be looked for through clinical intervention.

In short, family members' time and space management helps us to identify both present and past obstacles they encounter, as well as the resources available to them. But there is more; these dimensions also help to direct family support interventions. Some families do not need specific care because they already have it and their members are able to cope with the evil–illness–death of their loved ones. Gratitude for what has been given and what has been received helps lay a compassionate veil over the defects and wrongs of the previous generations that ultimately affect us all because we are all part of mankind. However, other families rest in the balance, awaiting a sign or presence that will acknowledge the value of recognition. To be able to identify recognition and make it work, clinicians must immerse themselves in the family's pain and sorrow and ascertain its resources. Still other families reveal their deeply rooted tragic situation from the very start. The elderly person's serious illness is like a bolt of lightning that rends the pain of intergenerational exchange, bathing it in an icily objective light. Even in such cases, however, it is worthwhile trying to find some positive aspect of the bond. Even a tiny seed, such as acknowledging pain, looking for plausible reasons for it, or considering if even a tiny amount of good has been done in the intergenerational exchange, might blossom in time. We could talk about damage prevention if it were not for the fact that intergenerational relationship is not the same as an infection to be cured. Life has to be lived, and while we are alive it is always possible to do something in terms of acknowledgement, even when family ties are painful and despairing.

FLIGHT AND TRANSITION

Living space and time to live. Life space and life time. We live in places, we move around in spaces, we share our language and culture with others—our beliefs in our relationship with nature (Mother Earth), between human beings, and between human beings and God. Rites, ceremonies, and practices highlight the peculiar characteristics of each culture. At times, however, we have to leave our life space–time. This *flight*—leaving one's homeland—leads to an adventurous and perilous existence. Flight is a traumatic event, but it is supported by deficiencies that force one forward.

The Israelites left Egypt to free themselves from slavery. There are various types of slavery: economic (poverty, lack of resources, and opportunity), political (discrimination, repression, terror), social (war, religious persecution, ethnic cleansing), and family (abuse by previous generations, unfair differences between members). A number of motives underlie the trauma flight, and they have a common objective: to shed the shackles of oppression while also cultivating the elective feeling of hope.

And so, by leaving our homeland (mother/stepmother) we also leave behind a shared heritage of language and culture. Will we be able to find a welcoming mother-land? Will it be possible to build a new linguistic and cultural heritage? Or will we be forced to enclose ourselves into our own space-world and build an enclave in a foreign land?

The fate of migrants is influenced by the reactions of those who already occupy the new lands and have given them expression through their own language and culture. If there exists "the other" from the migrant's point of view, there also exists "the other" from the point of view of whoever receives him. The "other" may be seen as a stranger, a foreigner, a barbarian, but also as a fellow-creature and a person in need.

Most psychosocial research on migration has focused on individuals and
their ethnic origins and has neglected the family origins of migrants and the
dynamics of the family to which they belong. Boyd (1989) shed light on the
stereotype of the single immigrant without any family ties and identified the
presence of both migratory chains and family mandates. The emigrant usually
chooses a country where he can count on the support of relatives and fellow
countrymen. But the migratory chain can give rise to a family diaspora, in the
sense that its members migrate toward different countries.

The theme of "family mandate" helps us to understand why some and not
all members of a family necessarily migrate. Frieze et al. (2004) believe that the
underlying reasons for the individual's choices to migrate lie in personal motivation. For example, the migrant might show a strong desire to succeed and to
put himself to the test, and is less concerned about interpersonal relationships.

Berry (1997) studied the acculturation strategies that guide foreigners in
their encounters with the country of adoption and its culture. These strategies
can be traced back to two fundamental issues—cultural maintenance and contact and participation in the new culture—and may result in assimilation of the
new culture, separation of the cultures (avoidance of confrontation with the
new culture), integration, (reexpression and recomposing of personal identity)
or in marginalization (the failure of the encounter).

Other studies of a clinical nature (Aktar, 1991; Grinberg & Grinberg, 1984)
have described the stages that migrants go through and the specific feelings that
characterize these stages. The initial stage is characterized by sorrow over loss
of family times and fear of the unknown. This stage is followed by ability to
bear sorrow (the mourning process) and integration into the new environment,
characterized by reawakening of desire and the ability to plan for the future.

As can be seen, these studies have an "individualistic principle" in common
that separates the person from his or her generational context, and they focus
on the individual's period of adjustment. In order to understand migration, we
believe, it is necessary to look at it from the family point of view and in terms
of *crisis*.

Migration can involve an entire nation, a race, groups, and families. The
history of mankind is the history of a migratory people, of often forceful
occupation of new lands, and of flight from one's own land in search of a new
one. We concentrate on migration as a family venture that gives rise to conflict
between intergenerational feelings of loyalty and the need to change the status
quo. This situation may presage a new family identity, but it can also mean a
loss of identity, with all its consequences. It will be future generations who
confirm whether the migration has been a success or a failure.

Sluzky (1979) made the most important study of migration from the family
viewpoint. Defining the stages of the migration process, Sluzky says of the
preparatory stage that if there is a positive reason underlying the decision to
migrate, such as to make a better living, then the pain is not so strong and the

sadness and regrets are manageable. With regard to the actual act of migration, he underlines how most cultures lack prescribed rituals to support the transition; the journey can at times be a brief transition but at others, longer times and journeys across many countries are required. It is, therefore, likely that migrants are left to deal with the painful act of migration alone, and they react by trying to create a bond with people going through the same experience. According to the author, migration styles vary from family to family. There are those who soon make the break with their homeland, those who hope to return to their homeland, and those who prepare the terrain for new arrivals.

The first period of adaptation to the new environment is characterized by overcompensation, in which the satisfaction of primary needs takes precedence, so that deeper conflicts and unease remain dormant. However, this situation is not possible in the second, decompensation or crisis stage, a stormy period characterized by conflicts and difficulties, if not actual crisis in the family's functioning. Sluzky stresses the importance of the family's ability to cope with the fundamental transition task, that of seeking a new balance between the need to safeguard family continuity in terms of identity and that of penetrating the new culture. Often it is children and their various of forms of intergenerational protest who bring on the family's identity crisis.

As Sluzky says, migrations that alternate departures from and reunions with members of the same family nucleus are extremely common. This is the most common situation in Italy and other European countries.[3] So, the overcompensation and decompensation stages are milestones in highly complex processes whose effects can lead to intergenerational and infragenerational conflicts.

More recently, Dumon (1992) highlighted the fundamental role of the migrant family. This is linked to the decision to migrate and the strategies employed to deal with problems as they arise. In all cases, the reciprocal obligations created between the migrant and those that remain in the homeland are crucial. In this sense, the migrant's remittance of money to the family of origin plays a social as well as an economic role.

We would now like to stress how migration sunders the flow of time. There are recognizable premigration and postmigration periods. Keeping memories alive—as well as practices, rules of life, and customs ranging across gender and generational relationships through to the preparation of food—is a typical family task. Its aim is to guarantee belonging, which is crucial to personal identity. In the succession of generations, memories can fade so that rituals lose focus and gradually disappear. Without their core symbolic meanings, rituals and customs become meaningless and even ridiculous. Even after several generations, however, the need to belong reemerges in some family members,

---

[3] There are over 100 different nationalities and races present in Italy at this time, and about 10 with a very high representation: Rumania, *Morocco,* Albania, Ukraine, China, *the Philippines,* Poland, Tunisia, Senegal, *Ghana,* India, *Brazil,* Peru, Ecuador, Egypt, Sri Lanka. Immigrants from the United States total over 40,000. The countries in italics are discussed here.

who go in search of their origins and try to reconstruct their family history. Evidence of this is provided in the many Internet sites dedicated to researching family origins and reconstructing family histories.

We now outline the first dimension that influences migration as a family enterprise: the bond with one's origins. This bond entails a specific generational task, which is custody of heritage.[4] As we saw in chapter 3, this consists of keeping the memory of the origins alive and in remaining loyal to one's maternal and paternal families of origin without denying their traumas and failures. Custody of heritage emerges at crucial moments in family life, and migration is one of these. Because this custody is of a generational nature, it should be considered over a period of at least three generations.

The bond with one's origins, and the hardships endured through custody of the heritage, do not occur in a void, but in the space–time continuum of encounter with the other culture. Here we come to the second dimension: The encounter with the other culture produces either openness or closure in migrants, acknowledgement or nonacknowledgement of the host culture and its organizations (schools, hospitals, welfare). As we saw in chapter 3, both family and society share the generative–degenerative process of the relationship, and are therefore faced with the problem of responsibility for their actions and the positive or negative effect they can have on each other. In this context, we have talked about caring about plurality. On the family side, this care is voiced through a sense of belonging that transcends blood ties and family history—the sense of belonging to a community and to a society. In society, care is expressed through acknowledgement of the ethnic, family, and cultural differences and the pursuit of shared values that transcend them, including the value of human life, and the shared experience of belonging to the human race on Mother Earth.

In our of studies of migration (Cigoli & Gozzoli, 2003; Cigoli, Gozzoli, & Tamanza, 2003; Gozzoli & Regalia, 2005), we interviewed 100 parent couples from the Maghreb, Brazil, Ghana, and the Philippines who had lived in Italy for at least 6 years and had children aged between 3 and 10 years.

We used the Family Interview and selected the following variables as indicators: for the bond with origins, the quality of the memory and how generational exchange occurs; in assessing the success of the transition, whether family members value what they have received as "hereditary baggage" and accept its failures and painful aspects, ensuring themselves of a resource to help them reorganize family identity through encounter with the culture of the host country. On the other hand, idealization of origins weighs down hereditary

---

[4] The difference between *"caring about recognition"* and *custody of heritage,* which moreover are connected, lies in the fact that the former operates in the exchange between family members and different generations, whereas the latter goes through and transcends the life exchanges over time, becoming a family task generation after generation.

baggage, while belittlement of origins adds deficiencies to the baggage and forces family members to seek new roots.

For the encounter with the other, the crucial variables are perception of help received and the acknowledgement of the host community. Here the criterion adopted to assess the success of the transition is perception of help given not only by fellow countrymen but also by the host community, and this, together with gratitude, creates a meeting point for the two cultures. On the other hand, the exploitation of the migrant, both by fellow countrymen and the host country, represents a problem, as does the feeling of losing identity to the host country. Another problem is the compelling need of the migrant family to have a motherland, and life models to look up to and feel a part of. This tempers criticism and enhances acknowledgement of cultural differences.

The instruments used for the study were the Family Interview and Family Life Space (FLS). The interviews focused on the migratory process (the economic–political situation of the country of origin), motives for leaving and the decision to leave, and the choice of target country (Italy).[5] Other topics include life in the new country (friends and other support, difficulties encountered, the relationship with the cultural models propounded), intergenerational relationships (with families of origin and current family), and forecasts of the future and future plans (possible life scenarios for oneself and the new generation).

In the FLS, each parent couple was asked to represent family members, the most significant events in family life, and other presences, such as, for example, reference groups or services the family has contact with. The FLS was done twice, first for the family situation (now) and then for what the couple thought of their family life in the past (then), so that the family's past and present are included in the drawing.[6] Figure 8.3 shows how the two dimensions intersect to produce specific relationship shapes.

In the *active space,* origins are represented as carriers of identity resources and family members have the mental space for encounter with the other culture. The *critical space* is in two different ways: first, as the obstacle of encountering the other culture (negative and evil attributions, pain over nonacknowledgement); and second, the tie with one's origins (deficient, or overtraumatic).

In the *gridlock* area there is an ominous intersection between the tie with origins and encounter with the other culture. These are family situations where "extremes touch," in the sense that the parent couple refuses the other culture and at the same time has to defend itself from deficient origins in some way (idealization, angry disparagement). Through its characteristic variables, the

---

[5] Italy is chosen for a wide variety of reasons: as a place of well-being, presence of fellow countrymen, high quality health and social services (and at low cost); the value given to the family, which is also due to the presence of the Catholic Church. This is also true for families of other religions such as Islam. In some cases, however, people are forced to come to Italy as a second-best choice instead of going to other destinations (Northern Europe and the United States).

[6] In this case, the FLS is a faithful reproduction of the couple's original drawing.

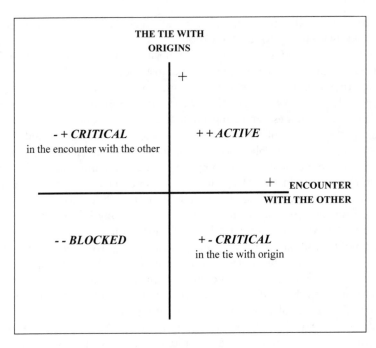

FIG. 8.3. Dimensions of family migration.

model identifies the areas with the greatest problems for the migrant family and helps us to define where and how to direct psychosocial and clinical support.

Table 8.1 summarizes the data collected from the hundred couples according to the model. In brief, we can see that a considerable number of the parent couples are faced with the difficulty of linking ties with origins to encounter with the other culture. On the other hand, critical ties respond best to support interventions that also involve the relative ethnic communities (for a cross-cultural approach highlighting similarities and differences between ethnic groups, see Murray, Smith, & Hill, 2001), and this is one of the purposes of our

TABLE 8.1
Typology of Immigrant Parent Couple

Tie	Active	Critical With Respect to the Encounter With the Other	Critical With Respect to the Origins	Gridlocked
Morocco	8	8	2	7
Brazil	5	5	10	5
Ghana	5	8	3	9
The Philippines	16	5	2	2
	34	26	17	23

research. Our study does not analyze representative samples of the different cultures by comparing given variables using self-report instruments prepared by the researchers, but attempts to outline features of the family relationship based on meetings with the parent couple, in order to provide support in the difficulties they encounter.

Our research to date (the ongoing project considers other ethnic groups, including Pakistanis and Chinese) shows that migrant families may depend on certain types of resources rather on others, and that they are prone to certain efforts rather than others. For example, parent couples from Morocco trace their identity roots to Islamic culture. Kinship is the matrix of social relationships, and loyalty to kin is taken for granted and not called into question by the decision to leave; in fact, the mandate to do so actually comes from the family. There is also the shared conviction that each family member must undertake the course set down for him by God. In gender relationships, it is an established rule that the woman should leave her parent-family to enter her husband's, so she is the "good" that ratifies the pact between the two families. It is rare for "roots" to be questioned and deprived of value, and more likely that these families will withdraw into their cultural identity in fear of and opposition to the other culture.

Parent couples from Brazil show highly individualistic emancipatory features and needs. Couples have their own models of male and female roles, but share the objective of maintaining family unity. Consequently, married couples try to leave together or are reunited within a short time. In some cases, the departure may be against the wish of others and seen as flight from a stifling situation. It is the women particularly who urge departure and change. So loyalty conflicts are either experienced intensely or rejected, while expectations of the new world are high.

Parent couples from Ghana have strong ties with their fellow countrymen and their evangelical communities. The relationship with their origins is generally strong. When normal or more serious problems arise, they protect their origins by idealizing them. On the other hand, encounter with the other culture is critical, and external relationships are more or less instrumental (i.e., linked to family needs: health services, schools), whereas the real provider of aid and services is the religious community to which they belong. Couples generally lack self-esteem, and they often feel victims of suspicion and intolerance in their host country. Black skin can, therefore, become a sign of segregation and ostracism.

For Filipino couples, the tie with origins is a resource expressed in the parents' desire to preserve and transmit their culture to their children. This does not exclude the fact, that as well as appreciating their origins (the search for harmony, solidarity, and respect), they may also be critical of both the economic situation aspects and gender relationships in their country. Essentially, they feel close to the culture of the host country and in times of need, they turn to either the host country or their country of origin, depending on the problems they encounter. In all cases, they were reserved and took a certain pride in not depending on the services of the host society.

Let us now look at the family histories of parent couples. We deliberately chose one gridlock situation and two critical situations that enable us to understand better what the obstacles are. How *does* one cross over to the other shore?

Unpicked Fruit

Nabjib (31 years old) decided to leave Morocco for Italy, and lived there for 8 years before he met Malika (29 years old). He progressed gradually, taking a course in Italian and then finding a permanent job and moving into a house. He got engaged to Malika during a holiday in Morocco. Two years later they were married and Nabjib brought Malika to Italy. Today they have a 5-year-old son, Javier. Nabjib is a laborer, as he was in Casablanca, and his wife, who was a nurse, now works as cleaning lady for a family.

The Interview.   The interview took place in a relaxed atmosphere, with mint tea and a tray of pastries on the table. The home was very comfortable, and full of typical articles from Morocco and photographs of the desert.

Nabjib described what coming to another country has meant for them and the families they left behind. Their hopes were based on new financial opportunities that would guarantee a better future for themselves and their siblings, parents, and children. Personal growth—getting to know the world and learning a new language, for example—was also an objective. We learned that the family mandate had been responsibly undertaken, and was also seen as a source of support and a demonstration of trust.

Nabjib encountered many difficulties on arriving in Italy and during the following years felt he was the object of suspicion, disapproval, and mistrust *"because no-one knows who you are. . . ."* All this led the couple to review their expectations and become more cautious and reserved with the other culture. *"In our country, everyone shakes hands. . . . They are all more open, more friendly. In this country, everyone judges you, maybe they're afraid, but we're not doing anything bad!"* The next comment is clear: *"I don't think we want to remain here. You're a foreigner in Italy, and you always will be. If Javier goes down to the courtyard to play, the other children hit him. We have to go down to tell them to stop."* Life progresses between work, the home, one or two Moroccan friends, and many phone calls to the family back home. Relationships with Italian colleagues are few and far between.

The great difference the couple found between the two cultures is in hospitality. Hospitality is sacred in Morocco, as in all of Africa; a relative or acquaintance can turn up at any time and be sure of a welcome. The dangers of travel, the great distances covered, and the strong sense of family ties makes everyone who knocks at the door a welcome visitor. Consequently, Nabjib and Malika see Italian invitation rituals, and the obligation to give warning of one's arrival beforehand, as rather complex. The other great difference is in the relationship between generations. The couple was worried that the host culture does not teach respect for adults and the elderly.

Both spouses say they feel extremely homesick and often see their future as bleak. Their greatest resource is their parents who *"listen to us and give us the strength to continue because they comfort us by saying that there are always difficulties in life and they have to be faced. The important thing is not to be alone and to believe that everything we do means something."* Having friends to turn to is also an important source of support.

The Family Life Space. The picture of the present (now) is rather bare and shows an indistinct grouping of all the elements in the center of the circle (Fig. 8.4). Special attention is given to those who have remained in the fatherland (parents, siblings, friends), domestic items such as perfumes, and good food. The only other representation is a larger circle that takes up the entire family life space. It represents the difficulties encountered in Italy. Malika says they feel like a shriveling piece of fruit that cannot give its juice to anyone because nobody wants to risk eating it.

In the drawing of the past (then), the space and boundary of the circle contains many elements that indicate an intense social and family life (parties, friends, walks, the beach, school and work friends, visits to holy cities). The ties are mostly positive. The difficult tie is the one with Morocco's economic situation.

Comparison of the two drawings reveals the impoverishment of elements and ties in the transition from past to present, as if the couple were withdrawing into themselves as protection against an inhospitable external world.

Family Interweaving. Nabjib and Malikas' family and cultural origins are a resource that helps them to face the many challenges of migration. The encounter with the other culture is a major difficulty for them. The more distant they feel, the more suspicion is created. More particularly, it is the relationship between the generations, and children's lack of respect for adults and the elderly, that disturb the couple. The image of shriveled, unpicked fruit is a good image of the impossibility of exchange. The tie with their origins has become an easy refuge that further hinders cultural exchange. The most suitable intervention in this type of situation is not by single couple, but by groups of family-couples that can compare their situations with other groups and families in the other culture. The aim is to respect differences in traditions while opening the way to an encounter of couple and family relationship values.

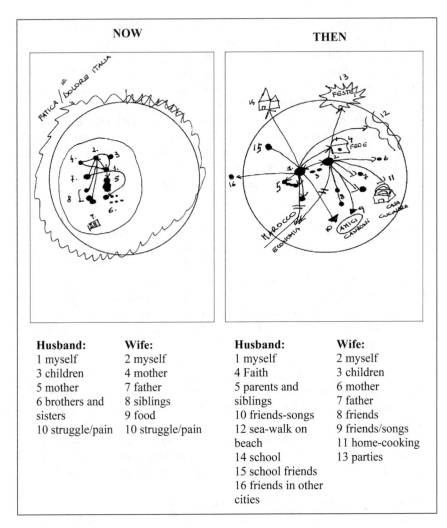

Husband:	**Wife:**	**Husband:**	**Wife:**
1 myself	2 myself	1 myself	2 myself
3 children	4 mother	4 Faith	3 children
5 mother	7 father	5 parents and	6 mother
6 brothers and	8 siblings	siblings	7 father
sisters	9 food	10 friends-songs	8 friends
10 struggle/pain	10 struggle/pain	12 sea-walk on	9 friends/songs
		beach	11 home-cooking
		14 school	13 parties
		15 school friends	
		16 friends in other	
		cities	

FIG. 8.4.   FLS: Nabjib & Malika.

Fertile Terrain

Esteban is 45 years old and came to Italy from Brazil over 10 years ago. Maria is 43 years old and arrived later, together with her youngest daughter who is now 10. The other two children, aged 15 and 21 years, were reunited with their family in 1995. The mother has a degree in Pedagogy, was the head of a school, and today works as a cleaner. Her husband was employed in a hospital in Brazil. When he came to Italy, he first worked for a cleaning company and now works as a social assistant in a community services cooperative.

The Interview.   The interview took place in the couple's home, which is tidy and full of objects. It is the wife who talks about the migration. The departure was opposed by both families, who could not understand the reason for it. Esteban's family did not reply to his letters and only contacted him when his mother died. Maria says over and over that for a long time she felt very lonely: *"We have to thank the Italians, our neighbors who helped us at the beginning . . . because our country has cut us off."*

Slowly, a picture emerges of a country that makes life impossible for its children-citizens: *"There's a moral crisis, an economic crisis and a political crisis. These crises forced us to leave. . . . There was neither flour or milk, those that did have such foods kept them and sold them at a very high price. Terrible, unmentionable things have happened even within our family, and I will never be able to forget them!"*

Life in Italy is considered positive in terms of both financial opportunities and local values. *"Latin people are very active and open. We are happy about this and the fact that our children have a lot of friends of different nationalities. We have tried to keep an open mind, getting used to the changes, and if you want to work, you can find people who will give you work!"*

Esteban and his wife have no intention of returning to Brazil because they much prefer living in this country. Even their circle of friends in Brazil has dwindled. *"Our children won't hear of returning: there are more opportunities here and more things to do. They're not at all homesick."* The spouses mention only two family resources: Maria's father and Esteban's younger sister, who both keep in touch and show interest in what has happened to them and their children. The only melancholy note is sounded when they recall the parties, dances, and music of Brazil.

The Family Life Space.   In the drawing of the present (now), the geometric center is occupied by the spouses and the children, from where positive elements of the new life context branch out (Fig. 8.5). These are Caritas, (the most important Catholic organization providing help to immigrants through active support and a major Study and Research Center), the hospital, Italian friends, cuisine, sport, travel, the parish, which are all defined as products of a good earth. The space occupied by the spouses is well balanced and the symbols are mutually recognized. Most of the ties are represented as positive except for the ties with some family members back home. The death of the mother is a negative element.

In the drawing of the past (then), the picture is extremely negative. There is a large number of insignificant conflictual ties to life in Brazil (crime, shootings, drugs, alcohol, illiteracy, moral crises . . .) that seem to crush the spouses and their children under their weight. Here, too, the psychological–geometric center is occupied by the couple, and below them by what gives them their strength: their values and their faith.

Family Interweaving. Ties with origins are seen as evil: The injustice and wrongs that have been suffered are difficult to justify. Consequently, it is felt that one has nothing to exchange with the other culture and the impulse is to take everything that the other culture has to offer. A space for reflection on the ties with one's origins needs to be created in order to balance the relationship between the two cultures. The origins are clearly deficient, but they do not correspond to either current family life or the country's current economic and moral condition. So specific values and features have to be looked for, even if it means digging into the past, in order to proffer an exchange to the other culture. Resources may even be discovered in memories of parties and dances. Here, too, intervention should take place through groups of couple-families

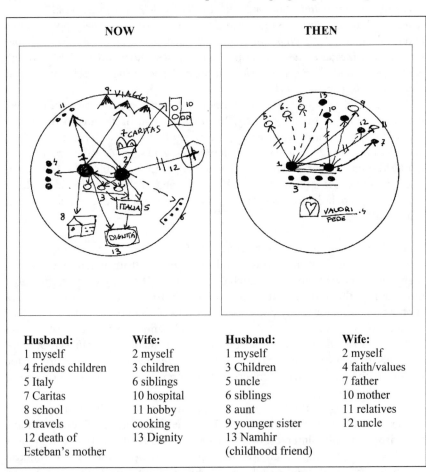

NOW		THEN	
Husband:	**Wife:**	**Husband:**	**Wife:**
1 myself	2 myself	1 myself	2 myself
4 friends children	3 children	3 Children	4 faith/values
5 Italy	6 siblings	5 uncle	7 father
7 Caritas	10 hospital	6 siblings	10 mother
8 school	11 hobby	8 aunt	11 relatives
9 travels	cooking	9 younger sister	12 uncle
12 death of	13 Dignity	13 Namhir	
Esteban's mother		(childhood friend)	

FIG. 8.5   FLS: Esteban & Maria.

that meet together to "think over their origins," looking for resources and working out their grief. Encounter with other couple-families of the host culture is not necessary as the family is already open to this.

Awaiting the Promised Land

Prince (38 years old) and his wife Marilyn (36 years old) come from Accra in Ghana. The husband arrived in Italy 10 years ago, and Marilyn, then his fiancée, came over 7 years ago. They have two children, Faustus, 7 years, and Joshua, 16 months. Prince's family broke up after death of his parents and because of his country's serious economic and political problems. He has a sister who lives in the United States, a brother in Nigeria, and another in Guinea, and his youngest sister is still in Ghana but is about to leave. Marilyn's mother has died, and she is the eldest of 11 siblings, all still living in Ghana.

Both spouses had a job before leaving Ghana. Prince graduated from high school and worked as an accountant for the Ministry of Social Affairs, and his wife was a cook at the Parliament cafeteria. On moving to Italy, they both had to settle for lower status jobs. Prince has been working in the same factory for 9 years without ever having obtained a promotion, while Marilyn worked for a family but had to leave when she had her first baby.

The Interview. The interview took place in an atmosphere of tension and embarrassment. The spouses continually apologized for their home, which *"is undignified and not how we would like it be to welcome our guests."* The husband, tense and nervous, starts with an agitated account of their migratory project. Prince tells us that, although proud of his origins and his country, he was forced to leave: *"Africa is a beautiful place . . . if you have money. I'm here just because there are so many economic problems there."* Their original destination was the United States, but they were unable to obtain a visa. So Italy, which at first was just a country of transit, became their home. After several years without a residence permit, he managed to legalize his status and found a job. At this point, Marilyn was able to join him.

The following years were dramatic, however. They were driven from one town to the next. For 4 years, they slept on chairs or makeshift beds. Marilyn had to cope with these conditions during her first pregnancy and in the first few months after giving birth. The people they met did not offer support, and were a threat and an obstacle. *"We didn't have a home, they kept sending us away saying they didn't have room. They threw us out of our home with our first son who was only two weeks old."* At the same time, the desire to reach the United States is increasing: *"In Italy, if you are a foreigner, you remain a foreigner forever. You will always feel left out. In the USA on the other hand, you are welcomed. . . . We want to go there as soon as possible."*

Not even the city council helped the couple: *"They don't inform us of our rights . . . there's no baby food and the nursery school is threatening to take Faustus off the cafeteria list if we don't pay the bill."* Prince and Marilyn refuse second-hand clothes (*"because perhaps the previous owner died of cancer or of AIDS"*) and free medicine from their pediatrician. The only help they accept is money sent by their sister in the United States.

The spouses are saddened that they cannot help to support the families they left behind in any way. They left believing they would be able to improve their condition, and their parents believed they would help the family, but they have found themselves struggling for survival. Consequently they feel ashamed and do not deem themselves worthy even of returning home. Their nostalgia for the past is very strong, with tinges of idealization. At the same time, there is a strong desire to leave and go to new places that are *"more favorable and more welcoming, where people acknowledge and appreciate you, not like here,"* although there does not seem to be any definite project at this time.

The Family Life Space. In the drawing of the present (now), the space within the circle is divided into two, with the top part occupied by the husband, and the bottom by the wife (Fig. 8.6). The two drawings do not touch, but reflect each other like mirrors. There is Jesus, a number of family members, and everyday items to do with finance and standard of living (money, car, bank, clothes . . .). The outside and the boundary are empty. Both spouses have drawn a stylized figure to represent themselves. They link to Jesus, and hierarchically to all the other family members. The whole gives a picture of a network with positive ties. According to the spouses, this drawing is a good representation of the Ghanaian tribe.

The drawing of the past (then) is not very different from the previous one, except for the fact that it is simpler and has more empty space. The spouses again represent themselves as two stylized figures, together with members of their families of origin, though fewer in number. The tie-lines are all positive. The other references (cinema, park, friendship, beach . . .) indicate that life back home was better. The wife, however, who occupies the lower space, has drawn herself on top of her little world in which she includes only her father and her aunt-mother. She does not include either the mother or the numerous siblings, whereas she does connect to the school because it taught her what she likes best, cooking. As the spouses then go on to relate, the wife is the eldest of 11 children and was left to her own devices as a child. The only care she received was from the school and from her aunt. Her husband connects himself to his parents and his elder sister, who was a mother for him and who still provides help from the United States.

What strikes one when looking at the drawing is the void in the center of the circle, representing the transition from "now" to "then," that highlights the crucial family problem: the lack of "care" or a project to unite people.

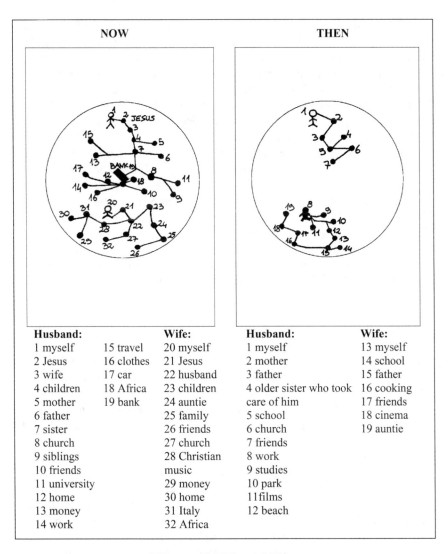

FIG. 8.6   FLS: Prince & Marilyn.

Family Interweaving. They escaped from the critical economic and political conditions of their country to go the United States, but now Prince and Marilyn are trapped in a country they have no love for and that they experience as hostile and dangerous. They have been in a stalemate situation for some time now. The land where they live is uninhabitable (rejecting and infecting), nor can they return to their homeland because of their shame over failing to help to their families. All that remains is the dream of going to the United States, the true destination and the Promised Land. However, there is no definite project for realizing this dream, although there is resentment against others in general (*"We shouldn't expect anything from anyone because everyone thinks for himself, we have to look after ourselves"*) and some practical conception of their relationship with others. The two FLS times are useful for "scratching the surface." The idealized destination has turned out to be a place of deprivation and ties that crumble away. The logical outcome of all this is the philosophy of "every man for himself."

Prince and Marilyn have certainly suffered great pain in this "transit country" on their way to the Promised Land. The bond with their origins is equally painful, and the representation of the relationship with the other is represented as one of exploitation, exactly like the exploitation they claim to be victims of.

Prince and Marilyn cannot get help directly from the Italian social services because the latter are part of the "kingdom of evil." But they can get help from the community of fellow countrymen with whom, moreover, they have difficulty in maintaining concrete relations. It is within such a context that a cultural counseling service needs to be set up, with a mediator from the same culture as Prince and Marilyn (Ciola & Rosenbaum, 2003; Moro, 2002).

ADAMAH

The migratory enterprise is studded with the usual difficulties and dangers of family identity and its renewal, and the price to pay is always high. Identity when encountering an "alien by culture," that is, an alien in terms of beliefs, values, rituals and practices, has always been a formidable challenge, as our examples confirm. However, there are differences between ethnic groups with regard to available resources and in the difficulties to be faced. Furthermore, each family has its idiosyncrasies, in the sense that each is a carrier not only of a culture, but also of a specific generational history. Just as the concept of family cannot be the sum of its members, so the family cannot be the same as the culture it belongs to. The cases we presented help us to understand this specificity, which is the result of historical and cultural encounter and the tripartite difference between gender, generations, and lineage.

For example, within the Brazilian ethnic group, it is the women who are most often the leading figures in the migratory project, which later extends to the partner and the entire family. Within the Moroccan ethnic group, there is a distinct dividing line between the man's field of action and the woman's, and it is the former who is responsible for the family's relationships with the outside world. Ghanaian women, although numerous and active, are heavily restricted by religion, whereas Filipino women take their bearings from their own culture as well as opening up to the new one. In all cases, family relationships do not reproduce the culture of origin but reinterpret and incorporate it on the basis of the generational exchange that has been experienced.

The result of the encounter of these differences is generational, as is the offspring's relationship with both the generations that precede them and the new cultural context—a relationship that can reveal the success or failure of the migratory enterprise. Offspring are "resemblers," but who do they resemble? Who do they take after? Whose heirs are they? These are fundamental "family" questions. In Western culture, the resemblance of a son or daughter is looked for in physical features and personality characteristics, whereas in African and other cultures, resemblance is a matter of lineage. Sons and daughters are like strangers who need to be invited to stay and to be affiliated. From whom did they get their souls? What do they have to offer the family? Without resemblance, there is no belonging. The children may have been born in the new land, or may have arrived there at an early age or even as adolescents, but they are still offspring—"resemblers" and heirs to cultural traditions. They do not develop on their own: Their minds and mental development are linked to the family matrix and its history, both with regard to the bond with their origins and to the openness or closure to encounter with the other. In this sense, experiences and memories of preceding generations and their expectations are written in their DNA, so to speak. Can children become "resemblers" of a foreign culture, and if so, which aspects of it? And how does this resemblance relate to generational and cultural resemblance?

In the biblical myth, Adamah is the interior Mother-Earth. Frye (1983) says the Bible is the "great code" of literature, and as such influences our creative imagination. Just like the exterior Mother-Earth, interior Mother-Earth needs to be cultivated so that fruit can issue from the seed; but the seed can be lost and remain dry and barren. Parasiticism and exploitation, failure to acknowledge the other, and exaltation of one's own culture are the pitfalls that dot the path toward the migrant family's new interior land.

Let us now examine the purpose of the undertaking, which is not to integrate "different identities" but to acknowledge one's own and others' identity and get people talking about difference. This is also evident in "mixed" couples whose members come from different cultures. To live with the other we need, at a certain point, to acknowledge difference (Gozzoli & Regalia, 2005). There is something in the other that cannot be integrated, something that must be accepted as such. Not everything lies within the realm of the reason that understands, guides, and coordinates our knowledge.

The maze you lose yourself in is always just round the corner. It could be parents' fears of losing their power, the pride of children who belittle and deride their parents' knowledge (the other side of the coin is shame of one's difference), or social pressure forcing cultures to adapt to consumerism and globalization.

We are now in a position to identify the milestones of the migratory process. The first is the *transferability of the Mother-Land*. If we have not experienced it, we need to recreate it, and if we lived it, we must take it with us, like the Lares and Penates, to make it blossom again. Only then can we feel we have done the "right thing" and have trust and hope in the renewal of our origins. The second milestone is the *feeling of justice* in exchanges with the other culture. What has the family given and proffered to its host country? And what has it received back? It is impossible not to put weights on the scale. If the feeling of injustice is all too real, acknowledgement of the other is impracticable. There is no connecting bridge or line, and forms of hatred like resentment, malice, and revenge will have the upper hand. If, on the other hand, the family members acknowledge that the exchange is just, even if limited, then the difference with the other culture becomes negotiable. Bridges are built and both our similarities and differences—which, as we have said, should be accepted as such—are acknowledged. It is the impossibility of dealing with cultural differences that spreads social exclusion, produces ghettos and exploitation, and the eliminates the other through terror regimes and ethnic cleansing. The frightening repetition of this breakdown throughout human history is both shocking and discouraging, but this does not mean we should give up doing good. Migrant families, with their specific cultural matrices and processes, teach us that the symbolic triangle of *faith, hope,* and *justice* invariably encourages acknowledgement of self and other.

References

Ackerman, N. W. (1958). *The psychodynamics of family life*. New York, NY: Basic Books.

Ainsworth, M. D. S., Blehar, M. C., Waters, E., & Wall, S. (1978). *Patterns of attachment: A psychological study of the Strange Situation*. Hillsdale, NJ: Lawrence Erlbaum Associates.

Aktar, S. (1991). *Immigration and identity. Turmoil, treatment and transformation*. Northvale, NJ: Jason Aronson Inc.

Alberoni, F. (1968). *Statu Nascenti* [Growing state of mind]. Bologna: Il Mulino.

Alberti, L. B. (1960). I libri della famiglia [Family books]. *Opere Volgari* [Vulgar literary works]. Bari: Laterza. (Original work published c. 1435)

Alighieri, D. (2000). *The divine comedy* (Rev. ed., J. F. Cotter, Trans.). Stony Brook, NY: Forum Italicum. (Original work written 1307)

Allen, T. D., Herst, D. E. L., Brack, C. S., & Sutton, M. (2000). Consequences associated with work-to-family conflict: A review and agenda for future research. *Journal of Occupational Health Psychology, 5*, 278–308.

Amato, P. (1999). Children of divorced parents as young adults. In E. M. Hetherington (Ed.), *Coping with divorce, single parenting, and remarriage* (pp. 147–164). Mahwah, NJ: Lawrence Erlbaum Associates.

Amerio, P. (2004). *Problemi umani in comunità di massa* [Human problems in mass communities]. Torino: Einaudi.

Anderson, S. A., & Sabatelli, R. M. (1992). The differentiation in the Family System Scale (DIFS). *The American Journal of Family Therapy, 20*(1), 77–89.

Andolfi, M. (Ed.). (1988). *La famiglia trigenerazionale* [The trigeneration family]. Roma: Bulzoni.

Angyal, A. (1941). A logic of systems. In F. E. Emery (Ed.), *Systems thinking* (pp. 27–40). Middlesex, UK: Penguin Books.

Arcand, D. (2003). *Les invasions barbares* [The barbarian invasions]. Miramax Films.

Arditti, J. A., & Prouty, A. M. (1999). Change, disengagement and renewal: Relationship dynamics between young adults and their fathers after divorce. *Journal of Marital and Family Therapy, 25*, 61–81.

Arendt, H. (1958). *The human condition*. Chicago, IL: University of Chicago Press.

Ariès, P. (1960). *Centuries of childhood*. New York, NY: Vintage Books. (Original work published 1960)

Aristotle. (2002). *Nicomachean ethics* (C. J. Rowe, Trans.). Oxford, UK: Oxford University Press.

Arnett, J. J. (2000). Emerging adulthood: A theory of development from the late teens through the twenties. *American Psychologist, 55*, 469–480.

Aron, L. (1995). The internalized primal scene. *Psychoanalytie Dial, 2*, 195–237.

Bank, S. P., & Kahn, M. D. (1982). *The sibling bond*. New York, NY: Basic Books.

Barnes, H. L., & Olson, D. H. (1982). Parent–adolescent communication. In D. H. Olson, H. Mc-Cubbin, H. L. Barnes, A. Larsen, M. Muxen, & C. M. Wilson (Eds.), *Family inventories* (pp. 55–70). St. Paul, MN: University of Minnesota.

Bateson, G. (1936). *Naven.* Stanford, CA: Stanford University Press.

Bateson, G. (1972). *Steps to an ecology of mind.* San Francisco, CA: Chandler Press.

Bateson, G. (1979). *Mind and nature: A necessary unity.* New York, NY: Dutton.

Beavers, W. R. (1982). Healthy, midrange, and severely dysfunctional families. In F. Walsh (Ed.), *Normal family processes* (pp. 45–66). New York, NY: Guilford.

Beavers, W. R. (1985). *Successful marriage.* New York, NY: Norton.

Bedford, V. (1989). Ambivalence in adult sibling relationships. *Journal of Family Issue, 10,* 211–224.

Bellah, R. N., Madsen, R., Sullivan, W. M., Swidler, A., & Tipton, M. (1991). *The good society.* New York, NY: Knopf.

Belsky, J., & Pensky, E. (1988). Marital change across the transition to parenthood. *Marriage and Family Review, 12,* 133–156.

Belsky, J., & Rovine, M. (1990). Patterns of marital change across the transition to parenthood: Pregnancy to three years postpartum. *Journal of Marriage and the Family, 52,* 5–19.

Bengston, V., & Allen, K. (1993). The life course perspective applied to families over time. In P. G. Boss, W. J. Doherty, R. LaRossa, W. R. Schumm, & S. K. Steinmetz (Eds.), *Sourcebook of family theories and methods: A contextual approach* (pp. 469–504). New York, NY: Plenum Press.

Benjamin, J. (1995). *Like subjects, love objects: Essays on recognition and sexual difference.* New Haven, CT: Yale University Press.

Benveniste, E. (1969). *Le vocabulaire des institutions européennes* [Dictionary of European institutions]. Paris: Les Editions de Minuit.

Berry, J. W. (1997). Immigration, acculturation, and adaptation. *Applied Psychology: An International Review, XLVI*(1), 5–34.

Blieszner, R., & Hamon, R. R. (1992). Filial responsibility: Attitudes, motivators, and behaviors. In J. W. Dwyer & R. T. Coward (Eds.), *Gender, families, and elder care* (Sage focus editions, Vol. 138, pp. 105–119). Thousand Oaks, CA: Sage.

Blum, H. P. (1996). The secret seed of hatred in a delinquent adolescent. In S. Rangell R. Moses-Hrushovski (Eds.), *Psychoanalysis and the political border: Essays in honor of Rafael Moses* (Vol. 112–137, pp. 35–48). Madison, CT: International Universities Press.

Bocchi, G., & Ceruti, M. (Eds.). (1985). *La sfida della complessità* [The complexity challenge]. Milano: Feltrinelli.

Bodenmann, G. (1995). A systemic-transactional conceptualization of stress and coping in couples. *Swiss Journal of Psychology, 54*(1), 34–49.

Bodenmann, G. (1997). Dyadic coping. A systemic transactional view of stress and coping among couples: Theory and empirical findings. *European Review of Applied Psychology, 47,* 137–140.

Bohannan, L. (1973). The six stations of divorce. In M. E. Lasswell & T. E. Lasswell (Eds.), *Love, marriage, and family: A developmental approach* (pp. 475–489). Glenview, IL: Scott Foresman.

Bonnie, H. (2002). Invisible fathers: Child development and family dynamics after heterologous insemination. *Praxis der Kinderpsychologie und Kinderpsychiatrie, 51*(2), 118–125.

Booth, A., & Amato, P. R. (2001). Parental predivorce relations and offspring postdivorce well-being. *Journal of Marriage and the Family, 63,* 197–212.

Boscolo, L., & Bertrando, P. (1996). *Terapia sistemica individuale* [Individual systemic therapy]. Milano: Raffaello Cortina Editore.

Boss, P. G., Doherty, W. J., LaRossa, R., Schumm, W. R., & Steinmetz, S. K. (Eds.). (1993). *Sourcebook of family theories and methods: A contextual approach.* New York, NY: Plenum Press.

Bossard, J. H., & Boll, E. S. (1956). *The large family system: An original study in the sociology of family behavior.* Philadelphia, PA: University of Pennsylvania Press.

Boszormenyi-Nagy, I., & Spark, G. (1973). *Invisible loyalties: Reciprocity in intergenerational family therapy.* New York, NY: Harper & Row.

Boszormenyi-Nagy, I., & Spark, G. (1986). *Between give and take.* New York, NY: Brunner/Mazel.

Bowen, M. (1976). Family reaction to death. In P. Guerin (Ed.), *Family therapy: Theory and practice* (pp. 335–348). New York, NY: Gardner Press.

Bowen, M. (1978). *Family therapy in clinical practice.* New York, NY: Jason Aronson.

Boyd, M. (1989). Family and personal networks in international migration: Recent developments and new agendas. *International Migration Review, XXIII*(3), 638–670.

Bradbury, T. N., & Fincham, F. D. (1990). Attributions in marriage: Review and critique. *Psychological Bulletin, 107,* 3–33.

Brand, A. E., & Brinich, P. M. (1999). Behavior problems and mental health contacts in adopted, foster and nonadopted children. *Journal of Child Psychology and Psychiatry, 40*(4), 1221–1229.

Branje, S. J. T., van Aken, M. A. G., & van Lieshout, C. F. M. (2002). Relational support in families with adolescents. *Journal of Family Psychology, 16*(3), 351–362.

Bray, J. H., Maxwell, S. E., & Cole, D. (1995). Multivariate statistics for family psychology research. *Journal of Family Psychology, 9*(2), 144–160.

Breunlin, D. C. (1988). Oscillation theory and the family development. In C. J. Falicov (Ed.), *Family transition* (pp. 133–155). New York, NY: Guilford.

Brewer, M. B. (1991). The social self: On being the same and different at the same time. *Personality and Social Psychology Bulletin, 17*(5), 475–482.

Brodzinsky, D. M., & Schechter, M. D. (Eds.). (1990). *The psychology of adoption.* New York, NY: Oxford University Press.

Brodzinsky, D. M., Smith, D. W., & Brodzinsky, A. B. (1998). *Children's adjustment to adoption.* Thousand Oaks, CA: Sage.

Buckley, W. (1976). *Sociology and modern systems theory.* Englewood, NJ: Prentice-Hall.

Bydlowsky, M. (1994). Desiderio di un bambino, desiderio di gravidanza. Evoluzione delle pratiche di procrezione [Wish for a child, wish for pregnancy. Evolution of procreation practices]. In S. Lebovici & F. Weil-Halpern (Eds.), *Psicopatologia delle prima infanzia* [Early childhood psychopathology] (Vol. 1, pp. 33–42). Torino: Bollati Boringhieri.

Byng Hall, J. (1995). *Rewriting family scripts.* New York, NY: Guilford.

Caprara, G. V., Pastorelli, C., Regalia, C., Scabini, E., & Bandura, A. (2004). Impact of adolescents' filial self-efficacy on quality of family functioning and satisfaction. *Journal of Research on Adolescence, 15*(1), 71–97.

Caprara, G. V., Regalia, C., Scabini, E., Barbaranelli, C., & Bandura, A. (2004). Assessment of filial, parental, marital, and collective family efficacy beliefs. *European Journal of Psychological Assessment, 20*(4), 247–261.

Carrà Mittini, E. (Ed.). (1999). *Una famiglia, tre famiglie. La famiglia giovane nella trama delle generazioni* [One family, three families. The young family in the generation plot]. Milano: Unicopli.

Carson, R. C., Butcher, J. N., & Coleman, J. C. (1988). *Abnormal psychology and modern life* (5th ed.). Glenview, IL: Scott Foresman & Co.

Cartwright, C., & Seymur, F. (2002). Young adults' perceptions of parents' response in stepfamilies: What hurts? What helps? *Journal of Divorce & Remarriage, 37*(3–4), 123–141.

Cassidy, J., & Shaver, P. (Eds.). (1999). *Handbook of attachment: Theory, research, and clinical applications.* New York, NY: Guilford Press.

Centro Studi e Ricerche sulla Famiglia. (2000). *La famiglia tra le generazioni* [The family among generations]. Privately produced educational video.

Ceruti, M. (1995). *Evoluzione senza fondamenti* [Evolution without foundations]. Bari: Laterza.

Chatel, M. M. (1993). *Malaise dans la procréation* [Procreative disease]. Paris: Albin Michel.

Cherlin, A., Scabini, E., & Rossi, G. (1997). Still in the nest: Delayed home leaving in Europe and the United States. *Journal of Family Issues, 18*(6), 572–575.

Chun, Y. J., & MacDermid, S. M. (1997). Perceptions of family differentiation, individuation, and self-esteem among Korean adolescents. *Journal of Marriage and the Family, 59*(2), 451–462.

Cicirelli, V. G. (1995). *Sibling relationships across the life span.* New York, NY: Plenum Press.

Cicirelli, V. G. (2002). *Older adults' views on death.* New York, NY: Springer.

Cigoli, V. (1992). *Il corpo familiare. L'anziano, la malattia, l'intreccio generazionale* [The family body. The elderly, illness, and the generational plot]. Milano: Franco Angeli.

Cigoli, V. (1994). *Tossicomania. Passaggi generazionali e intervento di rete* [Drug addiction. Generational exchanges and social services interventions]. Milano: Franco Angeli.

Cigoli, V. (1997). *Intrecci familiari. Realtà interiore e scenario relazionale* [Family plots. Inner reality and relational scenery]. Milano: Raffaello Cortina Editore.

Cigoli, V. (1998–2000). Quadri di famiglia: Dalla pittura romana alla pittura del Novecento. [Family paintings: From Roman to 20th century painting]. Privately produced educational CD.

Cigoli, V. (1998a). *Psicologia della separazione e del divorzio* [Psychology of separation and divorce]. Bologna: Il Mulino.

Cigoli, V. (1998b). Più stirpi e una comune dimora [Different lineages and a common abode]. In D. Bramanti & R. Rosnati (Eds.), *Il patto adottivo. L'adozione internazionale di fronte alla sfida dell'adolescenza* [The adoptive pact. The international adoption facing the adolescence challenge] (pp. 209–226). Milano: Franco Angeli.

Cigoli, V. (2000). *Il vello d'oro. Ricerche sul valore famiglia* [The golden fleece. Research on the value of the family]. Cinisello Balsamo: San Paolo.

Cigoli, V. (2001). Il corpo familiare. Scenario rappresentazionale e azione generazionale [The family body. Representational scenery and generational action]. *Interazioni, 2,* 29–42.

Cigoli, V. (2002). Confini, gerarchia, traingolarità: per una clinica delle famiglie ricomposte [Boundaries, hierarchy, triangularity: For a clinic intervention on step families]. *Interazioni, 1,* 11–25.

Cigoli, V. (2003a). La coppia tra scenari di origine e nuova nascita [The couple among origin scenarios and a new birth]. In M. Andolfi & V. Cigoli (Eds.), *La famiglia di origine. L'incontro in psicoterapia e in formazione* [The family of origin. The encounter in psychotherapy and training] (pp. 125–146). Milano: Franco Angeli.

Cigoli, V. (2003b). Contro l'enfasi della mediazione familiare. Il dover disporre dell'altro e il poter negoziare con l'altro nella coppia genitoriale divorziata [Contrasting the emphasis on family mediation. Disposing about the other and negotiating with the other within the divorced parental couple]. *Terapia Familiare, 72,* 1–22.

Cigoli, V., & Galimberti, C. (1983). *Psicoanalisi e ricerca sui sistemi in terapia familiare* [Psychoanalysis and systems research in family therapy]. Milano: Franco Angeli.

Cigoli, V., Galimberti, C., & Mombelli, M. (1988). *Il legame disperante. Il divorzio come dramma di genitori e figli* [The never-ending bond. The divorce as drama for parents and children]. Milano: Raffaello Cortina Editore.

Cigoli, V., Giuliani, C., & Iafrate, R. (2002). Il dolore del divorzio: adolescenti e giovani adulti tra riavvicinamento e distacco alla storia familiare [The divorce pain: Adolescents and young adults between reapproaching and detachment to the family story]. *Psicologia Clinica dello Sviluppo, 3,* 423–442.

Cigoli, V., & Gozzoli, C. (2003). Representar y vivir el espacio de vida familiar en familias migrantes: una confrontación intercultural [Representing and living the family life space in migrant families: An intercultural confrontation]. In D. Borobio (Ed.), *Familia e interculturalidad* [Family and interculture] (pp. 433–461). Salamanca: Ed. Universidad Pontificia Salamanca.

Cigoli, V., Gozzoli, C., & Tamanza, G. (2003). Processus de trasmission des valeurs dans la dinamique inter-generationnelle [The family transmission process of the values]. In C. Rodet (Ed.), *La transmission dans la famille: secrets, fictions et ideaux* [The transmission within the family: Secrets, fictions and ideals] (pp. 363–370). Paris: Harmattan.

Cigoli, V., Marta, E., Gozzoli, C., & Tamanza, G. (2003). Generatività familiare [Family generativity]. In S. Di Nuovo & S. Buono (Eds.), *Famiglie con figli disabili. Valori, crisi evolutiva, strategie di intervento* [Families with handicapped children. Values, developmental crisis, intervention strategies] (pp. 13–49). Catania: Città Aperta.

Cigoli, V., Marta, E., Gozzoli, C., & Tamanza, G. (in press). *L'intervista generazionale* [The generational interview]. Milano: Franco Angeli.

Ciola, A., & Rosenbaum, F. (2003). Girotondi a tre [Ring-around-the-rosy of three members]. In E. Scabini & G. Rossi (Eds.), *Rigenerare i legami: la mediazione nelle relazioni familiari e comunitarie* [Regenerate ties: Mediation in family and community relationships] (pp. 299–313). Milano: Vita e Pensiero.

Clark, M. S., & Mills, J. (1993). The difference between communal and exchange relationships: What it is and is not. *Personality and Social Psychology Bulletin, 19*(6), 684–691.

Clark, M. S., & Reis, H. T. (1988). Interpersonal processes in close relationships. *Annual Review of Psychology, 39,* 609–672.

Cohen, N. J., Coyne, J. C., & Duvall, J. D. (1996). Parents' sense of "entitlement" in adoptive and nonadoptive families. *Family Process, 35,* 441–456.

Cole, D. A., & Jordan, A. E. (1989). Assessment of cohesion and adaptability on component family dyads: A question of convergent and discriminant validity. *Journal of Counseling Psychology, 36*(4), 456–463.

Cole, M. (1996). *Cultural psychology.* Boston, MA: Harvard University Press.

Coleman, J. S. (1990). *Foundations of social theory.* Cambridge, MA: Harvard University Press.

Cook, W., & Dreyer, A. (1984). The Social Relations Model: A new approach to the analysis of family–dyadic interaction. *Journal of Marriage and the Family, 46,* 679–687.

Cooley, C. H. (1909). *Social organization.* Oxford, UK: Scribners.

Cooper, C. R., Grotevant, H. D., & Condon, S. (1983). Individuality and connectedness in the family as a context for adolescent identity formation and role-taking skill. *New Directions for Child Development, 22,* 43–59.

Cordon, J. A. (1997). Youth residential independence and autonomy: A comparative study. *Journal of Family Issues, 18,* 576–607.

Crohan, S. (1996). Marital quality and conflict across the transition to parenthood in African American and White couples. *Journal of Marriage and the Family, 58,* 933–944.

Davies, B., Reimer, J. C., & Martens, N. (1994). Family functioning and its implications for palliative care. *Journal of Palliative Care, 10,* 29–36.

Deal, J. E. (1995). Utilizing data from multiple family members: A within-family approach. *Journal of Marriage and the Family, 57*(4), 1109–1121.

Dermer, B., & Hutchings, B. (2000). Utilizing movies in family therapy: Applications for individuals, couples, and families. *American Journal of Family Therapy, 28*(2), 163–180.

De Rougemont, D. (1963). *Love declared: Essays on the myths of love.* New York, NY: Pantheon Books. (Original work published 1961)

de St. Aubin, E., & McAdams, D. P. (1995). The relations of generative concern and generative action to personality traits, satisfaction/happiness with life and ego development. *Journal of Adult Development, 2,* 99–112.

de St. Aubin, E., McAdams, D. P., & Kim, T. C. (Eds.). (2003). *The generative society: Caring for future generations.* Washington, DC: American Psychological Association.

Detienne, M. (1972). *Les jardins d'Adonis* [Adonis' gardens]. Paris: Gallimard.

Dicks, H. V. (1967). *Marital tensions: Clinical studies toward a psycho-analitic theory of interaction.* London, UK: Routledge & Kegan Paul.

Di Vita, A. M., & Calderaro, G. (Eds.). (2001). *La tutela degli affetti* [Protecting affections]. Milano: Unicopli.

Doane, J. A., & Diamond, D. (1994). *Affect and attachment in the family.* New York, NY: Basic Books.

Doherty, W. J. (1995). *Soul searching: Why psychotherapy must promote moral responsibility.* New York, NY: Basic Books.

Doherty, W. J., Boss, P. G., LaRossa, R., Schumm, W. R., & Steinmetz, S. K. (1993). Family theories and methods: A contextual approach. In P. G. Boss, W. J. Doherty, R. LaRossa, W. R. Schumm, & S. K. Steinmetz (Eds.), *Sourcebook of family theories and methods: A contextual approach* (pp. 3–30). New York, NY: Plenum Press.

Dolezel, L. (1988). *Occidental poetics: Tradition and progress*. Lincoln, NE: University of Nebraska Press.

Dollahite, D. C., Slife, B. D., & Hawkins, A. J. (1998). Family generativity and generative counseling: Helping families to keep faith with the next generation. In D. P. McAdams & E. de St. Aubin (Eds.), *Generativity and adult development: How and why we care for the next generation* (pp. 449–481). Washington, DC: American Psychological Association.

Donati, P. (1989). *La famiglia come relazione sociale* [Family as social relationship]. Milano: Franco Angeli.

Donati, P. (1991). *Secondo rapporto sulla famiglia in Italia* [Second report on family in Italy]. Cinisello Balsamo: Edizioni Paoline.

Donati, P. (1998). *Manuale di sociologia della famiglia* [Handbook of family sociology]. Bari: Laterza.

Dumon, W. A. (1992). Famiglia e movimenti migratori [Family and migration movements]. In E. Scabini & P. Donati (Eds.), *La famiglia in una società multietnica* [The family in a multiethnic society] (pp. 27–53). Milano: Vita e Pensiero.

Dunn, J., & Plomin, R. (1991). Why are siblings so different: The significance of differences in sibling experiences within the family. *Family Process, 30*, 271–283.

Eisler, I., Dare, C., & Szmuckler, G. I. (1988). What's happened to family interaction research? An historical account and a family systems viewpoint. *Journal of Marital and Family Therapy, 14*, 45–65.

Emery, R. (1994). *Renegotiating family relationship: Divorce, child custody and mediation*. New York, NY: Guilford.

Epstein, N. B., & Santa Barbara, J. (1975). Conflict behavior in clinical couplet: Interpersonal perceptions and stable outcomes. *Family Process, 14*, 51–66.

Erikson, E. H. (1964). *Insight and responsibility*. New York, NY: Norton.

Erikson, E. H. (1968). *Identity: Youth and crisis*. New York, NY: Norton.

Erikson, E. H. (1982). *The life cycle completed*. New York, NY: Norton.

Eyre, R. (Director). (2001). *Iris*. Miramax Films.

Fairbairn, W. R. D. (1952). *Psychoanalitic studies of the personality*. London, UK: Tavistock.

Falicov, C. J. (1988). *Family sociology and family therapy contributions to the family development framework: A comparative analysis and thoughts on future trends*. New York, NY: The Guilford Press.

Feetham, S. L. (1988). *Developing programs of research of families*. Paper presented at the University of Pennsylvania School of Nursing, Philadelphia, PA.

Fiese, B. H., & Kline, C. A. (1992). Dimensions of family rituals across two generations: Relation to adolescent identity. *Family Process, 31*, 151–162.

Fiese, B. H., & Kline, C. A. (1993). Development of the family ritual questionnaire: Initial reliability and validation study. *Journal of Family Psychology, 6(3)*, 290–299.

Finch, J. (1989). *Family obligations and social change*. Cambridge, MA: Polity Press.

Fincham, F. D. (2000). The kiss of the porcupines: From attributing responsibility to forgiving. *Personal Relationships, 7*, 1–23.

Fincham, F. D., & Beach, S. R. (2002). Forgiveness in marriage: Implications for psychological aggression and constructive communication. *Personal Relationships, 9*, 239–251.

Fincham, F. D., Beach, S. R. H., & Davila, J. (2004). Forgiveness and conflict resolution in marriage. *Journal of Family Psychology, 18*, 72–81.

Fincham, F. D., & Bradbury, T. N. (1987). The impact of attributions in marriage: A longitudinal analysis. *Journal of Personality and Social Psychology, 53*, 510–517.

Fincham, F. D., & Bradbury, T. N. (1993). Marital satisfaction, depression, and attributions: A longitudinal analysis. *Journal of Personality and Social Psychology, 64*, 442–452.

Fincham, F. D., Harold, G., & Gano-Phillips, S. (2000). The longitudinal relation between attributions and marital satisfaction: Direction of effects and role of efficacy expectations. *Journal of Family Psychology, 14*, 267–285.

Fincham, F. D., Paleari, G., & Regalia, C. (2002). Forgiveness in marriage: The role of relationship quality, attributions and empathy. *Personal Relationships, 9,* 27–37.

Fisher, J. V. (1999). *Uninvited guest: Emerging from narcissism towards marriage in psychoanalytic therapy with couples.* London, UK: Karnac Books.

Fisher, L., Kokes, R. F., Ransom, D. C., Philips, S. L., & Rudd, P. (1985). Alternative strategies for creating "relational" family data. *Family Process, 24,* 213–224.

Fivaz, E., & Corboz, A. (1999). *The primary triangle. A developmental systems view of mother, father, and infants.* New York, NY: Basic Books.

Fletcher, G. J. O., & Fincham, F. J. (1991). Attribution process in close relationships. In G. J. O. Fletcher & F. J. Fincham (Eds.), *Cognition in close relationships* (pp. 7–35). Mahwah, NJ: Lawrence Erlbaum Associates.

Fornari, F. (1981). *Il codice vivente* [The living code]. Torino: Bollati Boringhieri.

Foulkes, S. H. (1957). *Group analytic psychotherapy: Methods and principles.* New York, NY: Gordon and Breach.

Framo, J. L. (1992). *Family of origin therapy.* New York, NY: Brunner/Mazel.

Freud, S. (1895). A project for a scientific psychology. *Standard Edition, 1,* 283–397.

Freud, S. (1912). On the universal tendency to debasement in the sphere of love. *Standard Edition, 11,* 179–190.

Freud, S. (1913). Totem and taboo. *Standard Edition, 13,* 1–161.

Freud, S. (1914). An introduction to narcissism. *Standard Edition, 14.*

Frieze, I. H., Boneva, B. S., Sarlija, N., Horvat, J., Ferligoj, A., Kogovsek, T., et al. (2004). Psychological differences in stayers and leavers: Emigration desires in central and eastern European university students. *European Psychologist, IX*(1), 15–23.

Frye, N. (1967). *Fools of time: Studies in Shakespearean tragedy.* Toronto: University of Toronto Press.

Frye, N. (1983). *The myth of deliverance: Reflections on Shakespeare's problem comedies.* Toronto: University of Toronto Press.

Fuhrman, T., & Holmbeck, G. (1995). A contextual-moderator analysis of emotional autonomy and adjustment in adolescence. *Child Development, 66*(3), 793–811.

Furlong, A., & Cartmel, F. (1997). *Young people and social change.* Buckingham, UK: Open University Press.

Gardner, R. (1989). *Parental alienation syndrome.* New York, NY: Cresskill.

Gill, M. (1982). *The analysis of transference.* New York, NY: International University Press.

Girard, R. (1972). *La violence et la sacré* [Violence and the sacred]. París: Grasset.

Girard, R. (2003). *Le sacrifice* [The sacrifice]. Paris: Bibliothèque Nationale de France.

Giuliani, C., Iafrate, R., & Rosnati, R. (1998). Relationships within peer-group in adolescents from intact and divorced families. *Contemporary Family Therapy, 20*(1), 93–105.

Gloger, T., Gabriele, S., & Huerkamp, M. (1998). Relationship change at the transition to parenthood and security of infant–mother attachment. *International Journal of Behavioral Development, 22,* 633–655.

Godbout, J. (1992). *L'esprit du don* [The spirit of the gift]. Montreal: Editions du Boreal.

Goetting, A. (1986). The developmental tasks of siblings over the life cycle. *Journal of Marriage and the Family, 48,* 703–714.

Gold, D. (1989). Generational solidarity: Conceptual antecedents and consequences. *American Behavioral Scientist, 33,* 19–32.

Gold, D., Woodbury, M., & George, L. (1990). Relationship classification using grade of membership analysis: A typology of sibling relationships in later life. *Journal of Gerontology, 45,* 43–51.

Goldberg, A. E., & Perry-Jenkins, M. (2004). Division of labor and working-class women's well-being across the transition to parenthood. *Journal of Family Psychology, 18*(1), 225–236.

Goldbeter-Merinfeld, E. (1997). La place absents dans les familles [Nowhere places within families]. *Cahiers de Psychologie Clinique, 8,* 63–79.

Goldbeter-Merinfeld, E. (1998). Devils et fantômes [Mournings and ghosts]. *Cahiers Critique de Térapie Familliale, 20*, 51–57.

Goldscheider, F. (1997). Recent changes in U.S. young adult living arrangements in comparative perspective. *Journal of Family Issues, 18*, 708–724.

Golombok, S., Brewaeys, A., Cook, R., Giavazzi, M. T., Guerra, D., Mantovani, A., et al. (1996). The European study of assisted reproduction families: Family functioning and child development. *Human Reproduction, 11*, 2324–2331.

Golombok, S., & MacCallum, F. (2003). Practitioner review: Outcomes for parents and children following non-traditional conception. What do clinicians need to know? *Journal of Child Psychology and Psychiatry and Allied Disciplines, 44*(3), 303–315.

Gonzales, R., & Griffin, D. (1997). On the statistics of interdependence: Treating dyadic data with respect. In S. Duck (Ed.), *Handbook of personal relationships: Theory, research and interventions* (pp. 271–302). New York, NY: John Wiley & Sons.

Goodnow, J. J. (1997). Parenting and the transmission and internalization of values: From social–cultural perspectives to within-family analyses. In J. E. Grusec & L. Kuczynski (Eds.), *Parenting and children's internalization of values: A handbook of contemporary theory* (pp. 333–361). New York, NY: John Wiley & Sons.

Goolishian, H. A., & Anderson, H. (1992). Some afterthoughts on reading Duncan and Held. *Journal of Marital and Family Therapy, 18*, 35–37.

Gottman, J. M. (1982). Temporal form: Toward a new language for describing relationships. *Journal of Marriage and the Family, 44*(4), 943–964.

Gottman, J. M. (1994). *What predicts divorce?* Mahwah, NJ: Lawrence Erlbaum Associates.

Gottman, J. M., & Levenson, R. (1992). Marital processes predictive of later dissolution: Behavior, psychology, and health. *Journal of Personality and Social Psychology, 63*, 221–233.

Gouldner, A. W. (1960). The norm of reciprocity. *American Sociological Review, 25*, 161–178.

Gozzoli, C., & Regalia, C. (2005). *Migrazioni e famiglia: percorsi, legami, interventi psicosociali* [Family and migrations: Routes, ties, psychosocial interventions]. Bologna: Il Mulino.

Gozzoli, C., & Tamanza, G. (1998). *Il Family Life Space: L'analisi metrica del disegno* [Family Life Space: The drawing metric analysis]. Milano: Franco Angeli.

Graber, J., & Brooks-Gunn, J. (1999). Sometimes I think that you don't like me: How mothers and daughters negotiate the transition into adolescence. In M. Cox & J. Brooks-Gunn (Eds.), *Conflict and cohesion in families: Causes and consequences* (pp. 207–242). Mahwah, NJ: Lawrence Erlbaum Associates.

Greco, O. (1999). *La doppia luna. Test dei confini e delle appartenenze familiari* [The Double Moon: Test for family boundaries and belongings]. Milano: Franco Angeli.

Greco, O., & Iafrate, R. (2001). *Figli al confine. Una ricerca multimetodologica sull'affido familiare* [Children at the boundary. A multi-methodological research on family foster care]. Milano: Franco Angeli.

Greco, O., Ranieri, S., & Rosnati, R. (2003). *Il percorso della famiglia adottiva. Strumenti per l'ascolto e l'accompagnamento* [The route of the adoptive family: Instruments for listening and accompanying]. Milano: Unicopli.

Greco, O., & Rosnati, R. (1998). Alla ricerca di un patto adottivo [Searching an adoptive pact]. In D. Bramanti & R. Rosnati (Eds.), *Il patto adottivo. L'adozione internazionale di fronte alla sfida dell'adolescenza* [The adoptive pact. International adoption in front of the adolescent challenge] (pp. 172–208). Milano: Franco Angeli.

Green, R. J., & Werner, P. (1996). Intrusiveness and closeness–caregiving: Rethinking the concept of family enmeshment. *Family Process, 35*(2), 115–136.

Grinberg, L., & Grinberg, R. (1984). A psychoanalytic study of migration: Its normal and pathological aspects. *Journal of the American Psychoanalytic Association, 32*, 13–38.

Guglielmetti, C., & Greco, O. (2003). *Family rituals in the transition to parenthood.* Unpublished manuscript.

Guglielmetti, C., & Marta, E. (2003). La matrice familiare dell'impegno di giovani volontari: Uno studio esplorativo [The family matrix in young-adult volunteers: An explorative study]. In E. Marta & E. Scabini (Eds.), *Giovani Volontari* [Young Volunteers] (pp. 196–230). Firenze: Giunti.

Guthrie, W. K. C. (1968). *The Greeks and their gods.* Methuen, UK: University Paperback.

Hadley, T., Jacob, T., Milliones, J., Caplan, J., & Spitz, D. (1974). The relationship between family developmental crisis and the appearance of symptoms in a family member. *Family Process, 13*(2), 207–214.

Hahn, C. S. (2001). Review: Psychosocial well-being of parents and their children born after assisted reproduction. *Journal of Pediatric Psychology, 26*(8), 525–538.

Haley, J. (1973). *Uncommon therapy: The psychiatric techniques of Milton Erickson.* New York, NY: Norton.

Hamon, R., & Blieszner, J. (1990). Filial responsibility expectations among adult child–older parent pairs. *Journal of Gerontology, 45,* 110–112.

Hawley, D. R., & Dehaan, L. (1996). Toward a definition of family resilience: Integrating life-span and family perspectives. *Family Process, 35*(3), 283–298.

Haws, W. A., & Mallinckrodt, B. (1998). Separation-individuation from family of origin and marital adjustment of recently married couples. *American Journal of Family Therapy, 26*(4), 293–306.

Hegel, G. F. (1978). *Lineamenti di filosofia del diritto* [Principles of law philosophy] (F. Messineo, Trans.). Roma-Bari: Laterza. (Original work published 1821)

Héritier, F. (1996). *Masculin, féminin. La pensée de la différence* [Male and female. The thought about difference]. Paris: Edition Odile Jacob.

Herlihy, D. (1985). *Medieval household.* Cambridge, MA: Harvard University Press.

Hetherington, E. M. (1999). *Coping with divorce, single parenting, and remarriage.* Mahwah, NJ: Lawrence Erlbaum Associates.

Hetherington, E. M., Reiss, D., & Plomin, R. (Eds.). (1992). *Nonshared environment.* Mahwah, NJ: Lawrence Erlbaum Associates.

Hill, R. (1949). *Family under stress.* New York, NY: Harper & Row.

Hill, R. (1970). *Family development in three generations.* Cambridge, MA: Schenkman.

Hinde, R. A. (1979). *Toward understanding relationships.* London, UK: Academic Press.

Hinde, R. A. (1995). A suggested structure for a science of relationships. *Personal Relationships, 2,* 1–15.

Hinde, R. A. (1997). *Relationships: A dialectical perspective.* Cambridge, UK: Psychology Press.

Hurni, M., & Stoll, G. (1998). *La haine de l'amour. La perversion du lien* [The hate of loving. The tie perversion]. Paris: L'Harmattan.

Huston, T. L., & Vangelisti, A. (1995). How parenthood affects marriage. In M. Fitzpatrick & A. Vangelisti (Eds.), *Explaining family interactions* (pp. 147–176). Thousand Oaks, CA: Sage.

Iacovou, M., & Berthoud, R. (2001). *Young people's lives: A map of Europe.* Colchester, UK: University of Essex.

Johnson, S. (1755). *A dictionary of the English language.* London, UK: Longman.

Jones, J., Christensen, A., & Jacobson, N. S. (2000). Integrative behavioral couple therapy. In F. M. Dattilio & L. J. Bevilacqua (Eds.), *Comparative treatments for relationship dysfunction* (pp. 186–209). New York, NY: Springer.

Jurkovic, G. J. (1998). *Lost childhoods. The plight of the parentified child.* New York, NY: Brunner/ Mazel.

Jurkovic, G. J., Thirkield, A., & Morrell, R. (2001). Parentification of adult children of divorce: A multidimensional analysis. *Journal of Youth and Adolescence, 30*(2), 245–257.

Kaes, R. (1989). Filiation et affiliation [Filiation and affiliation]. *Gruppo, 1,* 23–46.

Kancyper, L. (1997). *La confrontación generacional. Estudios psicoanalitico* [The generational comparison. A psychoanalytic study]. Buenos Aires: Editorial Paidós.

Kandinsky, W. (1926). *Punkt und Linie zur Fläche* [Dot, line and surface]. München: Bauhaus-Bücher.

Karney, B. R., & Bradbury, T. N. (2000). Attributions in marriage: State or trait? A growth curve analysis. *Journal of Personality and Social Psychology, 78*(2), 295–309.

Kaslow, F. W. (1980). Stages of divorce: A psychological perspective. *Villanova Law Review, 4/5,* 718–751.

Kaslow, F. W. (1987). Stages in the divorce process. In F. W. Kaslow & L. L. Schwartz (Eds.), *The dynamics of divorce: A lifecycle perspective* (pp. 23–37). New York, NY: Brunner/Mazel.

Kelley, H. H., Berscheid, E., Christensen, A., Harvey, J. H., Huston, T. L., Levinger, G., et al. (2002). *Close relationships.* New York, NY: Percheron Press.

Kelley, H. H., & Thibaut, J. W. (1978). *Interpersonal relations: A theory of interdependence.* New York, NY: John Wiley & Sons.

Kelly, J. B., & Emery, R. (2003). Adjustment following divorce: Risk and relience perspectives. *Family Relations, 52,* 352–362.

Kenny, D. A., & Judd, C. M. (1986). Consequences of violating the independence assumption in analysis of variance. *Psychological Bulletin, 99*(3), 422–431.

Kernberg, O. (1995). *Love relations: Normality and pathology.* New Haven, CT: Yale University Press.

Kerr, M., Stattin, H., & Trost, K. (1999). To know you is to trust you: Parents' trust is rooted in child disclosure of information. *Journal of Adolescence, 22,* 737–752.

Klapisch-Zuber, C. (1985). *Women, family and ritual in Renaissance Italy.* Chicago, IL: University of Chicago Press.

Klock, S. C., & Maier, D. (1991). Psychological factors related to donor insemination. *Fertility and Sterility, 56,* 489–495.

Koestler, A. (1978). *Janus: A summary up.* New York, NY: Vintage Books.

Kog, E., Vertommen, H., & Vandereycken, W. (1987). Minuchin's psychosomatic family model revised: A concept validation study using a multitrait approach. *Family Process, 26*(2), 235–253.

Kolevzon, M. S., Green, R. G., Fortune, A. E., & Vosler, N. R. (1988). Evaluating family therapy: Divergent methods, divergent findings. *Journal of Marital and Family Therapy, 14*(3), 277–286.

Kotre, J. (1984). *Outliving the self: Generativity and the interpretation of lives.* Baltimore, MD: Johns Hopkins University.

Kotre, J., & Kotre, K. B. (1998). Intergenerational buffers: "The damage stops here." In D. P. McAdams, & E. de St.Aubin (Eds.), *Generativity and adult development: How and why we care for the next generation* (pp. 367–389). Washington, DC: American Psychological Association.

Kramer, B. J. (1993). Marital history and the prior relationship as predictors of positive and negative outcomes among wives caregivers. *Family Relations, 42,* 367–375.

Kramer, B. J., & Lambert, J. D. (1999). Caregiving as a life course transition among older husbands: A prospective study. *Gerontologist, 39*(6), 658–667.

Kubler Ross, E. (1969). *On death and dying.* New York, NY: McMillan.

Kurdek, L. A. (1993). Nature and prediction of changes in marital quality for first-time parent and nonparent husbands and wives. *Journal of Family Psychology, 6,* 255–265.

L'Abate, L. (1994). *A theory of personality development.* New York, NY: John Wiley & Sons.

L'Abate, L. (1997). *The self in the family.* Atlanta, GA: Georgia State University.

Lanz, M. (1998). Dall'adolescenza alla giovinezza: continuità e cambiamenti [From adolescence to youth: continuity and changes]. *Età Evolutiva, 61,* 56–63.

Lanz, M., Iafrate, R., Rosnati, R., & Scabini, E. (1999). Parent–child communication and adolescents' self-esteem in separated, inter-country adoptive and intact-nonadoptive families. *Journal of Adolescence, 22,* 785–794.

Lanz, M., & Rosnati, R. (1995). La comunicazione familiare: Uno studio sulle famiglie con adolescenti [Family communication: A study on families with an adolescent]. *Ricerche di Psicologia, 3*(19), 81–98.

Lanz, M., Rosnati, R., Iafrate, R., & Marta, E. (1999). Significant others in Italian families with late adolescents. *Psychological Reports, 84,* 459–466.

Lanz, M., Rosnati, R., Marta, E., & Scabini, E. (2001). Adolescents' future: A comparison of adolescents' and their parents' views. In J. E. Nurmi (Ed.), *Navigating through adolescence: European perspective* (pp. 169–198). New York, NY: Routledge.

Lee, G. R., Netzer, J., & Coward, R. (1994). Filial responsibility expectations and patterns of intergenerational assistance. *Journal of Marriage and the Family, 56,* 559–565.

Lee, G. R., Netzer, J. K., & Coward, R. T. (1995). Depression among older parents: The role of intergenerational exchange. *Journal of Marriage and the Family, 57*(3), 823–833.

Lemaire, G. (2002). Divorzi all'acqua di rose ["Light" divorces]. *Interazioni, 1,* 26–40.

Levi-Strauss, C. (1969). *The elementary structure of kinship.* Boston, MA: Beacon. (Original work published 1967)

Levy-Shiff, R., Goldsmith, I., & Har-Even, D. (1991). Transition to parenthood in adoptive families. *Developmental Psychology, 27*(1), 131–140.

Levy-Shiff, R., Vakil, E., Dimistovsky, L., Abramovitz, M., Shahar, N., Har-Even, D., et al. (1998). Medical, cognitive, emotional, and behavioral outcomes in school-age children conceived by in-vitro fertilization. *Journal of Clinical Child Psychology, 3,* 320–329.

Levy-Shiff, R., Zoran, N., & Shulman, S. (1997). International and domestic adoption: Child, parents, and family adjustment. *International Journal of Behavioral Development, 20*(1), 109–129.

Lewin, K. (1951). *Field theory in social science: Selected theoretical papers.* New York, NY: Harper & Row.

Li, L. W., & Seltzer, M. M. (2003). Parent care, intergenerational relationship quality, and mental health of adult daughters. *Research on Aging, 25*(5), 484–504.

Lieberman, M. A., & Fisher, L. (1999). The impact of a parent's dementia on adult offspring and their spouses: The contribution of family characteristics. *Journal of Mental Health and Aging, 5*(3), 207–222.

Lo Verso, G. (Ed.). (1998). *La mafia dentro* [Mafia insight]. Milano: Franco Angeli.

Luhmann, N. (1982). *Liebe als Passion* [Love and passion]. Frankfurt: Suhrkamp.

Lynch, D. (1999). *The straight story.* Walt Disney Pictures.

MacDermid, S., Huston, T., & McHale, S. (1990). Changes in marriage associated with the transition to parenthood: Individual differences as a function of sex-role attitudes and changes in the division of household labor. *Journal of Marriage and the Family, 52,* 475–486.

Magnusson, D., & Törestad, B. (1993). A holistic view of personality: A model revisited. *Annual Review of Psychology, 44,* 427–452.

Main, M., Kaplan, N., & Cassidy, J. (1985). Security in infancy, childhood, and adulthood: A move to the level of representation. *Monographs of the Society for Research in Child Development, 50*(1–2), 66–104.

Mantovani, G. (2000). *Exploring borders.* London, UK: Routledge.

Margola, D., & Molgora, S. (2002). Quando il lavoro interferisce con la vita familiare. Risultati di uno studio diadico [When work interferes with family life. Results from a dyadic family research]. *Ricerche di Psicologia, 25*(4), 117–141.

Margola, D., & Rosnati, R. (2003). Die schwierige Vereinbarung von Familie und Beruf: Eine italienische Studie [Coping with the demanding reconciliation between family and work: Evidence from Italy]. *Zeitschrift für Familienforschung, 3,* 220–237.

Markman, H. J., Floyd, F. J., Stanley, S. M., & Storaalsi, R. D. (1988). Prevention of marital distress: A longitudinal investigation. *Journal of Consulting and Clinical Psychology, 56,* 210–217.

Markman, H. J., Renick, M. J., Floyd, F. J., Stanley, S. M., & Clements, M. (1993). Preventing marital distress through communication and conflict management training: A 4- and 5-year follow-up. *Journal of Consulting and Clinical Psychology, 61*(1), 70–77.

Marta, E. (1997). Parent–adolescent interactions and psycho-social risk in adolescents: An analysis of communication, support, and gender. *Journal of Adolescence, 20,* 106–120.

Marta, E., & Pozzi, M. (in press). Young volunteers, family and social capital: From the care of family bonds to the care of community bonds. In M. Hofer, A. Sliwka, & M. Dietrich (Eds.), *Perspectives on citizenship education: Theory–research–practice.* Munster, NY: Waxmann.

Mauno, S., & Kinnunen, U. (1999). The effects of job stressors on marital satisfaction in Finnish dual-earner couples. *Journal of Organizational Behavior, 20*(6), 879–895.

Mauss, M. (1950). *The gift: The form and reason for exchange in archaic societies.* New York, NY: Norton & Co. (Original work published 1950)

McAdams, D. P. (2001). Generativity in midlife. In M. Lackman (Ed.), *Handbook of midlfe development* (pp. 395–443). New York: Wiley.

McAdams, D. P., & de St. Aubin, E. (1992). A theory of generativity and its assessment through self-report, behavioral acts, and narrative themes in autobiography. *Journal of Personality and Social Psychology, 62*(6), 1003–1015.

McAdams, D. P., & de St. Aubin, E. (1998). *Generativity and adult development: How and why we care for the next generation.* Washington, DC: American Psychological Association.

McAdoo, H. P. (1993). *Family ethnicity: Strength in diversity.* Thousand Oaks, CA: Sage.

McGoldrick, M., & Carter, E. A. (1982). The family life cycle. In F. Walsh (Ed.), *Normal family processes* (pp. 167–195). New York, NY: Guilford.

McGoldrick, M., Heiman, M., & Carter, B. (1993). The changing family life cycle: A perspective on normality. In F. Walsh (Ed.), *Normal family processes* (pp. 405–443). New York, NY: Guilford.

McWhinnie, A. (1996). Outcomes for families created by assisted conception programmes. *Journal of Assisted Reproduction and Genetics, 4,* 363–365.

Mejerchol'd, V. E. (1962). *La rivoluzione teatrale* [The theatre revolution]. Roma: Editori Riuniti.

Meltzer, D., & Harris, M. (1983). *Child, family and community: A psycho-analytical model of learning process.* Paris: Organization for Economic Co-operation and Development.

Michaels, G. Y., & Goldberg, W. A. (1988). The transition to parenthood: Current theory and research. *Cambridge studies in social and emotional development* (pp. 1–20). New York, NY: Cambridge University Press.

Miller, A. (1991). *Il bambino negato* [The denied child]. Milano: Garzanti.

Miller, B. C., Fan, X., Christen, M., Grotevant, H. D., & van Dulmen, M. (2000). Comparison of adopted and nonadopted adolescents in a large, nationally representative sample. *Child Development, 71,* 1458–1473.

Minuchin, S. (1998). Where is the family in narrative family therapy? *Journal of Marital and Family Therapy, 24*(4), 397–418.

Mitchell, S. A. (2002). *Can love last? The fate of romance over time.* New York, NY: Norton.

Morin, E. (1986). *La méthode. III. La connaissance de la connaissance* [The method. III. Knowledge of knowledge]. Paris: Edition du Senil.

Morin, E. (2001). *La Méthode. V. L'humanité de l'humanité. Tome 1. L'identité humain* [The method. V. Humanity of humanity. Volume 1. The human identity]. Paris: Edition du Senil.

Moro, M. R. (2002). *Genitori in esilio. Psicopatologia e migrzioni* [Parents in exile. Psychopathology and migrations]. Milano: Raffaello Cortina Editore.

Moss, B. F., & Schwebel, A. I. (1993). Defining intimacy in romantic relationships. *Family Relations, 42,* 31–37.

Mostwin, D. (1981). Life Space Ecological Model of Family Treatment. *International Journal of Family Psychiatry, 2,* 75–94.

Murray, W. M., Smith, E. P., & Hill, N. E. (2001). Race, ethnicity, and culture in studies of families in context. *Journal of Marriage and the Family, 63,* 911–914.

Niccol, A. (Director). (1997). *Gattaca.* Columbia Pictures.

Nicolas, G. (1991). Le don rituel, face voilée de la modernité [The ritual gift, the hidden face of modernity]. *Revue de MAUSS, 12,* 7–29.

Noack, P., Hofer, M., & Youniss, J. (1998). *Psychological responses to social changes.* Berlin: Walter de Gruyter.

Noller, P., & Callan, V. J. (1991). *The adolescent in the family.* Florence, KY: Routledge.

Norsa, D., & Zavattini, G. (1997). *Intimità e collusione* [Intimacy and collusion]. Milano: Raffaello Cortina Editore.

Nye, F. I. (1979). Choice, exchange and the family. In W. R. Burr, R. Hill, F. I. Nye, & I. Reiss (Eds.), *Contemporary theories about the family* (Vol. 2, pp. 1–17). New York, NY: Free Press.

Oliveri, M. E., & Reiss, D. (1982). Family styles of construing the social environment: A perspective on variation among nonclinical families. In F. Walsh (Ed.), *Normal family processes* (pp. 94–114). New York, NY: Guilford.

Olson, D. H. (1972). The powerlessness of family power: Empirical and clinical considerations. In J. H. Masserman (Ed.), *Science and psychoanalysis: The dynamics of power.* New York, NY: Grune & Stratton.

Olson, D. H. (1976). *Treating relationships.* Lake Mills, IA: Graphic.

Olson, D. H. (1993). Circumplex model of marital and family systems: Assessing family functioning. In F. Walsh (Ed.), *Normal family processes* (2nd ed., pp. 104–137). New York, NY:Guilford.

Olson, D. H., & Larsen, A. (1990). Capturing the complexity of family systems: Integrating family theory, family scores, and family analysis. In T. W. Draper & A. C. Marcos (Eds.), *Family variables: Conceptualizations, measurement and use. New perspectives on family* (pp. 19–47). Thousand Oaks, CA: Sage.

Olson, D. H., Russell, C. S., & Sprenkle, D. H. (1983). Circumplex model of marital and family system: Theoretical update. *Family Process, 22,* 69–83.

Palacios, J., & Sánchez-Sandoval, Y. (in press). Beyond adopted/non-adopted comparisons. In D. Brodzinsky & J. Palacios (Eds.), *Psychological issues in adoption: Theory, research and application.* Westport, CT: Praeger.

Paleari, G., Regalia, C., & Fincham, F. D. (2005). Marital quality, forgiveness, empathy, and rumination: A longitudinal analysis. *Personality and Social Psychology Bulletin, 31,* 295–300.

Pape Cowan, C., & Cowan, P. (1992). *When partners become parents.* New York, NY: Basic Books.

Parke, R. (1995). Fathers and families. In M. Bornstein (Ed.), *Handbook of parenting, Vol. 3: Status and social conditions of parenting* (pp. 27–63). Mahwah, NJ: Lawrence Erlbaum Associates.

Parsons, T., & Shils, E. A. (1959). *Toward a general theory of action.* Cambridge, MA: Harvard University Press.

Paul, N. L. (1980). Now and the past: Transgenerational analysis. *International Journal of Family Psychiatry, 1,* 235–248.

Pelligra, V. (2002). Fiducia Relazionale [Relational trust]. In P. L. Sacco & S. Zamagni (Eds.), *Complessità relazionale e comportamento economico. Materiali per un nuovo paradigma di razionalità* [Relational complexity and economic behavior. Matters for a new relational paradigm] (pp. 291–335). Bologna: Il Mulino.

Pina, D., & Bengston, B. (1993). The division of household labor and wives's happiness: Ideology, employment, and perception of support. *Journal of Marriage and the Family, 55,* 901–912.

Pincus, L., & Dare, C. (1978). *Secrets in the family.* London, UK: Faber & Faber.

Pontalti, C. (1993). Famiglia e cultura degli affetti [Family and sentiments culture]. In P. Donati (Ed.), *Terzo rapporto sulla famiglia in Italia* [Third report on family in Italy] (pp. 123–160). Cinisello Balsamo: Edizioni Paoline.

Pontalti, C. (1994). Matrice familiare e matrice gruppale: struttura e interconnessione [Family matrix and group matrix: Structure and interconnection]. *Ecologia della Mente, 17*(1), 7–12.

Pozzi, M. (2003). *What goes around comes around. What's beyond a volunteer's choices? A longitudinal study among young-adults.* Unpublished doctoral thesis, Catholich University, Milano.

Pratt, M. W., Danso, H. A., Arnold, M. L., Norris, J. E., & Filyer, R. (2001). Adult generativity and the socialization of adolescents: Relations to mothers' and fathers' parenting beliefs, styles, and practices. *Journal of Personality, 69*(1), 89–120.

Priel, B., Melamed-Hass, S., Besser, A., & Kantor, B. (2000). Adjustment among adopted children: The role of maternal self-reflectiveness. *Family Relations, 49*(4), 389–396.

Racamier, J. C. (1992). *Le génie des origines* [The origin genius]. Paris: Payot.

Rangell, L., & Hrushovski, R. (1996). *Psychoanalysis at the political border: Essays in honor of Rafael Moses.* Madison, CT: International University Press.

Raush, H. L., Barry, W. A., Hertel, R. H., & Swain, M. A. (1974). *Communication and conflict in marriage.* San Francisco, CA: Jossey-Bass.

Reiss, D., & Oliveri, M. E. (1984). Family concepts and their measurement: Things are seldom what they seem. *Family Process, 23,* 33–48.

Reiss, D., & Oliveri, M. E. (1991). The family's conception of accountability and competence: A new approach to the conceptualization and assessment of family stress. *Family Process, 30,* 193–213.

Rempel, J. K., Holmes, J. G., & Zanna, M. P. (1985). Trust in close relationships. *Journal of Personality and Social Psychology, 49*(1), 95–112.

Revenson, T. A., Kayser, K., & Bodenmann, G. (Eds.). (2005). *Couples coping with stress: Emerging perspectives on dyadic coping.* Washington, DC: American Psychological Association.

Romano, E., & Bouley, J. C. (1988). La coppia: terapeuta dell'individuo [Couple as the therapist of the individual]. In M. Andolfi, C. Angelo, & C. Saccu (Eds.), *La coppia in crisi* [Couple in crisis] (pp. 233–247). Roma: Istituto Terapia Familiare.

Rosnati, R., & Marta, E. (1997). Parent–child relationships as protective factors in preventing adolescents' psycho-social risk in adoptive and non-adoptive families. *Journal of Adolescence, 20,* 617–631.

Rossi, A., & Rossi, P. (1990). *Of human bonding: Parent–child relations across the life course.* New York, NY: Aldine De Gruyter.

Rossi, G. (2003). *La famiglia in Europa* [Family in Europe]. Roma: Carocci.

Ruble, D., & Seidman, E. (1996). Social transitions: windows into social psychological processes. In T. Higging & A. Kruglanski (Eds.), *Social psychology: Handbook of basic principles* (pp. 830–856). New York, NY: Guilford.

Rusbult, C. E. (1980). Commitment and satisfaction in friendship. *Representative Research in Social Psychology, 11,* 96–105.

Rusbult, C. E., Bissonnette, V. L., Arriaga, X. B., & Cox, C. L. (1998). Accommodation processes during the early years of marriage. In T. N. Bradbury (Ed.), *The developmental course of marital dysfunction* (pp. 44–73). New York: Cambridge University Press.

Sager, C. J., Kaplan, H. S., Grunlach, R. H., Kremer, M., Lenz, R., & Royce, J. R. (1972). The marriage contract. In C. J. Sager & E. S. Kaplan (Eds.), *Progress in group and family therapy* (pp. 483–497). Oxford, UK: Brunner/Mazel.

Sampson, R. J. (1992). Family management and child development: Insights from social disorganization theory. In J. McCord (Ed.), *Advances in criminology theory, vol. 3* (pp. 63–93). New Brunswick, NJ: Transaction Books.

Sampson, R. J. (1999). What "community" supplies. In R. Ferguson & W. T. Dickens (Eds.), *Urban problems and community development* (pp. 241–292). Washington, DC: Brooking Institution Press.

Sasaki, T. (2003). Generativity and the politics of intergenerational fairness. In E. de St. Aubin, D. P. McAdams, & T. C. Kim (Eds.), *The generative society: Caring for future generations* (pp. 211–219). Washington, DC: American Psychological Association.

Scabini, E. (1995). *Psicologia sociale della famiglia* [Family social psychology]. Torino: Bollati Boringhieri.

Scabini, E. (2000a). New aspects of family relations. In C. Violato, E. Oddone-Paolucci, & M. Genuis (Eds.), *The changing family and child development* (pp. 3–24). Aldershot, UK: Ashgate.

Scabini, E. (2000b). Parent–child relationship in Italian families: Connectedness and autonomy in the transition to adulthood. *Psicologia: Teoria e Pesquisa, 16*(1), 23–30.

Scabini, E. (2001). Adolescenti e relazioni familiari [Adolescents and family relationships]. In A. Cavalli & C. Facchini (Eds.), *Scelte cruciali. Indagine Iard su giovani e famiglie di fronte alle scelte alla fine della scuola secondaria* [Crucial choices. IARD report on young and families facing choices at the end of the secondary school] (pp. 171–227). Bologna: Il Mulino.

Scabini, E., & Cigoli, V. (1997). Young adult families: An evolutionary slowdown or a breakdown in the generational transition? *Journal of Family Issues, 18*(6), 608–626.

Scabini, E., & Cigoli, V. (1998). The role of theory in the study of family psychopathology. In L. L'Abate (Ed.), *Family psychopathology. The relational roots of dysfunctional behavior* (pp. 13–34). New York, NY: Guilford.

Scabini, E., & Cigoli, V. (2000). *Il famigliare. Legami, simboli e transizioni* [The familyness. Ties, symbols, and transition]. Milano: Raffaello Cortina Editore.

Scabini, E., & Cigoli, V. (2004). How do young adult children deal with parental divorce: A generational prospect. *Journal of Family Psychotherapy, 15*(1/2), 219–234.

Scabini, E., & Donati, P. (1988). *La famiglia "lunga" del giovane adulto* ["Long" family with the young adult, Vol. 7]. Milano: Vita e Pensiero.

Scabini, E., & Galimberti, C. (1995). Adolescents and young adults: A transition in the family. *Journal of Adolescence, 18*(5), 593–606.

Scabini, E., Lanz, M., & Marta, E. (1999). Psycho-social adjustment and family relationships: A typology of Italian families with a late adolescent. *Journal of Youth and Adolescence, 28*, 633–644.

Scabini, E., & Marta, E. (1996). Family with late adolescents: Social and family topics. In M. Cusinato (Ed.), *Research on family resources and needs across the world* (pp. 177–197). Milano: LED.

Scabini, E., Marta, E., & Lanz, M. (in press). *Transition to adulthood and family relations: An intergenerational perspective*. London, UK: Routledge.

Scabini, E., & Regalia, C. (1999). Benessere psichico, qualità dei legami e transizioni familiari [Psychic wellness, ties quality and family transitions]. In P. Donati (Ed.), *Famiglia e società del benessere. Sesto Raporto CISF sulla famiglia in Italia* [Family and wellness society. Sixth CISF report on family in Italy] (pp. 117–150). Cinisello Balsamo: San Paolo.

Scabini, E., & Rossi, G. (2000). *Dono e perdono nelle relazioni familiari e sociali* [Gift and forgiveness within family and society relationship]. Milano: Vita e Pensiero.

Scanzoni, J. (1972). *Sexual bargaining*. Chicago, IL: University of Chicago Press.

Sells, S. P., Smith, T. E., & Sprenkle, D. H. (1995). Integrating qualitative and quantitative research methods: A research model. *Family Process, 34*, 199–218.

Selvini Palazzoli, M. (1986). Towards a general model of psychotic family games. *Journal of Marital and Family Therapy, 12*(4), 339–349.

Sexton, C., & Perlman, D. (1989). Couple's career orientation, gender role orientation, and perceived equity as determinants of marital power. *Journal of Marriage and the Family, 51*, 933–941.

Shakespeare, W. (2001). *Anthony and Cleopatra*. Oxford, UK: Oxford University Press. (Original work published 1597)

Shanas, E. (1984). Old parents and middle-aged children: The four- and five-generation family. *Journal of Geriatric Psychiatry, 3*, 7–19.

Shapiro, J., Diamond, M., & Greenberg, M. (1995). *Becoming a father: Contemporary, social, developmental, and clinical perspectives*. New York, NY: Springer.

Sigafoss, A., Reiss, D., Rich, J., & Douglas, E. (1985). Pragmatics in the measurement of family functioning: An interpretative framework for methodology. *Family Process, 24*, 207–211.

Silverstone, B., & Hyman, H. (1982). *You and your aging parents*. New York, NY: Pantheon.

Singer, I. (1987). *The nature of love, vol. 3*. Chicago, IL: University of Chicago Press.

Sini, C. (1989). *I segni dell'anima: saggio sull'immagine* [The soul signs: Essay on image]. Bari: Laterza.

Sklovskij, V. (1976). *Teoria della prosa* [Prose theory]. Torino: Einaudi.

Sluzky, C. E. (1979). Migration and family conflict. *Family Process, 18*(4), 379–390.

Small, S., & Supple, A. (2001). Communities as systems: Is a community more than the sum of its parts? In A. Booth & A. C. Crouter (Eds.), *Does it take a village?: Community effects on children, adolescents, and families* (pp. 161–174). Mahwah, NJ: Lawrence Erlbaum Associates.

Snarey, J. (1993). *How fathers care for the next generation*. Cambridge, MA: Harvard University Press.

Snarey, J. (1998). Ego development and the ethical voices of justice and care: An Eriksonian interpretation. In P. Westenberg & A. Blasi (Eds.), *Personality development: Theoretical, empirical, and clinical investigations of Loevinger's conception of ego development* (pp. 163–180). Mahwah, NJ: Lawrence Erlbaum Associates.

Sobol, M. P., Delaney, S., & Earn, B. M. (1994). Adoptees' portrayal of the development of family structure. *Journal of Youth and Adolescence, 2,* 385–401.

Solnit, C., & Freud, A. (1973). *Beyond the best interest of the child.* London, UK: Free Press.

Spitze, G., & Ward, R. (2000). Gender, marriage, and expectations for personal care. *Research on Aging, 22*(5), 451–469.

Sprecher, S., & Felmlee, D. (1992). The influence of parents and friends on the quality and stability of romantic relationships: A three-wave longitudinal investigation. *Journal of Marriage and the Family, 54,* 888–900.

Sroufe, L. (1991). Assessment of parent–adolescent relationships: Implication for adolescent development. *Journal of Family Psychology, 5,* 21–45.

Sroufe, L., & Fleeson, J. (1988). The coherence of family relationships. In R. Hinde & J. Stevenson-Hinde (Eds.), *Relationships within the families: Mutual influences* (pp. 27–47). Oxford, MS: Clarendon Press.

Steinberg, L. (2001). We know some things: Parent–adolescent relationships in retrospect and prospect. *Journal of Research on Adolescence, 11,* 1–19.

Stierling, H. (1974). *Separating parents and adolescent.* New York, NY: Quadrangle.

Tajfel, H. (1981). *Human groups and social categories: Studies in social psychology.* Cambridge, MA: Cambridge University Press.

Takeshi, S. (2003). Generativity and the politics of intergenerational fairness. In E. de St. Aubin, D. P. McAdams, & T. C. Kim (Eds.), *The generative society: Caring for future generations* (pp. 211–219). Washington, DC: American Psychological Association.

Tamanza, G. (1998). *La malattia del riconoscimento. L'Alzheimer, le relazioni familiari, il processo di cura* [The recognition illness. Alzheimer, family relations, care process]. Milano: Unicopli.

Tashakkori, A., & Teddlie, C. (1998). *Mixed methodology.* Thousand Oaks, CA: Sage.

Théry, I. (1998). *Couple, filiation, et parenté aujourd'hui* [Couple, filiation, and kinship at present times]. Paris: Edition Odile Jacob.

Thibaut, J. W., & Kelley, H. H. (1959). *The social psychology groups.* New York, NY: John Wiley & Sons.

Turner, V. (1982). *From ritual to theatre: The human geniousness of play.* New York, NY: Performing Arts Journal Publications.

Ugazio, V. (1998). *Storie permesse, storie proibite. Polarità semantiche familiari e psicopatologia* [Allowed stories, prohibited stories. Family semantic polarities and psychopathology]. Torino: Bollati Boringhieri.

Van Gennep, A. (1909). *Les rites de passage* [The rites of passage]. Paris: Ferme.

Vernant, P. (1983). *Myth and thought among the Greeks.* London, UK: Routledge & Kegan. (Original work published 1965)

Veyne, P. (1985). De l'Empire Romain à l'an mil [From the Roman Empire to year 1000]. In P. Ariès & G. Duby (Eds.), *Histoire de la vie privée* [History of the private life] (Vol. 1, p. 360). Paris: Edition du Seuil.

Vignoles, V., Regalia, C., Manzi, C., Golledge, Y., & Scabini, E. (in press). Beyond self-esteem: Influence of multiple motives on identity construction. *Journal of Personality and Social Psychology.*

von Bertalanffy, L. (1968). *General system theory.* New York, NY: Braziller.

Vovelle, M. (1983). *La mort et l'Occident de 1300 a nos jours* [Death and the West from 1300 to our day]. Paris: Edition Gallimard.

Wallerstein, J. S., & Lewis, J. (1998). The long-term impact of divorce on children: A first report from a 25-year study. *Family and Conciliation Courts Review, 36,* 368–383.

Walsh, F. (1982). Conceptualizations of normal family functioning. In F. Walsh (Ed.), *Normal family processes* (pp. 3–44). New York, NY: Guilford.

Walsh, F., & McGoldrick, M. (1991). *Living beyond the loss: Death in the family.* New York, NY: Norton.

Wapner, S., & Craig-Bray, L. (1992). Person in environment transitions: Theoretical and method-ological approaches. *Environment and Behavior, 24*(2), 161–188.

Weaver, S., Clifford, M., Hay, D., & Robinson, J. (1997). Psychosocial adjustment to unsuccessful IVF and GIFT treatment. *Patient Education and Counseling, 31*, 7–18.

Wegner, G. C., & Jerrome, D. (1999). Change and stability in confidant relationships: Findings from the Bangor Longitudinal Study of Ageing. *Journal of Aging Studies, 13*(3), 269–294.

Whitaker, C., & Bumberry, W. (1987). *Dancing with the family. A symbolic-experiential approach.* New York, NY: Brunner/Mazel.

Whitbeck, L., Hoyt, D., & Huck, S. (1994). Early family relationships, intergenerational solidarity and support provided to parents by their adult children. *Journal of Gerontology: Social Science, 49*, 85–94.

White, M., & Epston, D. (1990). *Narrative means to therapeutic ends.* New York, NY: Norton.

Wilkinson, I. (1987). Family assessment: A review. *Journal of Family Therapy, 5*(4), 367–380.

Williamson, D. S. (1991). *The intimacy paradox.* New York, NY: Guilford.

Williamson, J. B., Kingson, E. R., & Watts-Roy, D. M. (1999). *The generational equity debate.* New York, NY: Columbia University Press.

Windle, M., & Dumenci, L. (1997). Parental and occupational stress as predictors of depressive symptoms among dual-income couples: A multilevel modeling approach. *Journal of Marriage and the Family, 59*, 625–634.

Winnicott, D. W. (1965). *The family and individual development.* London, UK: Tavistock.

Wolin, S. J., & Bennett, L. (1984). Family rituals. *Family Process, 23*, 401–420.

Worthington, E. (2001). *Five steps to forgiveness: The art and science of forgiving.* New York, NY: Crown.

Wynne Lymann, C. (1984). The epigenesis of relational systems: A model for understanding family development. *Family Process, 23*(3), 297–318.

Youniss, J., & Smollar, J. (1985). *Adolescent relations with mothers, fathers, and friends.* Chicago, IL: University of Chicago Press.

Zanetti, G. (1993). *La nozione di giustizia* [Justice notion]. Bologna: Il Mulino.

Zarit, S. H., & Eggebeen, D. J. (2002). Parent–child relationships in adulthood and later years. In M. H. Bornstein (Ed.), *Handbook of parenting, Vol. 1: Children and parenting* (2nd ed., pp. 135–161). Mahwah, NJ: Lawrence Erlbaum Associates.

Author Index

Subject Index